Learn pfSense 2.4

MW01089734

Get up and running with Pfsense and all the core concepts to build firewall and routing solutions

David Zientara

BIRMINGHAM - MUMBAI

Learn pfSense 2.4

Copyright © 2018 Packt Publishing

All rights reserved. No part of this book may be reproduced, stored in a retrieval system, or transmitted in any form or by any means, without the prior written permission of the publisher, except in the case of brief quotations embedded in critical articles or reviews.

Every effort has been made in the preparation of this book to ensure the accuracy of the information presented. However, the information contained in this book is sold without warranty, either express or implied. Neither the author, nor Packt Publishing or its dealers and distributors, will be held liable for any damages caused or alleged to have been caused directly or indirectly by this book.

Packt Publishing has endeavored to provide trademark information about all of the companies and products mentioned in this book by the appropriate use of capitals. However, Packt Publishing cannot guarantee the accuracy of this information.

Commissioning Editor: Gebin George
Acquisition Editor: Akshay Jethani
Content Development Editor: Abhishek Jadhav
Technical Editor: Mohd Riyan Khan
Copy Editor: Safis Editing
Project Coordinator: Jagdish Prabhu
Proofreader: Safis Editing
Indexer: Jagdish Prabhu
Graphics: Tom Scaria
Production Coordinator: Shraddha Falebhai

First published: July 2018

Production reference: 1310718

Published by Packt Publishing Ltd.
Livery Place
35 Livery Street
Birmingham
B3 2PB, UK.

ISBN 978-1-78934-311-3

www.packtpub.com

`mapt.io`

Mapt is an online digital library that gives you full access to over 5,000 books and videos, as well as industry leading tools to help you plan your personal development and advance your career. For more information, please visit our website.

Why subscribe?

- Spend less time learning and more time coding with practical eBooks and Videos from over 4,000 industry professionals

- Improve your learning with Skill Plans built especially for you

- Get a free eBook or video every month

- Mapt is fully searchable

- Copy and paste, print, and bookmark content

PacktPub.com

Did you know that Packt offers eBook versions of every book published, with PDF and ePub files available? You can upgrade to the eBook version at `www.PacktPub.com` and as a print book customer, you are entitled to a discount on the eBook copy. Get in touch with us at `service@packtpub.com` for more details.

At `www.PacktPub.com`, you can also read a collection of free technical articles, sign up for a range of free newsletters, and receive exclusive discounts and offers on Packt books and eBooks.

Contributors

About the author

David Zientara is a software engineer living in northern New Jersey. He has over 20 years of experience in IT.

In the mid-1990s, David became the lead software engineer for Oxberry LLC, a digital imaging company headquartered in New Jersey. In this capacity, he played a major role in developing a new software package for the company's equipment. In the mid-2000s, David took an interest in computer networking, an interest that led him to learn about m0n0wall and, eventually, pfSense.

About the reviewer

Alex Samm has +10 years of experience in the IT field, including system and network administration, EUCsupport, Windows and Linux server support, virtualization, programming, penetration testing, and forensic investigations.

Currently, he works at ESP Global Services, supporting contracts in North America, Latin America, and the Caribbean. He also lectures at the Computer Forensics and Security Institute on IT security courses, including ethical hacking and penetration testing. He recently reviewed Digital Forensics with Kali Linux, authored by Shiva Parasram published in December 2017, which covers forensics using Kali Linux.

> *I'd like to thank my parents Roderick and Marcia for their continued support in my relentless pursuit for excellence, ESP Management Vinod and Dianne, and CFSI's Shiva and Glen for their guidance and support.*

Packt is searching for authors like you

If you're interested in becoming an author for Packt, please visit `authors.packtpub.com` and apply today. We have worked with thousands of developers and tech professionals, just like you, to help them share their insight with the global tech community. You can make a general application, apply for a specific hot topic that we are recruiting an author for, or submit your own idea.

Table of Contents

Preface

As computer networks become ubiquitous, it has become increasingly important to both secure and optimize our networks. pfSense, an open-source router/firewall, provides an easy, cost-effective way of achieving this – and this book explains how to install and configure pfSense in such a way that even a networking beginner can successfully deploy and use pfSense.

This book begins by covering networking fundamentals, deployment scenarios, and hardware sizing guidelines, as well as how to install pfSense. The book then covers configuration of basic services such as DHCP, DNS, and captive portal and VLAN configuration. Careful consideration is given to the core firewall functionality of pfSense, and how to set up firewall rules and traffic shaping. Finally, the book covers the basics of VPNs, multi-WAN setups, routing and bridging, and how to perform diagnostics and troubleshooting on a network.

Who this book is for

This book is towards any network security professionals who want to get introduced to the world of firewalls and network configurations using Pfsense. No prior knowledge of PfSense is required.

What this book covers

Chapter 1, *Getting Started with pfSense*, discusses about a brief history of the pfSense project and the role it can play in a network and in the pfSense community

Chapter 2, *Installing pfSense*, discusses the role a pfSense router/firewall plays in a typical network considering the different deployment scenarios. The initial process is covered from the initial installion from either CD or USB memstick through the completion of the web GUI setup wizard

Chapter 3, *Configuring pfSense*, takes us through advanced options such as customizing the web GUI, SSH login, configuring additional interfaces, and IPv6 configuration along with how to back up, restore and update your pfSense system

Chapter 4, *Captive Portal*, describes how to set up a captive portal in pfSense, how to leverage the numerous options available, and how to implement different authentication options and how to use vouchers

Chapter 5, *Additional pfSense Services*, takes through services such as DNS, Dynamic DNS, NTP, and SNMP in detail along with their examples

Chapter 6, *Firewall and NAT*, covers using firewall rules to block and allow traffic, and how to use scheduling and aliases to make the process easier.

Chapter 7, *Traffic Shaping*, covers how to use traffic shaping, including traffic shaping using the wizard and manual configuration, as well as how to configure floating rules for traffic shaping, as well as options for deep packet inspection

Chapter 8, *Virtual Private Networks*, includes when and how to use virtual private networks (VPNs) to provide an encrypted tunnel. L2TP, IPsec and OpenVPN protocols are discussed, as well as how to set up both a peer-to-peer and client-server tunnel

Chapter 9, *Multiple WANs*, covers common scenarios for using multiple WANs, such as bandwidth aggregation and failover, and how to set up gateways and gateway groups in pfSense

Chapter 10, *Routing and Bridging*, discusses what routing and bridging are, when it is possible or necessary to employ them, as well as how to perform static and dynamic routing in pfSense

Chapter 11, *Diagnostics and Troubleshooting*, deals with what to do when pfSense does not function as expected. A step-by-step process for solving and documenting problems is outlined, common problems are enumerated, different diagnostic tools are discussed, and example problems are presented

To get the most out of this book

Some familiarity with Linux and/or BSD would be helpful, as well as access to a computer that is capable of running pfSense (any modern PC should do). The specifications for such a PC will be discussed in detail in the section regarding hardware sizing guidelines, but in brief, you will need a PC with a 64-bit, AES-NI-capable processor, 1 GB of RAM, and 1 GB of storage.

To get along with the book, you can find detailed technical requirement at the beginning of each chapter.

Conventions used

There are a number of text conventions used throughout this book.

`CodeInText`: Indicates code words in text, database table names, folder names, filenames, file extensions, pathnames, dummy URLs, user input, and Twitter handles. Here is an example: "There is a packet with a source address of `192.168.2.1`"

A block of code is set as follows:

```
html, body, #map {
  height: 100%;
  margin: 0;
  padding: 0
}
```

Any command-line input or output is written as follows:

```
ping: unknown host google.com
```

Bold: Indicates a new term, an important word, or words that you see onscreen. For example, words in menus or dialog boxes appear in the text like this. Here is an example: "To begin, navigate to **Firewall | Rules**."

 Warnings or important notes appear like this.

 Tips and tricks appear like this.

Get in touch

Feedback from our readers is always welcome.

General feedback: Email `feedback@packtpub.com` and mention the book title in the subject of your message. If you have questions about any aspect of this book, please email us at `questions@packtpub.com`.

Errata: Although we have taken every care to ensure the accuracy of our content, mistakes do happen. If you have found a mistake in this book, we would be grateful if you would report this to us. Please visit www.packtpub.com/submit-errata, selecting your book, clicking on the Errata Submission Form link, and entering the details.

Piracy: If you come across any illegal copies of our works in any form on the Internet, we would be grateful if you would provide us with the location address or website name. Please contact us at copyright@packtpub.com with a link to the material.

If you are interested in becoming an author: If there is a topic that you have expertise in and you are interested in either writing or contributing to a book, please visit authors.packtpub.com.

Reviews

Please leave a review. Once you have read and used this book, why not leave a review on the site that you purchased it from? Potential readers can then see and use your unbiased opinion to make purchase decisions, we at Packt can understand what you think about our products, and our authors can see your feedback on their book. Thank you!

For more information about Packt, please visit packtpub.com.

Getting Started with pfSense

1

As the internet approaches its fiftieth anniversary, networked computers have essentially become the norm across much of the world. Computer networks are commonplace, even within the home, and it is not uncommon for households to have multiple internet-connected devices—a trend that undoubtedly will only accelerate with the growing popularity of the **internet of things (IoT)**. With networks becoming part of our basic infrastructure, reliable networking equipment has become as essential as telephone exchanges and railways were to prior generations.

Even if you only have a home network, at a minimum, you will need a router to connect your private network with the public internet and a firewall to provide both ingress filtering (filtering for incoming traffic) and possibly egress filtering (for outgoing traffic). **pfSense** can perform both functions. In this chapter, we will introduce the pfSense project, explain how pfSense can help secure your network, and introduce you to the pfSense community, from which you can find out more about pfSense, and, hopefully, get answers to questions. Finally, we will briefly discuss the objectives of this book.

Reading this chapter should provide the reader with an understanding of the following:

- The pfSense project
- What pfSense can do
- The pfSense community
- The objectives of this book

Technical requirements

There are no particular technical requirements for this chapter, as it is simply an overview of pfSense and the book's objectives. Some familiarity with Linux and/or BSD would be helpful, as well as access to a computer that is capable of running pfSense (any modern PC should do); we will discuss the technical specifications in greater depth in the next chapter.

The pfSense project

pfSense runs on the FreeBSD operating system. FreeBSD is an offshoot from Berkeley UNIX—the University of California, Berkeley had acquired a license for AT&T UNIX in the 1970s. Students started to improve on this version of UNIX, and **Berkeley Software Distribution** (**BSD**) was founded as a project to make modifications to AT&T UNIX, as well as to distribute this modified version. This version, however, had proprietary AT&T source code in it, and BSD users thus had to obtain a license from AT&T to use it legally. In the late 1980s, however, work began on a project to eliminate AT&T code from BSD in order to produce an open source version of it, thus spawning the FreeBSD project. Since then, FreeBSD has gained a following among those seeking a stable and secure open source variant of UNIX that provides good performance.

pfSense is based on pf, which is OpenBSD's packet filter (itself designed as a replacement for Darren Reed's IPFilter, which OpenBSD had been using up to that point). pf was incorporated into OpenBSD distributions in 2001. pf is a command-line utility, and, as a result, several projects were launched to provide a graphical interface for the pf utility. **m0n0wall**, initially released in 2003, was the first successful attempt at providing a graphical front end for pf. pfSense, which began as a fork of this project, was another such project.

Version 1.0 of pfSense was released on October 4, 2006. Version 2.0 was released on September 17, 2011. Version 2.1 was released on September 15, 2013, and Version 2.2 was released on January 23, 2015. Version 2.3, released on April 12, 2016, phased out support for legacy technologies such as the **Point-to-Point Tunneling Protocol** (**PPTP**), **Wireless Encryption Protocol** (**WEP**) and single DES, and also provided a facelift for the web GUI.

Version 2.4, released on October 12, 2017, continues this trend of phasing out support for legacy technologies while also adding features and improving the web GUI. Support for 32-bit x86 architectures has been deprecated (however, security updates will continue for 32-bit systems for at least a year after the release of 2.4), while support for Netgate **Advanced RISC Machines** (**ARM**) devices has been added. A new pfSense installer (based on FreeBSD's **bsdinstall**) has been incorporated into pfSense, and there is support for the ZFS filesystem, as well as the **Unified Extensible Firmware Interface** (**UEFI**). pfSense now supports OpenVPN 2.4.x, and as a result, features such as AES–GCM ciphers can be utilized. In addition, pfSense now supports multiple languages; the web GUI has been translated into 13 different languages. At the time of writing, version 2.4.3, released on May 14, 2018, is the most recent version.

pfSense is not the only option if you are looking for open source firewall/router software—it is not even the only software making use of FreeBSD and pf. The m0n0wall project was discontinued in 2015, but there have been several m0n0wall forks since its end of life, including **t1n1wall** and **SmallWall**. Manuel Kasper, the developer behind m0n0wall, supports OPNsense, a project that forked from pfSense in 2015. There are also projects such as Shorewall, an open source firewall tool for Linux that builds on Netfilter.

Nevertheless, pfSense is currently the most popular open source firewall/router, and the developer community contributing to the project is strong. It is fairly easy to install and configure, and is useful in a variety of deployment scenarios.

What pfSense can do

To provide a general idea of the versatility of pfSense, consider the following use cases:

- You have a home network, and need a means of connecting the wireless devices in your house (such as computers, laptops, and tablets) to the internet. Therefore, you need a router (to connect your home network to the internet), a firewall (to perform ingress and egress filtering at the boundary between your private network and the internet), and a wireless access point (to enable wireless devices to connect to your home network). You will likely also want to have a DHCP server to assign IP addresses to devices on the network, and possibly **dynamic DNS** (**DDNS**) capabilities, so that you don't have to remember your public IP address when accessing your home network from the outside world. pfSense can perform all these functions.

- You have a **small office/home office** (**SOHO**) network, and you need to connect several computers in your company to the internet. You also want to provide a means of allowing customers to connect to the internet on the same connection, but you want to have some means of controlling their access to the network so they don't use up the bulk of available bandwidth. You also want to keep them from accessing the internal company network. Therefore, you need to have separate subnets for your internal network and for customers, a captive portal to control customers' access to your network, and possibly traffic shaping capabilities to limit the amount of bandwidth used by customers. Again, pfSense can perform all these functions.

- You are an administrator at a corporation that has an office in another city. You want to provide access to your local corporate network to workers in the remote facility, but you are concerned about confidential corporate information traveling over the public internet. A private WAN circuit is one possible option to allow remote users to connect securely to your network, but private WAN circuits are expensive. Therefore, you decide that the best option is to set up a peer-to-peer VPN connection between your local network and the remote site. You also want to have more than one internet connection, to provide redundancy when one of the connections goes down. As you might have guessed, pfSense allows you to set up VPN connections between networks, and to set up multiple WAN connections.

In short, pfSense can be used in a variety of scenarios, ranging from a simple home network with a handful of internet-connected devices to a corporate network with thousands of users. For those administering corporate networks, commercially available equipment with proprietary technology (such as Cisco switches and routers) may prove to be the better option. Such equipment often performs better under heavy load scenarios, offers integrated voice, video, and data services, and often comes bundled with technical support.

This book, however, is aimed primarily at beginners; therefore, it is generally assumed that the reader is more likely to set up a home network or SOHO network than a corporate network, in which case pfSense is generally a cost-effective, sensible option. There is a great deal of functionality built in to pfSense, and in many cases, when the base install does not provide the functionality you need, there are third-party packages available that do provide such functionality.

The pfSense community

There will be times when you encounter a problem that cannot be solved by referencing this book or by troubleshooting the problem yourself. Although this book provides a detailed procedure for troubleshooting in `Chapter 11`, *Diagnostics and Troubleshooting*, it is often expedient to refer the problem to those who are more knowledgeable about pfSense than you are. In such cases, you can turn to the online pfSense community.

The official pfSense forums have recently moved to Netgate's website, which has reorganized the forums and added several more (including many devoted to pfSense international support). Anyone can read the forums, but in order to post on the forums, you must register, which requires you to provide a name and email address. Participation in the official forums can be an effective way of resolving problems and increasing your knowledge of pfSense.

The forums can be found at `https://forum.netgate.com`.

Reddit has its own pfSense forum, and members of the pfSense development team often participate in this forum. Although Reddit isn't everyone's cup of tea, it is a good place to find out the latest pfSense news, ask questions, and (hopefully) get answers.

The Reddit pfSense forum can be found at `https://www.reddit.com/r/PFSENSE/`.

Also worth mentioning is the Spiceworks pfSense forum. Spiceworks is a professional network for the IT community. Although the company has its headquarters in Austin, Texas, it has an international presence as well. Their pfSense forum also has polls and how-to guides.

The Spiceworks pfSense forum can be found at `https://community.spiceworks.com/networking/pfsense`.

Finally, for those who find it easier to watch videos, there are many useful how-to video guides available online. An online search for the pfSense topic in which you need assistance will often turn up multiple videos, of varying degrees of complexity and clarity. YouTube is the most obvious place to look for such videos, although other video sites, such as Vimeo, also have pfSense-related content.

Objectives of this book

The purpose of this book is to explain the basics of pfSense—installing, configuring, and utilizing its services—to the networking beginner. This book does not presuppose any prior knowledge of networking, and thus some of the material is devoted to explaining networking basics. At the same time, this book focuses on pfSense fundamentals—not networking fundamentals—and if you find such explanations inadequate, it might behoove you to find a good networking primer to supplement your reading. For example, any of the popular review guides for the CompTIA's Networking+ exam should prove adequate.

The following are the main topics covered in this book:

- Installing and configuring pfSense
- Captive portal configuration
- Configuration of other basic services (DNS, NTP, SNMP, and so on)
- Firewall and NAT
- Traffic shaping
- VPNs
- Multiple WANs
- Routing and bridging
- Diagnostics and troubleshooting

This book is not aimed at intermediate users—it is aimed mainly at beginners setting up a home for their SOHO network. Therefore, some topics that would be more appropriate in a corporate network scenario have been omitted, such as load balancing and failovers. Other topics that might be worthy of a more extensive treatment in a more intermediate-level book, such as VLANs, have been scaled back somewhat. Also, although third-party packages are mentioned where appropriate, this book does not discuss such packages in any great depth.

Nonetheless, the reader should come away from this book with a basic understanding of how to utilize pfSense in the most common scenarios. If you feel you need to know more about pfSense than the information contained within this book, you might consider another book I authored, *Mastering pfSense*, which covers intermediate-level topics.

Summary

In this chapter, we introduced FreeBSD and the pfSense project, provided a brief overview of what pfSense can do, mentioned the online pfSense community, and looked at the objectives of this book. In the next chapter, we will provide a survey of the basics of networking, ways in which pfSense can be deployed in typical networks, the hardware requirements for pfSense, and how to install pfSense and do some basic configuration.

Questions

1. What OS is used to run pfSense?
2. What does pf stand for?
3. Name one open source alternative to pfSense.

Further reading

Hansteen, Peter N.M. (2014). *The Book of PF: 3rd Edition*. San Francisco, CA: No Starch Press. To my knowledge, the only comprehensive guide on pf, the command-line utility upon which pfSense is based.

Installing pfSense

2

As computer networks grow in size and complexity, there is an increasing role for applications that enable us to interconnect networks and filter network traffic. pfSense is one such application. This book endeavors to enable relative newcomers to the world of computer networking to utilize pfSense in building their own networks. In fact, by the end of this chapter, even a pfSense neophyte should be able to determine where to deploy pfSense within a network, which hardware to select, and how to install pfSense—everything that is needed to get a pfSense firewall/router up and running for the first time.

We assume that most readers of this book will be using pfSense on a home network or a **small office/home office** (**SOHO**) network, and we have tailored the content accordingly. Fundamental networking concepts will be described in some detail, as well as the pfSense functions and services that we think will be of interest to such users. But before we delve into this, we must first cover the basics of installing pfSense.

Reading this chapter should provide the reader with an understanding of the following concepts:

- Networking fundamentals
- A brief overview of the pfSense project
- Typical pfSense deployment scenarios
- Hardware sizing guidelines for pfSense
- Installing pfSense
- pfSense configuration using the command line and web GUI
- Additional setup options
- Enabling SSH login

Technical requirements

To follow along with this chapter, you will need a PC that's capable of running pfSense. The specifications for such a PC will be discussed in detail in the section regarding hardware sizing guidelines, but in brief, you will need a PC with a 64-bit, AES-NI-capable processor, 1 GB of RAM, and 1 GB of storage. You may also run pfSense in a virtual machine if your PC meets these requirements.

Networking fundamentals

Computer networking can be defined as an interconnection between two or more computers that allows the computers to share resources. This definition describes both the minimum requirement of having a network—at a minimum, there must be a physical means of connecting the computers—and the objective of networking, which is to share resources (examples include files, computational power, and many others).

The seven-layer OSI model

At this point, we will introduce a conceptual model that will hopefully clarify a number of basic networking concepts—the **Open Systems Interconnect** (**OSI**) reference model. This model was created by the **International Organization for Standards** (ISO) in 1978, and was revised in 1984. It divides networking into seven layers, as follows:

- **Physical**: This is simply the network's physical characteristics, including the hardware and network topology.
- **Data link layer**: This layer is responsible for getting data to the physical layer, as well as error detection, error correction, and hardware addressing. It also has two sublayers:
    - **Media Access Control (MAC)**: The MAC address, the 48 or 64-bit hardware address that's burned into the network card. It is defined at this sublayer, which also controls access to the device.
    - **Data link**: This sublayer is responsible for the error correction and flow-control capabilities of the layer.
- **Network**: The primary responsibility for this layer is to handle routing—that is, providing a means for network data to pass from one network to another. This functionality is provided via network protocols.

- **Transport**: This layer provides connection services between devices and ensures the reliable delivery of data via error checking, service addressing (making sure that data is passed to the right service), and segmentation (dividing data into packets). This layer also provides flow control by adding buffering and windowing (the size of a window determines how many packets can be sent before receiving an acknowledgment).
- **Session**: This layer is responsible for controlling the synchronization of data between applications on different nodes, which it does by establishing, maintaining, and breaking sessions.
- **Presentation**: This layer translates data from a format used by applications to one in which it can be transported across the network. This layer provides encryption, compression, and decompression functionality.
- **Application**: This layer takes data from the users and passes it on to lower layers of the OSI model.

If the full import of this model is not apparent yet, you needn't worry: different aspects of it will be revisited throughout this text. This section deals primarily with the first four layers of the OSI model, as they are the most relevant to your understanding of basic networking.

LANs, WANs, and MANs

Most early PC networks focused on interconnecting computers within a single physical location, such as an office or a college campus. Networks which span such a limited physical space are called **local area networks**, or **LANs**. Even then, however, there were networks that connected computers to other, far away computers, such as on another college campus, another company, or a corporate office in another city. Such networks are called **wide-area networks**, or **WANs**. There are also networks that, while they cover a larger area than a LAN, nonetheless cover a fairly limited geographic entity such as a single city. Such networks are usually designated as **metropolitan area networks** (**MANs**).

Client-server and peer-to-peer networking

We can also distinguish networks by their structure. Many early networks followed a **client-server** model, in which the network is partitioned between providers of resources, called **servers**, and multiple nodes requesting services, called **clients**. Management and authentication are also centralized on such networks. At the time, specialized server software required more powerful computers than the typical desktop user had, and this type of partitioning made sense.

Later on, as desktop computers became more powerful, **peer-to-peer** networks, in which workloads are divided between peers, became more prevalent. In such a network, each peer can be a consumer and a provider of resources, and there is no centralized administration.

Layers 1 and 2 — topology and data link protocols

Networks require physical connections between computers or nodes, and there are several options when it comes to network topology. Early networks often employed a **bus topology**, in which nodes are connected to a single cable which acts as a backbone. A terminating resistor at either end of the cable prevented signal reflection. This topology had many advantages. It was simple to implement, and could function even if one or more nodes went down. There were several disadvantages, however. A break at any point in the cable, or a missing terminating resistor, could bring down the whole network.

Another problem stemmed from the protocol used on these early bus networks. Most of these networks used **Ethernet**, a technology that's commonly used for networking, and which defines the cabling used, the structure of network data (the frame), and the means of sending data. Early Ethernet networks used a method of sending data called **carrier sense multiple access** with **collision detection** (**CSMA/CD**). This method entails the following: a node that has a frame ready for transmission waits until the medium is idle. When the medium is idle, the node transmits a frame. The problem is that other nodes might also be transmitting frames at the same time. Therefore, each node that transmitted a frame must monitor for a collision. If a collision is detected, the transmitting node must resend the frame. The node will remain idle for a random period of time (thus avoiding a situation in which two or more nodes are constantly resending frames and causing collisions). If the medium is still idle after this random idle period, the node resends the frame. If not, it waits until the medium is idle to resend.

This early method of transmitting data sent frames to every node on the network. It was left to the **network interface card** (**NIC**) to reject frames that were not addressed to it. This, as you might imagine, was a potential security issue. Any node on the network, using a device called an **Ethernet sniffer**, could eavesdrop on frames that were not addressed to that node.

Such a method solved the problem of ensuring that data eventually got to its destination, but as you might have guessed, collisions on such networks are unavoidable, and the number of collisions increases as more nodes are added. As a result, competing technologies emerged to address this issue. The most popular of these was IBM's **token ring network**. A token ring network has a ring topology, although the ring was a logical one; the physical network topology was that of a star, with nodes connected to a device called a **Multistation Access Unit** (**MAU**) that functioned like a ring. A special frame, known as a **token**, traveled around the ring, and in order for a node to send a frame, it must seize the ring. This eliminated the problem of collisions. When IBM first introduced token ring hardware, the standard had a speed of 4 **megabits per second** (**Mbps**). Although this would, at first glance, place it as a disadvantage of Ethernet, which by then had been upgraded from 2.94 Mbps to 10 Mbps, since token ring networks had no collisions, they were able to achieve throughput that was comparable to or even better than Ethernet. The introduction of the 16 Mbps token ring technology in 1988 gave it even more of an advantage.

In spite of this, token ring struggled to achieve a significant market share, and in the end, Ethernet was able to prevail by providing more speed. **Fast Ethernet**, the designation given for Ethernet standards that provided speeds of 100 Mbps, was introduced as **100BASE-T**. This standard required either Cat-3 or Cat-5 twisted-pair cabling, and instead of using a physical bus topology, all nodes connected to a hub and thus 100BASE-T had a physical star topology (the hub still functioned as a logical bus, however). The issue of collisions was solved by replacing hubs (which simply re-transmits frames to every port on the hub except the port on which the frame was received) with switches, which only transmit the frame to the destination device. Switches use a store-and-forward mechanism to send data, and each port on a switch forms its own collision domain.

Other layer 2 devices include **repeaters** and **bridges**. Repeaters are unintelligent devices that re-transmit network signals, allowing us to effectively increase the total range of a network. For example, if we have two 100Base2 networks, each of these networks can span a total distance of 185 meters. By putting a repeater between the two network segments, we could combine them into a single network and effectively double the size of the network to 370 meters.

Bridges, which can also be used to connect network segments, are more intelligent devices. Like a repeater, a bridge enables us to connect multiple network segments. However, a bridge has a forwarding database that it uses to determine whether a frame gets forwarded to another port on the bridge. At first, the database is empty, and when the bridge receives a frame, it floods all ports on the bridge with the frame. Over time, however, the bridge learns which nodes are connected to each port (or more accurately, connected to the segment that is connected to a port), and only bridge then only sends the frame to the correct port.

Layers 3 and 4 — network and transport

With the advent of switches, bridges, and repeaters, a single network can become quite large. Nonetheless, we may want to divide such a network into two or more separate networks for organizational reasons (for example, separate networks for sales and marketing departments, or, in a SOHO environment, a Wi-Fi network for customers, and a separate internal network for the company). We may also want to connect to other people's networks. In such cases, we need a network protocol.

 It is commonplace to use the term network to refer to either [a] a network in the proper sense—a single network separated from other networks by a router—or [b] generically, to refer to the networked computers under our administrative control. When used in the latter sense, a network could actually refer to multiple networks using the former definition. For the sake of clarity, in this book, we will use the terms subnet, local network, or network segment to refer to a network in the former sense, and use the term network to refer to a group of network segments under the administrative control of a single entity.

The **Internetwork Packet Exchange/Sequenced Packet Exchange (IPX/SPX)** protocol suite, which was introduced by Novell in 1983, gained a great deal of traction, primarily because it was the protocol suite used by Novell Netware, which was the most popular network operating system from the late 1980s through the mid-1990s. IPX is the network layer protocol, while SPX is the transport layer protocol, providing connection-oriented services between nodes.

As the internet grew in popularity, however, IPX/SPX began to lose ground to **Transmission Control Protocol/Internet Protocol (TCP/IP)**, the protocol suite used on the internet. IP is the network layer of the suite, providing routing and addressing capabilities, and TCP is the transport layer of the suite, providing connection-oriented services and error-checking. TCP and IP are often discussed as if they are inseparable, but in cases where low latency is more important than reliability, IP can be paired with **User Datagram Protocol (UDP)**, a connectionless protocol which does not provide error-checking capabilities. Today, TCP/IP is the dominant protocol suite for the network and transport layers.

You may have noticed that there is some redundancy in the OSI model—namely, that between layer 2 and layer 3, there are multiple ways of addressing a node. If you were wondering if there is a protocol that allows us to discover the link layer address associated with a network address, there is—it is called **Address Resolution Protocol (ARP)**, and it is a layer 2 protocol. We can also obtain the network address if we have the link layer address using **Reverse ARP**.

IP addressing

Because of the dominance of TCP/IP on modern networks, it is important to understand the address scheme used by IP. The original address structure called for 32-bit addresses, divided into four octets of 8 bits each. This form of addressing in known as IPv4. Thus, when expressed in base-10 form, the addresses are expressed as four base-10 numbers—for example, 192.168.1.1. IP addresses are further divided into a network address (or prefix) and a node address. The network address is the portion of the address that identifies each network it is, and can be determined by the subnet mask. For example, if our subnet mask is 255.255.255.0, then the first 24 bits of the address form the network portion of the address. Thus, our network address would be 192.168.1.0, and we would be able to determine whether nodes are on the same network or different networks.

In the early days of the internet, the network portion of an IP address was determined by the first octet of the address. Networks were divided into class A, B, and C networks, as indicated in the following table:

Class	First octet	Subnet mask	Maximum number of nodes
A	1 to 126	255.0.0.0	16,777,216
B	128 to 191	255.255.0.0	65536
C	192 to 223	255.255.255.0	256

Note that the actual maximum number of nodes is actually two fewer than indicated in the table, as we do not use addresses in which the node portion is all zeros (for example, 192.168.1.0), and addresses in which the node portion is all 255s (for example, 192.168.1.255), which are reserved for broadcast messages.

You may have noticed that class A, B, and C networks do not cover all possible first octets. This is because a portion of the address space was reserved for special purposes:

First octet	Description
127	Reserved for loopback addresses
224 to 239	Reserved for multicast addresses (former class D)
240 to 255	Reserved for future use (former class E)

Class A networks were reserved for large organizations, class B networks were reserved for medium-sized organizations, and class C networks were reserved for small organizations. Although this scheme was adequate, it had some shortcomings. For example, if we need 1 million addresses, it is too many addresses for a class B network, but significantly fewer addresses than a class A network. The broad alternatives in this case are acquiring a class A network (in which case, we would have more addresses than we need), or acquiring multiple class B networks.

Partially because of this inflexibility, and partially because this original address scheme did not anticipate the rapid growth of the internet, the **Internet Engineering Task Force (IETF)**, the group responsible for promoting and developing internet standards, saw the exhaustion of the IPv4 address space as an inevitability. Thus, the IETF adopted a two-pronged approach to solve this problem. The long-term solution was to increase the number of bits in the address from 32 bits to 128. This address scheme eventually became standardized as IPv6. The IETF also adopted two measures in 1993 that greatly increased the life span of IPv4: **private networks** and **classless subnetting**.

 A more detailed description of IPv6 addressing, and the differences between IPv6 and IPv4, can be found in Chapter 3, *Configuring pfSense*.

Private networks are networks that use private IP address space. These addresses cannot be routed through the public internet, and are designated by the **Institute of Electrical and Electronics Engineers'** (IEEE) **Request For Comments** (RFC) 1918. The designations are as follows:

Class	Address range	Maximum number of nodes
A	10.0.0.0 to 10.255.255.255	16,777,216
B	172.16.0.0 to 172.31.255.255	1,048,576
C	192.168.0.0 to 192.168.255.255	256

Classless subnetting, or **Classless Inter-Domain Routing** (CIDR), replaces the classful network design. As with classful networks, the most significant bits of the address form the network portion of the address (or prefix) and the least significant portion of the address represents the node address (or node identifier). But with classless subnetting, the network prefix is not determined by the first octet, but can be arbitrarily defined to meet our needs.

To demonstrate how this works, consider the case of the private class C network, 192.168.1.0. Assume that we need to have two smaller networks, each able to accommodate about 100 nodes. We could have two separate private class C networks (for example, 192.168.1.0 and 192.168.2.0), but unless we anticipate the rapid growth of our network, this would represent a waste of address space.

By dividing 192.168.1.0 into two networks, we can have two smaller networks without wasting address space. We can divide our original network, which could accommodate 254 nodes (256 minus 1 for the network identifier or zero minus 1 for the broadcast address) into two networks which can accommodate 126 nodes (128 minus 1 minus 1). The network prefix of the first network is 192.168.1.0/25, and the network prefix of the second network is 192.168.1.128/25. Note that we have extended the network prefix by one bit so that we can partition the network. Also note that now that we can arbitrarily define the number of bits in the prefix, the number of bits in the prefix might not align on an octet boundary, and therefore we must specify the number of bits in the prefix, which we do by appending a forward slash and the number of bits (in this case, /25). This is called **CIDR notation**.

Because of classless subnetting, we can have a maximum of 1,048,576 nodes on a class B private network. This is because we only need 12 bits for the 172.16.0.0 private network. By moving the boundary for the prefix from 16 bits to 12, this leaves 4 more bits for the node identifier, or 20 bits ($2^{20} = 1,048,576$).

It is worth noting that IPv4 has three different address types:

- **Unicast**: With this type of address, a single address is specified. Thus, these addresses are used for point-to-point communications.
- **Broadcast**: This is the opposite of a unicast address. By using a broadcast address, we can target everyone on a subnet instead of a single node. The broadcast address is typically the last address in a subnet; for example, 192.168.1.255 is the broadcast address for the 192.168.1.0 network.
- **Multicast**: With this type of address, a group of nodes can send and receive data between the members of the group at one time by sending it to the multicast IP address. All members of the multicast group have the same multicast address.

Whereas hubs and switches allow network traffic within a network segment, inter-network communication requires specialized hardware. Such hardware devices are called **routers**, and in most cases, a router forwards a packet to another router, since there are typically several steps (or hops) between the source and destination. It is commonplace to have a router at the boundary between a private network and the public internet. Since connecting to the public internet raises security concerns, it is also common to place a firewall—a network device that controls incoming and outgoing traffic—on this boundary as well. Some hardware devices (such as a pfSense device) can function as both a firewall and a router, although a network may also have a dedicated firewall and a dedicated router.

If a node is communicating with a node on the same network segment, it can find the node via ARP without having to use a router. If the node is not on the local network, however, there are two ways the sending node can find a route to it. It might have a statically configured route to the host, otherwise known as a **static route**, in its routing table. If not, however, it can send the packet to the default gateway, assuming that a default gateway is configured. Such a gateway enables nodes to communicate with nodes on other network segments and other networks.

 In general, hubs operate on the physical layer of the OSI model; switches operate on the data link layer, and routers operate on the network layer. There are, however, devices known as **layer 3 switches**, which incorporate some routing functions.

Although this section is by no means an exhaustive guide to networking fundamentals, we have at least outlined the world of networking as it exists today. Ethernet is the dominant standard for networking hardware, and **Gigabit Ethernet** has supplanted Fast Ethernet as the de facto standard. On the networking and transport levels, TCP/IP is the dominant standard and although the roll out of IPv6 has been a slow one, it is gradually replacing IPv4.

Typical pfSense deployment scenarios

Once you have decided to add a pfSense system to your network, you need to consider how it is going to be deployed on your network. pfSense is suitable for a variety of networks, from small to large ones, and can be employed in a variety of deployment scenarios. In this section, we will cover the following possible uses for pfSense:

- Perimeter firewall
- Router
- Switch
- Wireless router/wireless access point

As this book is aimed at beginner pfSense users, we will mainly focus on the first two items, as these are the most common uses of a pfSense device. We will, however, briefly discuss the latter two items.

The most common way to add pfSense to your network is to use it as a perimeter firewall. In this scenario, your internet connection is connected to one port on the pfSense system, and your local network is connected to another port on the system. The port connected to the internet is known as the WAN interface, and the port connected to the local network is known as the LAN interface.

If pfSense is your perimeter firewall, you may choose to set it up as a dedicated firewall, or you might want to have it perform the double duty of a firewall and a router. You may also choose to have more than two interfaces in your pfSense system (known as optional interfaces). In order to act as a perimeter firewall, however, a pfSense system requires at least two interfaces: a WAN interface (to connect to outside networks), and a LAN interface (to connect to the local network).

The perimeter firewall performs two broad functions. The first, monitoring and controlling inbound traffic, should be fairly obvious. Allowing certain traffic on certain ports, while blocking all other traffic, is a core function of all firewalls. The second, monitoring and controlling outbound traffic, might seem less obvious, but is also important. Outbound web traffic tends to pass through the firewall unchallenged. This, however, leaves our network vulnerable to malware that targets web browsers. To protect our networks against such threats, we need to monitor outbound traffic as well.

It is commonplace to set up the networks behind the firewall with a split architecture, with assets that are accessible from the internet being kept separate from the rest of the network. In such cases, the internet-accessible resources are placed on a separate network, which is generally referred to as the **demilitarized zone** (**DMZ**). If your network requires such a setup, you can easily do this with pfSense as your perimeter firewall, as we will see later.

In more complex network setups, your pfSense system may have to exchange routing information with other routers on the network. There are two types of protocols for exchanging such information: distance vector protocols obtain their routing information by exchanging information with neighboring routers; routers use link-state protocols to build a map of the network in order to calculate the shortest path to another router, with each router calculating distances independently. pfSense is capable of running both types of protocols. Packages are available for distance vector protocols such as **Routing Information Protocol** (**RIP**) and **RIPv2**, and link-state protocols such as **Border Gateway Protocol** (**BGP**). These protocols will be discussed in greater detail in Chapter 10, *Routing and Bridging*.

Another common deployment scenario is to set up pfSense as a router. In a home or SOHO environment, firewall and router functions are often performed by the same device. In mid-sized to large networks, however, the router is a device that's separate from that of the perimeter firewall.

In larger networks which have several network segments, pfSense can be used to connect these segments. Traditionally, using a router to connect multiple networks requires multiple network interfaces on the router. However, with VLANs, we can use a single network interface card to operate in multiple broadcast domains via 802.1q tagging. VLANs are often used with the ever-popular router on a stick configuration, in which the router has a single physical connection to a switch (this connection is known as a trunk), with the single Ethernet interface divided into multiple VLANs, and the router forwarding packets between the VLANs. One of the advantages of this setup is that it only requires a single port, and, as a result, it allows us to use pfSense with systems where adding another NIC would be cumbersome or even impossible: for example, a laptop or certain thin clients. We will cover VLANs in greater depth in Chapter 3, *Configuring pfSense*.

In most cases, where pfSense is deployed as a router on mid-sized and large networks, it will be used to connect different LAN segments; however, it could also be used as a WAN router. In this case, pfSense's function would be to provide a private WAN connection to the end user.

It is possible to have pfSense function as a switch. This can be done by bridgin[g]
interfaces and thus bypassing the packet filtering capabilities of pfSense. This
not recommended, however, for several reasons. A dedicated switch can be p   a
fraction of the cost of a pfSense device (for example, a 5-port gigabit Ethernet
purchased for less than 15 U.S. dollars). These switches will likely outperforr
since pfSense is limited by the bus speed of the expansion bus on which the r
reside. Finally, there is an administrative overhead involved in using pfSens
while commercially available unmanaged switches are designed to be plug-
Managed switches can be more difficult to configure, but the pay off of usir   es
is that they support more advanced features such as VLANs. For these reas
generally not recommended that you use pfSense as a switch.

Another possibility is using pfSense as a **wireless access point (WAP)**/router. `i`   e
done by adding a wireless network card to one of the expansion slots on your pf.
system. If you decide to go this route, you will want to check the FreeBSD **Hardware**
Compatibility List (HCL) to make sure that the wireless card you use is compatible with
pfSense.

One way to add wireless capabilities to your network without having to worry about
hardware compatibility issues, however, is to use a commercially available wireless access
point or wireless router and connect it to your pfSense device. If you use a router, you will
likely want to operate it in wireless access point mode, if it has one. You can then configure
pfSense to run a DHCP server on the interface to which the WAP or router is connected.
Nodes connecting to the WAP or wireless router will then be able to obtain an IP address
from pfSense's DHCP server.

Hardware requirements and sizing guidelines

Once you have decided where to deploy pfSense on your network, you should have a
clearer idea of what your hardware requirements are. As a minimum, you will need a CPU,
motherboard, memory (RAM), some form of disk storage, and at least two network
interfaces (unless you are opting for a router on a stick setup, in which case you only need
one network interface). You may also need one or more optional interfaces.

Minimum requirements

The starting point for our discussion on hardware requirements is pfSense's minimum specifications. As of January 2016, the minimum hardware requirements are as follows (these specifications are from the official pfSense site, `https://www.pfsense.org/`):

- **CPU**: 500 MHz (1 GHz recommended)
- **RAM**: 512 MB (1 GB recommended)

 pfSense requires a 64-bit Intel (x86-64) or AMD (amd64) CPU. pfSense 2.5 will require a processor that supports AES-NI encryption and decryption, so take that into account when choosing a CPU. There are three separate images available: CD, CD on a USB memstick, and an image for the Netgate SG-3100 system. The active default console for the CD and USB memstick images is VGA, while the active default console for the Netgate image is serial. The NanoBSD images (for embedded systems, which had the serial console as their default) were deprecated with the release of pfSense 2.4. The serial console can be enabled on images which default to VGA via the web GUI by navigating to **System | Advanced**.

A pfSense installation requires at least 1 GB of disk space. If you are installing to an embedded device, you can access the console either by a serial or VGA port. A step-by-step installation guide for the pfSense Live CD can be found on the official pfSense website at: `https://doc.pfsense.org/index.php/Installing_pfSense`.

Version 2.3 eliminated the Live CD, which allowed you to try out pfSense without installing it onto other media. If you really want to use the Live CD, however, you could use a pre-2.3 image (version 2.2.6 or earlier). You can always upgrade to the latest version of pfSense after installation.

Installation onto either a **hard disk drive** (**HDD**) or an SSD is the most common option for a full install of pfSense, whereas embedded installs typically use CF, SD, or USB media. A full install of the current version of pfSense will fit onto a 1 GB drive, but will leave little room for installation of packages or log files. Any activity that requires caching, such as running a proxy server, will also require additional disk space.

The last installation option is installation onto an embedded system using the Netgate ADI image. Netgate currently sells the SG-3100, which is advertised as an appliance that can be used in many deployment scenarios, including firewalls, LAN or WAN routers, VPN appliances, and DHCP or DNS servers. It targets small and medium-sized businesses and may appeal to home and business users seeking a reliable firewall appliance with a low total cost of ownership. Storage (without upgrading) is limited to 8 GB of eMMC flash, which would limit which packages could be installed.

Hardware sizing guidelines

The minimum hardware requirements are general guidelines, and you may want to exceed these minimums based on different factors. It may be useful to consider these factors when determining what CPU, memory, and storage device to use:

- For the CPU, requirements increase for faster internet connections. Guidelines for the CPU and network cards can be found at the official pfSense site at http://pfsense.org/hardware/#requirements. The following general guidelines apply: the minimum hardware specifications (Intel/AMD CPU of 500 MHz or greater) are valid up to 20 Mbps. CPU requirements begin to increase at speeds greater than 20 Mbps.
- Connections of 100 Mbps or faster will require PCI-E network adapters to keep up with the increased network throughput.

If you intend to use pfSense to bridge interfaces—for example, if you want to bridge a wireless and wired network, or if you want to use pfSense as a switch—then the PCI bus speed should be considered. The PCI bus can easily become a bottleneck. Therefore, in such scenarios, using PCI-e hardware is the better option, as it offers up to 31.51 GB/s (for PCI-e v. 4.0 on a 16-lane slot) versus 533 MB/s for the fastest conventional PCI buses.

If you plan on using pfSense as a VPN server, then you should take into account the effect VPN usage will have on the CPU. Each VPN connection requires the CPU to encrypt traffic, and the more connections there are, the more the CPU will be taxed. Generally, the most cost-effective solution is to use a more powerful CPU. But there are ways to reduce the CPU load from VPN traffic. Soekris has the vpn14x1 product range; these cards offload the CPU for computing-intensive tasks such as encryption and compression. AES-NI acceleration of IPSec also significantly reduces the CPU requirements.

If you have hundreds of simultaneous captive portal users, you will require slightly more CPU power than you would otherwise. Captive portal usage does not put as much of a load on the CPU as VPN usage, but if you anticipate having a lot of captive portal users, you will want to take this into consideration.

If you're not a power user, 512 MB of RAM might be enough for your pfSense system. This, however, would leave little room for the state table (where, as mentioned earlier, active connections are tracked). Each state requires about 1 KB of memory, which is less memory than some consumer-grade routers require, but you still want to be mindful of RAM if you anticipate having a lot of simultaneous connections. The other components of pfSense require 32 MB to 48 MB of RAM, and possibly more, depending on which features you are using, so you have to subtract that from the available memory in calculating the maximum state table size:

256 MB	~22,000 connections
512 MB	~46,000 connections
1 GB	~93,000 connections
2 GB	~190,000 connections

Installing packages can also increase your RAM requirements; **Snort** and **ntop** are two such examples. You should also probably not install packages if you have limited disk space. Proxy servers in particular use up a fair amount of disk space, which is something you should probably consider if you plan on installing a proxy server such as Squid.

The amount of disk space, as well as the form of storage you utilize, will likely be dictated by what packages you install, and what forms of logging you will have enabled. Some packages are more taxing on storage than others. Some packages require more disk space than others. Proxies such as Squid store web pages; anti-spam programs such as pfBlocker download lists of blocked IP addresses, and therefore require additional disk space. Proxies also tend to perform a great deal of read and write operations, therefore, if you are going to install a proxy, disk I/O performance is something you should likely take into consideration.

You may be tempted to opt for the cheapest NICs. However, inexpensive NICs often have complex drivers that offload most of the processing to the CPU. They can saturate your CPU with interrupt handling, thus causing missed packets. Cheaper network cards typically have smaller buffers (often no more than 300 KB), and when the buffers become full, packets are dropped. In addition, many of them do not support Ethernet frames that are larger than the **maximum transmission unit** (**MTU**) of 1,500 bytes.

NICs that do not support larger frames cannot send or receive jumbo frames (frames with an MTU larger than 1,500 bytes), and therefore they cannot take advantage of the performance improvement that using jumbo frames would bring. In addition, such NICs will often have problems with VLAN traffic, since a VLAN tag increases the size of the Ethernet header beyond the traditional size limit.

The pfSense project recommends NICs based on Intel chipsets, and there are several reasons why such NICs are considered reliable. They tend to have adequately sized buffers, and do not have problems processing larger frames. Moreover, the drivers tend to be well-written and work well with UNIX-based operating systems.

For a typical pfSense setup, you will need two network interfaces: one for the WAN and one for the LAN. If you do not configure **virtual LANs (VLANs)**, then each additional subnet (for example, for a guest network) will require an additional interface, as will each additional WAN interface. VLANs, which we will cover in Chapter 3, *Configuring pfSense*, enable us to have several subnets on the same interface. It should also be noted that you don't need an additional card for each interface added; you can buy a multiport network card (most of such cards have either two or four ports). You don't need to buy new NICs for your pfSense system; in fact, it is often economical to buy used NICs, and except in rare cases, the performance level will be the same.

If you want to incorporate wireless connectivity into your network, you may consider adding a wireless card to your pfSense system. As mentioned earlier, however, the likely better option is to use pfSense in conjunction with a separate wireless access point. If you do decide to add a wireless card to your system and configure it for use as an access point, you will want to check the FreeBSD hardware compatibility list before making a purchase.

Budget-priced options

Although it's generally a good idea to determine the minimum specifications of your pfSense system and then select hardware accordingly, you may have old hardware that can be re-purposed. In this section, we will briefly consider three such options, which will enable you to assemble a pfSense router/firewall on the most limited of budgets.

Using an old desktop system

If you have been using computers for any amount of time, you may have an old desktop that can be used with pfSense. Even if you do not, old desktop computers can be purchased relatively cheaply ($100 U.S. and under). For example, a brief web search resulted in me finding an HP Compaq 8100 Elite desktop system with the following specifications:

- Intel 64-bit i5-650 processor; 3.2 GHz
- 4 GB RAM
- 500 GB SATA hard drive
- DVD-RW drive
- Expansion slots: 1 PCI-e x1; 1 PCI-e x 4; 1 PCI-e x 1; 1 legacy (32-bit) PCI

As you can see, this system, which costs less than $100 U.S. (including shipping), easily meets the minimum requirements for a pfSense system. Three of the four expansion slots will accommodate a multi-port network interface card (there is also an on-board Ethernet interface). Moreover, the i5-650 supports AES-NI encryption (in fact, as a processor based on the Westmere microarchitecture, it is one of the oldest Intel processors that supports such encryption); therefore it will be compatible with pfSense 2.5.

There are drawbacks to using a desktop system such as this. The power consumption will be that of a typical desktop computer. In addition, the hard drive is a typical SATA drive; the **mean time between failures** (**MTBF**) for traditional hard drives is about three years, so the possibility of a hard drive failure is something to consider. Using a thin client rather than typical desktop computers addresses these two concerns, as their power consumption is lower than that of desktop systems; moreover, they typically have some form of flash storage or **solid-state drive** (**SSD**), which should be less likely to fail than a traditional hard drive. Still, using a desktop computer such as this for pfSense is a reasonably low-cost option.

Using a thin client

Thin clients are lightweight computers that are optimized for logging into remote servers, and they are ideal for situations in which much of the processing is going to be offloaded to the server. Their properties also make them ideal for use with pfSense for the following reasons:

- They utilize less power than most desktop computers. For example, an HP t5740e thin client uses 10.7 watts of power (according to HP's documentation) and it is not uncommon to see thin clients with power consumption at approximately this level.

- They are likely to use flash storage or an SSD, which is less likely to fail than an IDE or SATA hard drive.
- Because they are designed to connect to a server, they have built-in networking capabilities. A typical thin client will have a built-in Gigabit Ethernet interface, thus providing at least one of the two interfaces needed for a pfSense system.

There are drawbacks, however, to using a thin client. Disk space can be limited (sometimes to either 2 GB or 4 GB); therefore, if you plan on installing a lot of third-party packages or maintaining large log files, this may not be the best option. Moreover, unless you plan to use pfSense with a single Ethernet port (for more about this, see the next subsection), you will need to install a network interface card on your thin client, and the expansion options on thin clients are limited. Expansion modules for thin clients typically exist, but they may only accommodate low-profile cards. Furthermore, even when adding a network card is technically possible, sometimes unforeseen difficulties emerge. For example, I found an HP thin client that met the minimum pfSense specifications, installed the expansion module, and added a four-port network card to the expansion module, only to find that the unit overheated when the network card was installed. Using a thin client is probably the best option if you want to optimize for power consumption, but it is also an open invitation to various setbacks. Before you purchase a thin client for use with pfSense, you will definitely want to do your homework. Consulting online pfSense forums is not a bad idea, either.

Using an old laptop

You might be wondering if using an old laptop as a pfSense router is a good idea. In many respects, laptops are good candidates for being repurposed into routers. They are small, energy efficient, and when the AC power shuts off, they run on battery power, so they have a built-in uninterruptable power supply (UPS). Moreover, many old laptops can be purchased relatively cheaply at thrift shops and online.

There is, however, one critical limitation to using a laptop as a router: in almost all cases, they only have one Ethernet port. Moreover, there is often no realistic way to add another NIC, as there are no expansion slots that will take another NIC (some, however, do have PCMCIA slots that will take a second NIC). There are gigabit USB-to-Ethernet adapters (for USB 3.0), but this is not much of a solution. Such adapters do not have the reliability of traditional NICs. Most laptops do not have Intel NICs either; high-end business laptops are usually the exception to this rule.

There is a way to use a laptop with a single Ethernet port as a pfSense router, and that is to configure pfSense using VLANs. As mentioned earlier, VLANs, or virtual LANs, allow us to use a single NIC to serve multiple subnets. Thus, we can set up two VLANs on our single port: virtual LAN #1, which we will use for the WAN interface, and virtual LAN #2, which we will use for the LAN interface. The one disadvantage of this setup is that you must use a managed switch to make this work. Managed switches are switches that can usually be configured and managed as groups, they often have both a command-line and web interface for management, and they often have a wide range of capabilities, such as VLANs. Since unmanaged switches forward traffic to all other ports, they are unsuitable for this setup. You can, however, connect an unmanaged switch to the managed switch to add ports. Keep in mind that managed switches are expensive (more expensive than dual and quad port network cards), and if there are multiple VLANs on a single link, this link can easily become overloaded. In scenarios where you can add a network card, this is usually the better option. If you have an existing laptop, however, a managed switch with VLANs is a workable solution.

Installing pfSense

You will also want to download the MD5 checksum file in order to verify the integrity of the downloaded image. Verifying the integrity of downloads serves two purposes:

- It ensures that the download completed
- It safeguards against a party maliciously tampering with the images

In order to safeguard against the latter, however, be sure to download the checksum from a different mirror site than the site from which you downloaded the image. This provides an additional measure of security should an individual mirror site be compromised. Windows has several utilities for displaying MD5 hashes for a file. Under BSD and Linux, generating the MD5 hash is as easy as typing the following command:

```
md5 pfSense-LiveCD-2.4.3-RELEASE-amd64.iso
```

This command will generate the MD5 checksum for the 64-bit Live CD version for pfSense 2.4.3. Compare the resulting hash with the contents of the .md5 file that you downloaded from the pfSense website. Windows has several utilities for displaying SHA256 hashes for a file. Under BSD and Linux, generating the SHA256 hash is as easy as typing the following command:

```
shasum -a 256 pfSense-LiveCD-2.4.3-RELEASE-amd64.iso.gz
```

This command will generate the MD5 checksum for the 64-bit Live CD version for pfSense 2.4.3. Compare the resulting hash with the contents of the `.sha256` file you downloaded from one of the (other) mirrors. Under BSD and Linux, generating the MD5 hash is as easy as typing the following command:

```
md5 pfSense-LiveCD-2.4.3-RELEASE-amd64.iso
```

This command will generate the MD5 checksum for the 64-bit Live CD version for pfSense 2.4.3. Compare the resulting hash with the contents of the `.md5` file you downloaded from the pfSense website.

If you are doing a full install from the Live CD or memory stick, then you just need to write the ISO to the target media, boot from either the CD or memory stick, perform some basic configuration, and then invoke the installer.

Step-by-step installation guide

You can go through the following steps in order to install pfSense on your system:

1. Browse to the **Download** section of `https://www.pfsense.org/` and select the appropriate computer architecture (64-bit or Netgate ADI), the appropriate platform (live CD or memstick), and you should be presented with a list of mirrors. Choose the closest one for the best performance:
   - If the system hangs during the boot process, there are several options you can try. The first menu that appears, as pfSense boots, has several options. The last two options are **Kernel** and **Configure Boot Options**. **Kernel** allows you to select which kernel to boot from among the available kernels:
     - If you have a reason to suspect that the FreeBSD kernel being used is not compatible with your hardware, you might want to switch to the older version. **Configure Boot Options** launches a menu (shown in the preceding screenshot) with several useful options. A description of these options can be found at `https://www.freebsd.org/doc/en_US.ISO8859-1/books/ handbook/`. Toggling [A]CPI Support to off can help in some cases, as ACPI's hardware discovery and configuration capabilities may cause the pfSense boot process to hang. If turning this off doesn't work, you could try booting in Safe [M]ode, and if all else fails, you can toggle [V]erbose mode to On, which will give you detailed messages while booting.

- While booting, pfSense provides information about your hardware, including expansion buses that are supported, network interfaces found, and USB support. When this is finished, the graphical installer will launch and you will see the copyright and distribution notice.

2. Select **Accept** and press *Enter* to accept these terms and conditions and continue with the installation.

3. The installer then provides you with three options: **Install pfSense**, **Rescue Shell**, and **Recover config.xml**. In most cases, you can choose the first option and proceed with the installation. The **Rescue Shell** option launches a BSD shell prompt from which you can perform functions that might prove helpful in repairing a non-functional pfSense system. For example, you can copy, delete, and edit files from the shell prompt. If you suspect that a recent configuration change is what caused pfSense to break, however, and you saved the configuration file before making the change, the easiest way to fix your system may be to invoke **Recover config.xml** and restore pfSense from the previously saved `config.xml` file:

    - The next screen provides keymap options. Version 2.4.3 supports 99 different keyboard layouts, including both QWERTY and Dvorak layouts. Highlighting a keymap option and pressing *Enter* selects that option. There's also an option to test the default keymap, and an option to continue with the default keymap.

4. Select **Accept**, and press *Enter* when you have selected a keymap.

5. Next, the installer provides the following disk partitioning options: **Auto (UFS)**, **Manual**, **Shell**, and **Auto (ZFS)**. The first and last options allow you to format the disk with the **Unix File System** (**UFS**) and Oracle's **ZFS**, respectively:

    - In general, UFS is the tried-and-true file system, while ZFS was created with security in mind and incorporates many newer features such as file system-level encryption and data checksums.

    - **Manual**, as the name implies, allows you to manually create, delete, and modify partitions. There are several choices for partition types; you can even create an **Apple Partition Map** (**APM**) or a DOS partition, if that suits you. The **Shell** option drops you to a BSD shell prompt from which you can also manually create, delete, and modify partitions using shell commands.

6. If you chose ZFS, the next screen will present a series of options that allow you to further configure your ZFS volume. If not, skip to step 8:

- **Pool Type/Disks** allows you to select the type of redundancy. The default option is stripe, which provides no redundancy at all. The mirror option provides for duplicate volumes, in which the array continues to operate as long as one drive is functioning. The raid10 option combines mirroring and striping (it is an array of mirrored drives). It requires at least four drives; the array continues to operate if one drive fails; up to half the drives in the RAID can fail so long as they aren't all from the same subset.

- The next three options, **raidz1**, **raidz2**, and **raidz3**, are non-standard RAID options. Like RAID levels 5 though, they achieve redundancy through a parity stripe, although the parity stripes in Z1, Z2, and Z3 are dynamically sized. RAID-Z1 requires at least three disks/volumes and allows one of them to fail without data loss; RAID-Z2 requires four disks/volumes and allows two to fail; RAID-Z3 requires five disks/volumes and allows three to fail.

The installer will not let you proceed unless your RAID set has the minimum number of volumes for the configuration you selected.

7. If your ZFS RAID is configured correctly, the installer will then present you with a series of ZFS-specific options. You can change the pool Name (the default is `zroot`), toggle **Force 4K Sectors** on or off depending on whether or not you want sectors to align on 4K boundaries, and toggle **Encrypt Disks** on or off. You can also select a partition scheme for the system:

- The default is **GUID Partition Table** (**GPT**), but the legacy **Master Boot Record** (**MBR**) is also supported. You can set it up to boot in **BIOS mode**, **Unified Extensible Firmware Interface** (**UEFI**) mode, or, if your system supports it, both modes. UEFI-based systems, by specification, can only boot from GPT partitions, while some BIOS-based systems can boot from GPT partitions (and all BIOS-based systems can boot from MBR partitions). There is also support for the FreeBSD patch that fixes a bug that prevents GPT partitions from booting on some Lenovo systems (GPT and Lenovo Fix). You can also set the **Swap Size**, toggle **Mirror Swap** on or off, and toggle **Encrypt Swap** on or off.

8. After you have made all the desired modifications, you can proceed; the installer will format all selected volumes, extract the archive files, and install pfSense. You will also be given an option to open a shell prompt to make any final modifications. Otherwise, you can reboot the system and run the newly installed copy of pfSense:

- If you were unable to install pfSense onto the target media, you may have to troubleshoot your system and/or installation media. If you are attempting to install from the CD, your optical drive may be malfunctioning, or the CD may be faulty. You may want to start with a known good bootable disc and see if the system will boot off of it. If it can, then your pfSense disk may be at fault; burning the disc again may solve the problem. If, however, your system cannot boot off the known good disc, then the optical drive itself, or the cables connecting the optical drive to the motherboard, may be at fault.

- In some cases, however, none of the aforementioned possibilities hold true, and it is possible that the FreeBSD boot loader will not work on the target system. If so, then you could opt to install pfSense on a different system.

- Another possibility is to install pfSense onto a hard drive on a separate system, then transfer the hard drive into the target system. In order to do this, go through the installation process on another system as you would normally until you get to the **Assign Interfaces** prompt. When the installer asks if you want to assign VLANS, type **n**. Type `exit` at the **Assign Interfaces** prompt to skip the interface assignment. Proceed through the rest of the installation, and then power down the system and transfer the hard drive to the target system. Assuming that the pfSense hard drive is in the boot sequence, the system should boot pfSense and detect the system's hardware correctly. Then, you should be able to assign network interfaces. The rest of the configuration can then proceed as usual.

9. If you have not encountered any of these problems, the software should be installed on the target system, and you should get a dialog box telling you to remove the CD from the optical drive tray and press *Enter*. The system will now reboot, and you will be booting into your new pfSense installation for the first time.

Initial pfSense configuration

If the installation was successful, you should see a screen similar to the one shown in the following screenshot:

```
FreeBSD/amd64 (thewookie.thewookie.duckdns.org) (ttyv0)

VirtualBox Virtual Machine - Netgate Device ID: b3bd7fcb975cb1b874f0

*** Welcome to pfSense 2.4.3-RELEASE (amd64) on thewookie ***

 WAN (wan)        -> em0       -> v4/DHCP4: 10.0.2.15/24
 LAN (lan)        -> em1       -> v4: 172.16.1.2/16
                                 v6: 1234:5678:9a::1/48
 OPT_WAN (opt1)  -> em2       ->
 PFSYNC (opt2)   -> em3       -> v4: 10.0.10.10/24

 0) Logout (SSH only)              9) pfTop
 1) Assign Interfaces             10) Filter Logs
 2) Set interface(s) IP address   11) Restart webConfigurator
 3) Reset webConfigurator password 12) PHP shell + pfSense tools
 4) Reset to factory defaults     13) Update from console
 5) Reboot system                 14) Disable Secure Shell (sshd)
 6) Halt system                   15) Restore recent configuration
 7) Ping host                     16) Restart PHP-FPM
 8) Shell

Enter an option: █
```

The console menu in pfSense 2.4.3

Some of the initial configuration must be done at the console, while some aspects of the configuration, such as VLAN and DHCP setup, can be done from either the console or the web GUI. Configuration takes place in two phases. Some configuration must be done at the console, including interface configuration and interface IP address assignment. Some configuration steps, such as VLAN and DHCP setup, can be done both at the console and within the web GUI. On initial bootup, pfSense will automatically configure the WAN and LAN interfaces, according to the following parameters:

- Network interfaces will be assigned to device IDs **em0**, **em1**, and so on
- The WAN interface will be assigned to em0, and the LAN interface will be assigned to **em1**
- The WAN interface will look to an upstream DHCP server for its IP address, while the LAN interface will initially be assigned an IP address of **192.168.1.1**

You can, of course, accept these default assignments and proceed to the web G

UI, but chances are you will need to change at least some of these settings. If you need to change interface assignments, select 1 from the menu.

Configuration from the console

On boot, you should eventually see a menu identical to the one seen on the CD version, with the boot multi or single user options, and other options. After a timeout period, the boot process will continue and you will get an Options menu. If the default interface assignments are unsatisfactory, select **1** from the menu to begin interface assignment. This is where the network cards installed in the system are given their roles as WAN, LAN, and optional interfaces (OPT1, OPT2, and so on).

If you select this option, you will be presented with a list of network interfaces. This list provides four pieces of information:

- pfSense's device name for the interface (**fxp0**, **em1**, and so on)
- The MAC address of the interface
- The link state of the interface (up if a link is detected; down otherwise)
- The manufacturer and model of the interface (Intel PRO 1000, for example)

As you are probably aware, generally speaking, no two network cards have the same MAC address, so each of the interfaces in your system should have a unique MAC address:

1. To begin the configuration, select **1** and *Enter* for the Assign Interfaces option.
2. After that, a prompt will show up for VLAN configuration.
3. If you wish to set up VLANs, see `Chapter 3`, *pfSense Configuration*. Otherwise, type **n** and press *Enter*. Keep in mind that you can always configure VLANs later on.
4. The interfaces must be configured, and you will be prompted for the WAN interface first.
5. If you only configure one interface, it will be assigned to the WAN, and you will subsequently be able to log in to pfSense through this port. This is not what you would normally want, as the WAN port is typically accessible from the other side of the firewall.
6. When at least one other interface is configured, you will no longer be able to log in to pfSense from the WAN port. Unless you are using VLANs, you will have to set up at least two network interfaces.

In pfSense, network interfaces are assigned rather cryptic device names (for example, **fxp0**, **em1**, and so on) and it is not always easy to know which ports correspond to particular device names. One way of solving this problem is to use the automatic interface assignment feature:

1. To do this, unplug all network cables from the system, and then type a and press *Enter* to begin auto-detection.
2. The WAN interface is the first interface to be detected, so plug a cable into the port you intend to be the WAN interface. This process is repeated with each successive interface.
3. The LAN interface is configured next, and then each of the optional interfaces (OPT1, OPT2, and so on).
4. Once you have finished configuration, type y at the Do you want to proceed? prompt, or type n and press *Enter* to re-assign the interfaces.
5. Option two on the menu is **Set interface(s) IP address**, and you will likely want to complete this step as well. When you invoke this option, you will be prompted to specify which interface's IP address is to be set.
6. If you select the WAN interface, you will be asked if you want to configure the IP address via DHCP. In most scenarios, this is probably the option you want to choose, especially if pfSense is acting as a firewall. In that case, the WAN interface will receive an IP address from your ISP's DHCP server. For all other interfaces (or if you choose not to use DHCP on the WAN interface), you will be prompted to enter the interface's IPv4 address.
7. The next prompt will ask you for the subnet bit count. In most cases, you'll want to enter 8 if you are using a class A private address, 16 for class B, and 24 for class C, but if you are using classless subnetting (for example, to divide a class C network into two separate networks), then you will want to set the bit count accordingly.
8. You will also be prompted for the IPv4 gateway address (any interface with a gateway set is a WAN, and pfSense supports multiple WANs); if you are not configuring the WAN interface, you can just press *Enter* here.

 If auto-detection does not work, or you do not want to use it, you can always choose manual configuration. You can always reassign network interfaces later on, so even if you make a mistake in this step, the mistake can be easily fixed.

The advantages of IPv6 over IPv4 will be discussed fully in Chapter 3, *Configuring pfSense.*

We have now configured as much as we need to from the console (actually, we have done more than we have to, since we really only have to configure the WAN interface from the console). The remainder of the configuration can be done from the pfSense web GUI.

Configuration from the web GUI

The pfSense web GUI can only be accessed from another PC. If the WAN was the only interface that was assigned during the initial setup, then you will be able to access pfSense through the WAN IP address. Once one of the local interfaces is configured (typically the LAN interface), pfSense can no longer be accessed through the WAN interface. You will, however, be able to access pfSense from the local side of the firewall (typically through the LAN interface). In either case, you can access the web GUI by connecting another computer to the pfSense system, either directly (with a crossover cable) or indirectly (through a switch), and then typing either the WAN or LAN IP address into the connected computer's web browser.

If you enabled the LAN interface but did not enable DHCP on LAN, or if you are accessing the web GUI on another computer on the LAN network, you must statically set the IP address on that computer to a valid IP address for the LAN network (for example, if the LAN interface IP address is 192.168.1.1 and the LAN network is 192.168.1.0/24, set it to 192.168.1.2 or any number other than 1 for the last octet).

1. When you initially log in to pfSense, the default username/password combination will be admin/pfsense, respectively.
2. On your first login, the **Setup Wizard** will begin automatically.
3. Click on the **Next** button to begin configuration.
4. The first screen provides a link for information about a pfSense Gold Netgate Global Support subscription. You can click on the link to sign up to learn more, or click on the **Next** button.
5. On the next screen, you will be prompted to enter the hostname of the router as well as the domain. Hostnames can contain letters, numbers, and hyphens, but must begin with a letter. If you have a domain, you can enter it in the appropriate field.

6. In the **Primary DNS Server and Secondary DNS Server** fields, you can enter your DNS servers. If you are using DHCP for your WAN, you can probably leave these fields blank, as they will usually be assigned automatically by your ISP. However, your ISP's DNS servers may not be reliable. There are many third-party DNS servers available, including OpenDNS (`208.67.220.220` and `208.67.222.222`) and Google Public DNS (`8.8.8.8` and `8.8.4.4`). Uncheck the Override DNS checkbox if you want to use third-party DNS servers rather than the DNS servers used by your ISP. Click on **Next** when finished.

7. The next screen will prompt you for the **Network Time Protocol** (NTP) server as well as the local time zone. The NTP server configuration will be covered in greater detail in the next chapter; you can keep the default value for the server hostname for now. For the **Timezone** field, you should select the zone which matches your location and click on Next.

8. The next screen of the wizard is the WAN configuration page. If you need to make changes to the WAN configuration, see the detailed guide in the advanced WAN configuration. The two most common options most users will want to configure are the **Block RFC1918 Private Networks** and **Block Bogon Networks** checkboxes (in most cases, both should be checked). When you are done configuring WAN options, click on **Next**.

9. The next screen provides fields in which you can change the LAN IP address and subnet mask, but only if you configured the LAN interface previously. You can keep the default, or change it to another value within the private address blocks. You may want to choose an address range other than the very common 192.168.1.x in order to avoid a conflict. Be aware that, if you change the LAN IP address value, you will also need to adjust your PC's IP address, or release and renew its DHCP lease when you're finished with the network interface. You will also have to change the pfSense IP address in your browser to reflect the change.

10. The final screen of the pfSense **Setup Wizard** allows you to change the admin password, which you should do now. Enter the password, enter it again for confirmation in the next edit box, and click on **Next**. Later on, you can create another administrator account with a username other than admin and disable the admin account for additional security, unless you plan on setting up multiple firewalls for high availability, in which case you will need to retain the admin account.

11. On the following screen, there will be a **Reload** button; click on **Reload**. This will reload pfSense with the new changes.

12. Once you have completed the wizard, you should have network connectivity. Although there are other means of making changes to pfSense's configuration, if you want to repeat the wizard, you can do so by navigating to **System | Setup Wizard**. Completion of the wizard will take you to the pfSense dashboard.

Advanced WAN configuration

In most scenarios, you won't need to make any changes to the WAN in comparison to what was done at the console (at least initially; a multi-WAN setup is more involved, and will be discussed more fully in `Chapter 9`, *Multiple WANs*).

If you need to make changes, however, there are several options on this page:

1. For **Selected Type**, you have several options, but the most commonly used options are **DHCP** (the default type) or **Static**. If your pfSense system is behind another firewall and it is not going to receive an IP address from an upstream DHCP server, then you should probably choose Static. If pfSense is going to be a perimeter firewall, however, then **DHCP** is likely the correct setting, since your ISP will probably dynamically assign an IP address (this is not always the case, as you may have an IP address statically assigned to you by your ISP, but it is the more likely scenario).

2. The other choices are **Point-to-Point Protocol over Ethernet (PPPoE)** and **Point-to-Point Tunneling Protocol (PPTP)**. Your ISP may require that you use one of these options for the WAN interface; if you are not sure, check with them.

3. If you selected either **PPPoE** or **PPTP**, you will have to scroll down to the appropriate part of the page to enter parameters for these connections.

4. At a minimum, you will likely have to enter the **Username** and **Password** for such connections. In addition, PPTP requires that you enter a local IP address and a remote IP address.

5. The **dial-on-demand** checkbox for PPPoE and PPTP connections allows you to connect to an ISP, but only when a user requests data that requires an internet connection. Both PPPoE and PPTP support an Idle timeout setting, which specifies how long the connection will be kept open after transmitting data when this option is invoked. Leaving this field blank disables this function.

6. We can now turn our attention to the **General Configuration** section. The **MAC address** field allows you to enter a MAC address that is different from the actual MAC address of the WAN interface. This can be useful if your ISP will not recognize an interface with a different MAC address from the device that was previously connected, or if you want to acquire a different IP address (changing the MAC address will cause the upstream DHCP server to assign a different address).

7. If you use this option, make sure the portion of the address reserved for the **Organizationally Unique Identifier** (**OUI**) is a valid OUI—in other words, an OUI assigned to a network card manufacturer. (The OUI portion of the address is the first three bytes of a MAC-48 address and the first five bytes of an **Extended Unique Identifier** (**EUI**)-48 address.)

8. The next few fields can usually be left blank. **Maximum Transmission Unit** (**MTU**) allows you to change the MTU size if necessary. DHCP hostname allows you to send a hostname to your ISP when making a DHCP request, which is useful if your ISP requires this.

9. The **Block RFC1918 Private Networks** checkbox, if checked, will block registered private networks (as defined by RFC 1918) from connecting to the WAN interface. The **Block Bogon Networks** option blocks traffic from reserved and/or unassigned IP addresses. For the WAN interface, you should check both options unless you have special reasons for not invoking these options. Click the **Next** button when you are done.

> **Point-to-Point Protocol** (**PPP**) and **Layer 2 Tunneling Protocol** (**L2TP**) are also valid choices for the WAN configuration type. However, the **Setup Wizard** does not allow the user to select either of these. In order to select PPP or L2TP, navigate to **Interfaces** | **WAN** from the top menu, and select PPP or L2TP in either the IPv4 configuration type or IPv6 configuration type drop-down box (or both). Setup is similar to the setup for PPPoE and PPTP—you will have to enter a username and password—and in the case of PPP, you will also have to enter your ISP's phone number in the **Phone number** field.

Additional setup options

You can find several configuration options under **System** | **General Setup**. Most of these are identical to settings that can be configured in the **Setup Wizard** (**Hostname**, **Domain**, **DNS servers**, **Timezone**, and **NTP server**). There are two additional settings available:

1. The **Language** drop-down box allows you to select the web configurator language.

2. Under the **Web Configurator** section, there is a **Theme** drop-down box that allows you to select the theme. The default pfSense theme is perfectly adequate, but you can select another one here. There are several new theme options available for version 2.4, so if you have not tried these, you may want to do so.

pfSense 2.3 added new options to control the look and feel of the web interface and 2.4 has added some more; these settings are also found in the **Web Configurator** section of the **General Settings** page:

1. The top navigation drop-down box allows you to choose whether the top navigation scrolls with the page, or remains anchored at the top as you scroll.
2. The **Hostname** in the Menu option allows you to replace the Help menu title with the system name or fully qualified domain name (FQDN).
3. The **Dashboard Columns** option allows you to select the number of columns on the dashboard page (the default is 2).
4. The next set of options is **Associated Panels Show/Hide**. These options control the appearance of certain panels on the Dashboard and System Logs page. The options are:
   - **Available Widgets**: Checking this box causes the **Available Widgets** panel to appear on the dashboard. Prior to version 2.3, the **Available Widgets** panel was always visible on the dashboard.
   - **Log Filter**: Checking this box causes the **Advanced Log Filter** panel to appear on the **System Logs** page. **Advanced Log Filter** allows you to filter the system logs by time, process, PID, and message.
   - **Manage Log**: Checking this box causes the **Manage General Log** panel to appear on the **System Logs** page. The **Manage General Log** panel allows you to control the display of the logs, how big the log file may be, and the formatting of the log file, among other things.
   - **Monitoring Settings**: Checking this box causes the **Settings** section to appear on the **Status | Monitoring** page, which allows custom configuration of the interactive graph on that page.
5. The Require State Filter checkbox, if checked, causes the state table in **Diagnostics | States** to only appear if a filter is entered.
6. **Left Column Labels** allows you to select/toggle the first item in a group by clicking on the left column if checked.
7. The last three options on the page were added with version 2.4:
   - The **Alias Popups** checkbox, if checked, will disable showing the details of an alias in alias popups that appear when dragging the mouse over an alias on the **Firewall** page.
   - The **Login page color** drop-down box allows you to customize the login page color; the current default color is blue.

- Finally, the **Login hostname** checkbox, when checked, will display the hostname on the login page. Having the hostname on the login page can be a helpful reminder if you are managing a large network with several firewalls, but it also potentially gives away what network is being secured.

8. Click on **Save** at the bottom of the page to save any changes.

 Version 2.4.3 has added **cross-site request forgery** (**CSRF**) protection to its dashboard widgets.

SSH login

In the previous chapter, we referred several times to configurations that can be done at the pfSense console. The same functionality is available via remote SSH login, if you enable it:

1. To do so, navigate to **System** | **Advanced**. Make sure that the **Admin Access** tab is selected and scroll down to the **Secure Shell** section of the page.
2. Check the **Secure Shell Server** checkbox to enable SSH login.
3. If all you want to do is enable traditional login via the standard SSH port (22), then you can click on the **Save** button at the bottom of the page.
4. If you want to change the login port, you can do so by entering a port number other than 22 in the SSH port edit box. Changing the SSH port is a good additional security measure, especially if you plan on making SSH login accessible from the WAN side of the firewall.
5. If you set a strong password, SSH login should be pretty secure, but you can add another layer of security by checking **Disable password login for Secure Shell (RSA/ DSA key only)**. If you invoke this option, you must create authorized SSH keys for each user that requires SSH access.
6. The process for generating SSH keys differs, depending on what program and OS you use. One handy program for generating SSH keys is PuTTYgen, a companion to the PuTTY terminal program. This program can be downloaded from the following link: `https://www.chiark.greenend.org.uk/~sgtatham/putty/latest.html`.
7. PuTTYgen's interface takes the form of a dialog box. In the Parameters section at the bottom, you can select the type of key to generate (select either **RSA** or **DSA** to generate a valid SSH-2 key for pfSense) and the number of bits in the key.

8. When you are finished setting the parameters, click the **Generate** button in the **Actions** section to generate a public/private key pair. The program will request that you move the mouse over the top area of the dialog box to generate some entropy. When the key is generated, the dialog box should look similar to the following screenshot:

9. Click the **Save private key** button to save the private key; you will need this later to log in to pfSense. Once you have saved the private key, copy the public key in the textbox at the top of the dialog box to the clipboard.

10. The next step is to paste the public key into pfSense. From the web GUI, navigate to **System | User Manager**. Scroll down to the **Keys** section, and paste the public key into the Authorized SSH Keys edit box. Once you have done this, scroll to the bottom of the page and click on Save.

11. Now, you can launch PuTTY and configure your session. Enter the IP address of the pfSense system in the Host Name (or IP address) edit box. Enter the port in the Port edit box. Keep the default Connection Type on SSH.

12. In the left pane, navigate to **Connection | SSH | Auth** (you may have to expand **Connection and SSH** to reveal the **Auth** settings page). In the **Private key for authentication**: edit box, enter the full path and filename of the private key. This is the private key you saved previously.

13. You can now save the current configuration by clicking on Session at the top of the left pane, typing a name into Saved Sessions and clicking on Save, or you can just click on Open to connect to the pfSense console.

14. At the **login as:** prompt, type in the administrator username; the next prompt will be for the key's passphrase. Enter the passphrase and press *Enter*, and you should be logged into the console.

If you were unable to log in to the console, then you need to make sure that you went through the process correctly; namely, the following steps must have been completed:

1. Enabling SSH login in pfSense.
2. Generation of a valid SSH-2 public/private key pair.
3. Adding the public key to the list of authorized SSH keys for the administrator in pfSense.
4. Configuring PuTTY to log in to pfSense, remembering to add the private key to the SSH authorization options.

If there was a public/private key mismatch, make sure that the keys are correct and that there aren't any additional characters or white spaces in them.

Summary

In this chapter, we began by discussing networking basics using the seven-layer OSI model as a point of departure. Although not an exhaustive tutorial on networking, the first section should help provide a basic idea of where pfSense fits into the structure of a typical network. We also covered typical pfSense deployment scenarios as well as the hardware requirements and sizing guidelines. We also covered how to download and install pfSense and how to perform basic system configuration using both the console and the Setup Wizard in the web GUI. Finally, we covered some additional setup options, and how to enable SSH login.

In the next chapter, we will cover how to complete pfSense configuration, including how to add interfaces, how to set up pfSense as a DHCP server, how to set up VLANs, and how to back up and restore your system.

Questions

1. Identify all seven layers of the seven-layer OSI model of networking.
2. (a) On what layer does the IP portion of the TCP/IP protocol suite reside? (b) On what layer does TCP reside?
3. Identify the ranges of the Class A, B, and C private networks.
4. Identify the three types of IPv4 addresses.
5. A desktop system has the following specifications. Can the current version of pfSense be installed onto it?
    - Pentium 4 1.8 GHz; 32-bit processor
    - 2 GB RAM
    - 250 GB IDE drive
    - DVD-ROM optical drive
6. Identify the file system options that are available when installing pfSense.
7. Under what circumstances is it possible to login to the pfSense console through the WAN port? Assume that SSH login has not yet been enabled.
8. If you configured both the WAN and LAN interfaces from the console, but you did not set up a DHCP server on the LAN interface, what additional step must be done if you want access to the pfSense web GUI from a PC that's connected to the LAN port?
9. If you need to run the Setup Wizard again after the initial configuration, how can you do this?
10. Why is it generally a good idea to enable Block RFC1918 Private Networks on the WAN interface?

Further reading

- Hunt, C. (2002). TCP/IP network administration (3rd ed.). Sebastopol, CA: OReilly. *Chapter 1, Overview of TCP/IP*, provides a good summary of the seven-layer OSI model and the TCP/IP protocol architecture.
- Kurose, James F. and Ross, Keith W. (2000). Computer Networking: A Top-Down Approach Featuring the Internet. Boston: Addison Wesley. This book is organized around the seven-layer OSI model, so it is good supplemental reading for the part of this chapter which discusses that model.
- Y. Rekhter; B. Moskowitz; D. Karrenberg; G. J. de Groot; E. Lear (February 1996). Address Allocation for Private Internets (`https://tools.ietf.org/html/rfc1918`). Network Working Group IETF. This is the IETF's RFC defining private networks.

3
Configuring pfSense

In the previous chapter, we covered the installation of pfSense, as well as some basic configuration that should be enough to get your pfSense router/firewall up and running. There are some configuration steps, however, that while not strictly necessary, involve functionality that you may want to enable. You may want to utilize additional setup options, enable SSH login for non-console access to the command line, add interfaces, configure a DHCP server, or add VLANs. All of these steps are covered in this chapter. Since this chapter also involves IPv6 to a greater degree than in previous chapters, we will begin by briefly discussing IPv4 and IPv6 addressing.

Completing this chapter should provide you with an understanding of the following topics:

- IPv4 and IPv6 addressing
- Additional setup options
- SSH login
- How to add interfaces
- How to configure pfSense to act as a DHCP server
- How to add VLANs to a pfSense configuration

Technical requirements

All of the requirements for the previous chapter apply to this chapter. If you want to follow along with the sections on adding interfaces and configuring a DHCP server, it will help to have an additional network card to add to your pfSense system. If you set pfSense up in a virtual machine, the software should provide the ability to add virtual network cards to the machine. If you want to follow along with the section on VLANs, it is necessary to have one or more managed (in other words, VLAN-capable) switches.

IPv4 and IPv6 addressing

In order to communicate on a TCP/IP network, a node must have an IP address. TCP/IP currently supports two methods of addressing: IPv4 and IPv6. IPv5 was strictly an experimental addressing standard and was never formally adopted. As mentioned in the previous chapter, IPv4 was the first publicly used version of the Internet Protocol, and it called for addressing using four octets of 8 bits each, for a total of 32 bits. This allows for about 4.3 billion addresses. While this addressing scheme was adequate for its time, by the early 1990s it became clear that as more nodes connected to the internet, IPv4 address exhaustion was inevitable, even after classless addressing and private addresses were introduced to conserve IPv4 address space.

As a result, the IPv6 project began in the 1990s. IPv6 addressing uses 128 bits, and the standard size of an IPv6 subnet is 64 bits—the square of the size of the entire IPv4 address space. It can thus handle the growth of public networks, and the larger addresses make route aggregation easier, as well as enable special features.

An IPv6 address is divided into eight 16-bit sections, each separated by a colon. Each section is represented by a hexadecimal number. As a result, IPv6 addresses are said to be in colon-hexadecimal format (as opposed to the dotted-decimal format of IPv4 addresses). An IPv6 address can be further simplified by removing the leading zeroes within each 16-bit block. Furthermore, a contiguous set of 16-bit blocks that are all zeroes can be abbreviated as ::, known as the **double colon**. Putting these two rules to use, the address `2001:0db8:0a0b:12f0:0000:0000:0000:0001` can be simplified as `2001:db8:a0b:12f0::1`. It should be noted that you can only use the double colon once within an IPv6 address. Using the double colon twice would make it impossible to know how many zeroes are in an address.

IPv6 supports a number of different address types, as follows:

- **Unicast**: As you might have guessed, unicast addresses specify a single interface. Therefore, a uni-cast address represents a single line of communication with a host. Uni-cast addresses can be divided into a number of different categories:
    - **Global unicast**: These are the equivalent of IPv4 public addresses.
    - **Link-local**: These are addresses allocated for use on a single network. They are the IPv6 equivalent of IPv4 `169.254.0.0/16` **Automatic Private IP Addressing** (**APIPA**) addresses that are used for host-internal auto-configuration when other methods of address assignment are unavailable. IPv6 reserves `fe80::/10` for link-local uni-cast addressing.

- **Site-local**: These are the IPv6 equivalent of IPv4 private addresses. Site-local addresses do not interfere with global uni-cast addresses. As with IPv4 private addresses, routers do not forward site-local traffic to public networks. Site-local addresses are not automatically configured, and must be assigned via a stateless or stateful address configuration process (stateless configuration is a process by which hosts configure themselves, whereas stateful configuration involves the host getting configuration data from a server). The prefix for IPv6 site-local addresses is `fec0::/10`.

- **Multicast**: As with IPv4, multicast addressing, or multi-casting, involves sending and receiving data between groups of nodes. This is a middle ground between uni-casting (sending to a single node) and broadcasting (sending to every node on the network).
- **Anycast**: This method of addressing involves sending and receiving data to a single node in a multicast group.

Additional setup options

You can find several configuration options under **System | General Setup**. Most of these are identical to settings that can be configured in the **Setup Wizard** (Hostname, Domain, DNS servers, Timezone, and NTP server). There are two additional settings available:

1. The **Language** drop-down box allows you to select the web configurator language.
2. Under the **Web Configurator** section, there is a **Theme** drop-down box that allows you to select the theme. The default theme of pfSense is perfectly adequate, but you can select another one here. There are several new theme options available for version 2.4, so if you have not tried these, you may want to do so.

pfSense 2.3 added new options to control the look and feel of the web interface and 2.4 has added some more; these settings are also found in the **Web Configurator** section of the **General Settings** page:

1. The top navigation drop-down box allows you to choose whether the top navigation scrolls with the page, or remains anchored at the top as you scroll.
2. The **Hostname** in the **Menu** option allows you to replace the **Help** menu title with the system name or **fully qualified domain name** (FQDN).

3. The **Dashboard Columns** option allows you to select the number of columns on the dashboard page (the default is 2).

4. The next set of options is **Associated Panels Show/Hide**. These options control the appearance of certain panels on the **Dashboard** and **System Logs** page. The options are as follows:

   - **Available Widgets**: Checking this box causes the **Available Widgets** panel to appear on the **Dashboard**. Prior to version 2.3, the **Available Widgets** panel was always visible on the **Dashboard**.
   - **Log Filter**: Checking this box causes the **Advanced Log Filter** panel to appear on the **System Logs** page. The **Advanced Log Filter** allows you to filter the system logs by time, process, PID, and message.
   - **Manage Log**: Checking this box causes the **Manage General Log** panel to appear on the **System Logs** page. The **Manage General Log** panel allows you to control the display of the logs, how big the log file may be, and the formatting of the log file, among other things.
   - **Monitoring Settings**: Checking this box causes the **Settings** section to appear on the **Status** | **Monitoring page**, which allows custom configuration of the interactive graph on that page.

5. The **Require State Filter** checkbox, if checked, causes the state table in **Diagnostics** | **States** to only appear if a filter is entered.

6. **Left Column Labels** allows you to select/ toggle the first item in a group by clicking on the left column if it's checked.

7. The last three options on the page were added with version 2.4:

   - The **Alias Popups** checkbox, if checked, will disable showing the details of an alias in alias popups that appear when dragging the mouse over an alias on the **Firewall** page.
   - The **Login page color** drop-down box allows you to customize the login page color; the current default color is blue.
   - Finally, the **Login hostname** checkbox, when checked, will display the hostname on the login page. Having the hostname on the login page can be a helpful reminder if you are managing a large network with several firewalls, but it also potentially gives away what network is being secured.

8. Click on **Save** at the bottom of the page to save any changes.

 Version 2.4.3 has added **Cross-Site Request Forgery (CSRF)** protection to the dashboard widgets.

SSH login

In the previous chapter, we referred several times to configurations that can be done at the pfSense console. The same functionality is available via remote SSH login, if you enable it:

1. To do so, navigate to **System** | **Advanced**. Make sure that the **Admin Access** tab is selected and scroll down to the **Secure Shell** section of the page.
2. Check the **Secure Shell Server** checkbox to enable SSH login.
3. If all you want to do is enable traditional login via the standard SSH port (22), then you can click on the **Save** button at the bottom of the page.
4. If you want to change the login port, you can do so by entering a port number other than 22 in the SSH port edit box. Changing the SSH port is a good additional security measure, especially if you plan on making SSH login accessible from the WAN side of the firewall.
5. If you set a strong password, SSH login should be pretty secure, but you can add another layer of security by checking **Disable password login for Secure Shell (RSA/ DSA key only)**. If you invoke this option, you must create authorized SSH keys for each user that requires SSH access.
6. The process for generating SSH keys differs depending on what program and OS you use. One handy program for generating SSH keys is **PuTTYgen**, a companion to the PuTTY terminal program. This program can be downloaded here: https://www.chiark.greenend.org.uk/~sgtatham/putty/latest.html.
7. PuTTYgen's interface takes the form of a dialog box. In the **Parameters** section at the bottom, you can select the type of key to generate (select either **RSA** or **DSA** to generate a valid SSH-2 key for pfSense) and the number of bits in the key.

8. When you are finished setting the parameters, click the **Generate** button in the **Actions** section to generate a public/private key pair. The program will request that you move the mouse over the top area of the dialog box to generate some entropy. When the key is generated, the dialog box should look similar to the following screenshot:

9. Click the **Save private key** button to save the private key; you will need this later to log in to pfSense. Once you have saved the private key, copy the public key in the textbox at the top of the dialog box to the clipboard.

10. The next step is to paste the public key into pfSense. From the web GUI, navigate to **System** | **User Manager**. Scroll down to the **Keys** section, and paste the public key into the **Authorized SSH Keys** edit box. Once you have done this, scroll to the bottom of the page and click on **Save**.

11. Now, you can launch PuTTY and configure your session. Enter the IP address of the pfSense system in the **Host Name (or IP address)** edit box. Enter the port in the **Port** edit box. Keep the **Default Connection Type** on **SSH**.

12. In the left pane, navigate to **Connection | SSH | Auth** (you may have to expand Connection and SSH to reveal the **Auth settings** page). In the **Private key for authentication** edit box, enter the full path and filename of the private key. This is the private key you saved previously.

13. You can now save the current configuration by clicking on **Session** at the top of the left pane, typing a name into **Saved Sessions**, and clicking on **Save**, or you can just click on **Open** to connect to the pfSense console.

14. At the `login as:` prompt, type in the administrator username; the next prompt will be for the key's passphrase. Enter the passphrase and press *Enter*, and you should be logged into the console.

If you were unable to log in to the console, then you need to make sure that you have gone through the process correctly; namely, the following steps must have been completed:

1. Enabling SSH login in pfSense.
2. Generation of a valid SSH-2 public/private key pair.
3. Adding the public key to the list of authorized SSH keys for the administrator in pfSense.
4. Configuring PuTTY to log into pfSense, remembering to add the private key to the SSH authorization options.

If there was a public/private key mismatch, make sure that the keys are correct and that there aren't any additional characters or white spaces in them.

Adding interfaces

The basic configuration in `Chapter 2`, *Installing pfSense*, took us through configuration of the WAN and LAN interfaces. At some point, you will likely want to add at least one more interface, which is the topic of this section. There are two ways of adding an interface: from the console/SSH login, or (somewhat more conveniently) from the web GUI. The following procedure describes how to add an interface from within the web GUI.

Configuration of LAN-type interfaces

Configuration of an interface for use with a local network differs somewhat from configuration of a WAN interface (which will be used to provide access to public networks). First, we will consider the former case:

1. To add optional interfaces, navigate to the **Interfaces | Assignments** tab, which will show a list of assigned interfaces, and at the bottom of the table, there will be an **Available network ports** option.

2. There will be a corresponding drop-down box with a list of unassigned network ports. These will have device names such as `fxp0`, `em1`, and so on.

3. To assign an unused port, select the port you want to assign from the drop-down box, and click on the **+** button to the right.

4. The page will reload, and the new interface will be the last entry in the table. The name of the interface will be OPTx, where x equals the number of optional interfaces.

5. By clicking on the interface name, you can configure the interface:

   - Nearly all the settings here are similar to the settings that were available on the **WAN** and **LAN** configuration pages in the **pfSense Setup Wizard**.

   - Some of the options under the **General Configuration** section, that are not available in the **Setup Wizard**, are **Maximum Segment Size** (**MSS**) and **Speed and duplex**. Normally, **MSS** should remain unchanged, although you can change this setting if your internet connection requires it.

6. If you click on the **Advanced** button under **Speed and duplex**, a drop-down box will appear in which you can explicitly set the speed and duplex for the interface. Since virtually all modern network hardware has the capability of automatically selecting the correct speed and duplex, you will probably want to leave this unchanged.

7. The section at the bottom of the page, **Reserved Networks**, allows you to enable **Block private networks**, **loopback addresses**, and **Block bogon networks** via their respective check-boxes. Although these options are checked by default when configuring the WAN interface, we normally want to allow private networks on internal interfaces, so these options are normally not enabled when configuring non-WAN interfaces.

8. If you chose an option other than **Static** for the **Configuration Type**, then other options will appear.

Since it is unlikely that internal interfaces will be configured as non-static interfaces, further discussion of these options will take place in the next section on WAN configuration.

WAN configuration

The configuration done in the **Setup Wizard** will be enough to get you started. We won't have to do any additional configuration for the WAN interface. In case we need to make any changes, then we need to follow these steps:

1. Navigate to **Interfaces | WAN** in the main menu.
2. The most likely scenario is that your ISP will provide an IP address via DHCP, but many providers will provide you with a static IP address if you require one. In such cases, you will need to set your **Configuration Type** to **Static** and then enter your WAN IP address and CIDR under either the **Static IPv4 Configuration** or **Static IPv6 Configuration** (or possibly both, if you plan to have both an IPv4 and IPv6 address).
3. You will also need to specify your ISP's gateway, which you can do by clicking on the **Add a new gateway** button. A dialog box will appear in which you can enter the IP address and a description.
4. If you have selected **DHCP** as the configuration type, then there are several options in addition to the ones available in the **Setup Wizard**. Clicking on the **Advanced** checkbox in the **DHCP client configuration** causes several additional options to appear in this section of the page:
   - The first is **Protocol Timing**, which allows you to control DHCP protocol timings when requesting a lease. You can also choose several presets (**FreeBSD**, **pfSense**, **Clear**, or **Saved Cfg**) using the radio buttons on the right.
   - There is also a **Configuration Override** checkbox, which, if checked, allows you to specify the absolute path to a DHCP client configuration file in the **Configuration Override File** edit box. If your ISP supports pfSense, it should be able to provide you with a valid configuration override file. If the **Configuration Override** checkbox is not checked, there will be three edit boxes in this section under the checkboxes. The first is **Hostname**; this field is sent as a DHCP hostname and client identifier when requesting a DHCP lease. **Alias IPv4 address** allows you to enter a fixed IP address for the DHCP client. The **Reject Leases from** field allows you to specify the IP address or subnet of an upstream DHCP server to be ignored.

- The next section is **Lease Requirements and Requests**. Here, you can specify send, request, and require options when requesting a DHCP lease. These options are useful if your ISP requires these options. The last section is **Option Modifiers**, where you can add DHCP option modifiers, which are applied to an obtained DHCP lease.

5. Starting with pfSense version 2.2.5, there is support for IPv6 with DHCP (DHCP6). If you are running 2.2.5 or above, there will be a section on the page called **DHCP6 client configuration**.

6. Similar to the configuration for IPv4 DHCP, there are check-boxes for **Advanced Configuration** and **Configuration Override**.

7. Checking the **Advanced** checkbox in the heading of this section displays the Advanced DHCP 6 options:

   - If you check the **Information Only** checkbox on the left, pfSense will send requests for stateless DHCPv6 information.
   - You can specify **Send and Request** options, just as you can for IPv4.
   - There is also a **Script** field where you can enter the absolute path to a script that will be invoked on certain conditions.
   - The following options are for the **Identity Association Statement** checkboxes. The **NonTemporary Address Allocation** checkbox results in normal, that is, not temporary, IPv6 addresses to be allocated for the interface. The **Prefix Delegation** checkbox causes a set of IPv6 prefixes to be allocated from the DHCP server.
   - The next set of options, **Authentication Statement**, allows you to specify authentication parameters to the DHCP server. The **Authname** parameter allows you to specify a string, which in turn specifies a set of parameters. The remaining parameters are of limited usefulness in configuring a DHCP6 client, because each has only one allowed value, and leaving them blank will result in only the allowed value being used. If you are curious as to what these values are, the following table can help you out:

Parameter	Allowed value	Description
Protocol	Delayed	The DHCPv6 delayed authentication protocol
Algorithm	hmac-md5; HMAC-MD5; hmacmd5; or HMACMD5	The HMAC-MD5 authentication algorithm
rdn	Monocounter	The replay protection method; only monocounter is allowed

8. Finally, **Key info Statement** allows you to enter a secret key. The required fields are **key id**, which identifies the key, and **secret**, which provides the shared secret. **key name** and **realm** are arbitrary strings and may be omitted. **expire** may be used to specify an expiration time for the key, but if it is omitted, the key will never expire.

9. If you do not check the **configuration override** checkbox (in which case you will specify a configuration override file, similar to how this option works with DHCP over IPv4), there will be several more options in the **DHCP Client Configuration** section. Using IPv4 connectivity as the parent interface allows you to request an IPv6 prefix over an IPv4 link.

10. Requesting only an IPv6 prefix allows you to request just the prefix, not an address. **DHCPv6 Prefix Delegation** size allows you to specify the prefix length.

11. You can check the **Send IPv6** prefix hint to indicate the desired prefix length, **Debug** for debugging, and select **Do not wait for an RA (router advertisement)** and/or **Do not allow PD/Address release**, if your ISP requires it.

12. The last section on the page is identical to the interface configuration page in the **Setup Wizard**, and contains the **Block Private Networks** and **Block Bogon Networks** checkboxes. On WAN-type interfaces, these options should be checked, unless there is another private network on the other side of the WAN.

Adding a DHCP server

If you only have a few devices on your network, you could easily configure them with static IP addresses and not use a DHCP server at all. In such cases, internet connectivity will be established more quickly, since computers on the network won't have to go through the DHCP discovery-offer-request-acknowledge process. As the size of your network grows, however, a DHCP server becomes essential, as keeping track of statically assigned IP addresses will become far too cumbersome. Fortunately, configuring pfSense to act as a DHCP server is relatively easy, and can be done from either the console or the web GUI.

DHCP configuration at the console

DHCP configuration at the console can be done with the following steps:

1. At the console, select **Set interface(s) IP address** on the menu.
2. Select the interface on which you want to run the pfSense DHCP server (this is usually a LAN, but it could be any interface other than the WAN interface). You will be prompted for the interface's IPv4 IP address.
3. Type in the address (or leave the line blank for none) and press *Enter*.
4. The next prompt is for the subnet bit count. Type in the correct bit count and press *Enter*.
5. Next, you will be prompted for the upstream gateway address. You do not need to provide this information, so just press *Enter*. IPv4 address configuration is now complete.
6. The next prompt will be for the IPv6 address. If you have a small network, IPv6 configuration is not necessary, although there are some advantages to IPv6 configuration, such as the ability to assign addresses automatically, enhanced security, and even better mobility features. Enter an IPv6 address if you want to use IPv6 on the interface.
7. After you enter the IPv6 address, you will be prompted to enter the subnet bit count, so enter the bit count and press *Enter*. Since you don't need to specify an upstream gateway, you can press *Enter* there as well.
8. The next two prompts will ask you whether to start the DHCP server on IPv4 and IPv6, respectively. If you specify **y** for either one, you will be prompted to enter the address range for DHCP. Here, you can specify any valid address range for your subnet. Keep in mind that you don't have to start the DHCP server for IPv6 unless you want clients to have their IPv6 addresses assigned to them. Instead, you can utilize client address configuration.

Now that you have enabled DHCP at the console and assigned address ranges, you should be able to connect to your network via DHCP. Configuring networking on the client for DHCP will be different for each platform, but virtually all modern OSes allow you to select either static IP assignment or DHCP (if it's not explicitly called DHCP, it will likely be called **automatic IP assignment** or something similar). You may have to reset your network connection, but once you do, the DHCP server should assign you an IP address.

DHCP configuration in the web GUI

You can also set up your DHCP server in the web GUI, which includes many more options than the console does:

1. Navigate to **Services** | **DHCP Server**. There will be a separate tab for each non-WAN interface.
2. Click on the tab for the interface you want to configure.
3. In the **General Options** section, there is an **Enable** checkbox, which, as you probably guessed, enables the DHCP server on the interface.
4. There are also **Range** edit boxes where you can define the range of assigned addresses. If this is all you want to do (which is no more than the level of DHCP configuration the console provides), you can click on the **Save** button at the bottom of the page and the DHCP server will now be up and running.
5. One of the options added in version 2.4, the **BOOTP** checkbox, if checked, will cause the DHCP server to ignore BOOTP queries. BOOTP is a protocol by which networks can assign IP addresses to users. Like DHCP, it uses port 67 and port 68 to communicate. It also predates DHCP (it was originally defined in RFC 951 in September 1985, while DHCP was not defined until March 1997). Both BOOTP and DHCP are methods of automatic IP assignment. However, BOOTP differs from DHCP in several significant ways:
   - BOOTP uses the **User Datagram Protocol** (**UDP**), while DHCP uses the **Transport Control Protocol** (**TCP**).
   - BOOTP only works with IPv4 networks, while DHCP has been revised to support IPv6 networks.
   - BOOTP does not support DHCP, but the reverse is true: parts of BOOTP provide services to DHCP, and DHCP servers provide legacy BOOTP functionality.
   - Therefore, a DHCP server will normally also act as a BOOTP server. This can be problematic, however, because BOOTP leases do not have a maximum lease time by default (the original definition of BOOTP does not even include the lease concept). Therefore, BOOTP leases can easily exhaust the DHCP address pool. One possible solution is to just ignore BOOTP queries, which may seem like overkill, but it also eliminates the possibility of DHCP support for BOOTP ever being a problem. If you ever have problems with BOOTP queries, you can enable this option.

6. The **Ignore denied clients** checkbox, if checked, will cause pfSense to ignore denied clients rather than reject them. This, however, is not compatible with failover, because another pfSense system in the failover group will assume that the failure to respond to a DHCP request indicates a failure of the other system.

7. The **Additional Pools** section allows you to specify additional pools of addresses outside of the range specified in **General Options**:
    - You can add address pools by clicking on the **Add pool** button and entering the new range.
    - Once a new pool has been added, it will appear under the **Additional Pools** section, and you will be able to edit or delete the pool from the **DHCP Server** page.

8. You may want to set up your system so that only devices with certain MAC addresses receive DHCP leases. If so, check the **Deny unknown clients** checkbox.

9. You will then have to scroll down to the **Other Options** section and click on the **Advanced** button next to the **MAC Address Control** section.

10. In the **MAC Allow** edit box, specify the MAC addresses of the devices (as comma-separated values with no spaces) to which you want to allow access. If you want to deny access to certain devices, you can specify their MAC addresses in the **MAC Deny** edit box.

Be aware that MAC address control only provides a minimal level of security. A user who relies on auto-configuration to connect to the internet will be locked out, but a determined hacker can easily resort to MAC address spoofing, which, as you probably know, is one of pfSense's capabilities. Therefore, it's not a good idea to rely on MAC address control as a security measure.

DHCP static configuration

There may be devices on your network (for example, file servers and printers) which need to have the same IP address at all times. For these devices, you can rely on static mappings:

1. If you scroll down to the bottom of the page, you will find a section labeled **DHCP Static Mappings for this Interface**. Following this heading and to the right, there will be an **Add** button which will launch a page on which you can add a mapping.

2. The first setting on this page is **MAC Address**. Here, you must enter the MAC address of the device that is to receive a static mapping.

3. To the right of the **MAC Address** edit box, there is a **Copy My MAC** button that will copy the MAC address of the device currently being used to connect to pfSense; this is provided for your convenience.

4. The MAC address is the only field you must enter. If this is all you enter, this MAC address will be added to the list of allowed MAC addresses for the DHCP server. To obtain a static mapping for this device, you need to enter an IP address in the **IP Address** field.

A bug in pfSense prevented multiple MAC addresses being mapped to a single IP address. Version 2.4.3 fixed this bug, and so this is now possible.

5. There is also a **Hostname** field, in which you can specify the hostname, minus the domain. This field is optional, but, if specified, will be forwarded to the DNS server to help identify the client.

6. Another optional field is **Description**, which just allows you to enter a text description of the static mapping.

7. The **Client Identifier** field allows you to enter a client identifier string, which, when specified, is used along with the assigned network address by the DHCP server to identify the client, per RFCs 2131 and 6842.

8. In the **Servers** section, you can specify both WINS servers and DNS servers. WINS servers provide Windows with a means of mapping NetBIOS names to network addresses. If you don't have a WINS server on your network, you can leave this blank:

    - The **DNS Servers** fields need not be filled in most cases. If these fields are left blank and the DNS forwarder is enabled, pfSense will automatically assign itself as the DNS server for client PCs.
    - If the DNS forwarder is disabled and these fields are left blank, the default DNS servers specified in **System | General Setup** will be used. There are, however, circumstances in which you may want to override either the default DNS servers or the DNS forwarder:
        - When you need to specify custom DNS servers (for example, an Active Directory configuration in which the Active Directory has its own DNS servers).
        - If you are using the **Common Address Redundancy Protocol (CARP)** in conjunction with the DNS forwarder, you should specify the field. There are also fields for the primary domain name server IP address, as well as the DDNS key name and key secret.

With the release of version 2.4.3, several options have been added to the DHCP Dynamic DNS options. The **DDNS Hostnames** checkbox, if enabled, will force the dynamic DNS hostname to be the same as the configured hostname for static mappings, rather than the hostname supplied by the DHCP client. The **key algorithm** drop-down box provides several options for the server key encryption algorithm. **HMAC-SHA512** is the most secure of these options. The **DDNS Client Updates** drop-down box provides options for controlling who is allowed to update DNS. If it is set to **Allow**, the client is allowed to update DNS; the DHCP server is prevented from updating forward entries. If it is set to **Deny**, the DHCP server will do the updates and the client will not. If it is set to **Ignore**, then the DHCP server will do the update, but the client can also attempt an update, usually using a different domain name.

DHCPv6 configuration in the web GUI

As with DHCP configuration on IPv4 networks, DHCP configuration on an IPv6 network (DHCPv6) has many options. The DHCPv6 configuration page combines DHCPv6 and router advertisement configuration. This section will focus on options that are only available with DHCPv6 rather than options that are present in both DHCP and DHCPv6.

To configure DHCPv6, navigate to **Services** | **DHCPv6/RA**. Under **DHCPv6 Options**, there are several useful settings such as the **Prefix Delegation Range** option, the purpose of which is to delegate the ability to act as DHCPv6 servers to clients by assigning portions of the subnet to them. Consider one of the common IPv6 prefix examples: `fd12: 3456: 78: 9a::` with a subnet mask of `48`. The remaining bits are available for delegation, so we have an available range of `fd12: 3456: 789a::` to `1234: 5678: 9a: ffff:ffff:ffff:ffff:ffff`. We can delegate any subset of this range. The boundaries of the range indicated in the **DHCPv6 Prefix Delegation Size** must include the prefix delegation size, which indicates the CIDR of the client's subnets. In our previous example, we had a ULA with a prefix of `fd12: 3456: 789a::/ 48`. We set the prefix delegation range of `fd12: 3456: 789a: 0000::` to `fd12: 3456: 789a:ff00::` with a size of 56 if we want our clients to receive portions of the subnet. This would result in a maximum of 256 blocks of delegated addressed to be provided.

While it is possible to use a prefix longer than 64 bits, doing so is discouraged, since features such as **stateless address autoconfiguration** (**SLAAC**) depend on the DHCPv6 server advertising a prefix of 64 bits.

There is another tab on this page for **Router Advertisements** (**RA**). This enables an IPv6-capable router to advertise its presence to other routers, and keep other nodes informed of any changes in the network.

Understanding the RA configuration options requires an understanding of the RA flags. Two flags that are in every RA packet are the M flag and the O flag. The M flag stands for managed address configuration and it informs the host receiving the packet that there is a DHCPv6 server available and that the host should get its IPv6 address from this server. If the M flag is set to zero, then it means that the host should not look for a DHCPv6 server. The O flag stands for an other configuration and it tells the host that it should get other configuration information (for example, DNS) from the DHCP server.

In addition, many packets have an L flag and an A flag. The L flag tells the host that other devices with the same prefix as the prefix contained in the RA packet are on the same subnet. Therefore, they should communicate at the switch level and not send every packet to the router. The A flag tells the host to use the prefix inside the RA packet and the host's own MAC address to generate its own IPv6 address. Thus, the host should use SLAAC.

With this in mind, here is how these flag settings correspond to the router mode options:

	M flag	O flag	L flag	A flag
Router Only	0	0	0	0
Unmanaged	0	0	1	1
Managed	1	1	1	0
Assisted	1	1	1	1
Stateless DHCP	0	1	1	1

In addition to these options, there is also a **Disabled** option to completely disable router advertisements.

Most modern operating systems support both SLAAC and DHCPv6, so you should be able to choose either **Unmanaged** or **Managed** in most cases. If you are not sure which modes are supported on your systems, you can choose **Assisted** mode. The **Default valid lifetime** field defines the length of time in seconds that the prefix is valid for the purposes of on-link determination.

The **Default preferred lifetime** field defines the length of time in seconds that the addresses generated from the prefix via SLAAC remain preferred. The defaults are 86,400 seconds and 14,400 seconds, respectively.

The **RA Subnets** field allows you to specify subnets on which RA will take place. If no subnet is specified, the RA daemon will advertise on the subnet to which the router's interface is assigned. You must specify both the subnet and the CIDR mask. This option allows you to only perform RA on selected subnets.

The **DNS Servers** section allows you to specify different DNS servers than the default ones (the interface IP if **DNS Forwarder** or **Resolver** is enabled, or the servers configured on the **General** page if neither of these is enabled). In the **Domain search list**, you can specify an optional list, and there is also a **Use same settings as DHCPv6 server** checkbox if you just want the RA daemon to use the same DNS servers specified on the DHCPv6 tab.

DHCP and DHCPv6 relay

Especially in larger networks, it is possible that you don't want to run the DHCP server on your system, but instead want to pass on DHCP requests to another server. In this case, you can use the pfSense DHCP relay, which can be found by navigating to **Services** | **DHCP Relay**. In order to use the **DHCP Relay**, the DHCP server must be disabled on all interfaces. Note, however, that the DHCPv6 server may still be enabled. The reverse is also true: in order to use **DHCPv6 Relay**, you must disable the DHCPv6 server on all interfaces, but you do not have to disable the DHCP server.

If you later enable the DHCP server, the DHCP relay will be automatically disabled, and if you enable the DHCPv6 server, the DHCPv6 relay will be disabled.

To enable to the DHCP relay, refer to the following steps:

1. To enable the DHCP relay, check the **Enable** checkbox.
2. There is also an **Interface(s)** list box where you can select the interfaces on which the DHCP relay will be enabled. If you want the DHCP relay to append the circuit ID (the pfSense interface number) and the agent ID, you should check the **Append circuit ID** and **agent ID to requests** checkboxes.
3. The **Destination** server edit box allows you to specify the IP address of the DHCP server. You can specify more than one IP address; you can use the **Add** and **Delete** buttons to add/delete entries.

The DHCPv6 relay can be enabled by navigating to **Services** | **DHCPv6 Relay**. The settings for the DHCPv6 relay are identical to the settings for the DHCP relay.

DHCP and DHCPv6 leases

If you want to see what DHCP leases have been issued, navigate to **Status | DHCP Leases**. This page offers several pieces of information about active and inactive leases:

- The IP address of the lease.
- The MAC address of the client that has received the lease.
- The hostname of the client.
- A description of the client, if one is available.
- The start and end time of the lease.
- Whether the client is online, and the type of lease: static, active, or inactive. Static is for statically mapped DHCP leases; active and inactive are for dynamically allocated leases. Active denotes those clients that are using their leases, while inactive is for inactive clients whose DHCP leases have not yet expired.

To find out what DHCPv6 leases have been issued, navigate to **Status | DHCPv6 Leases**. All of the information about DHCP leases that the **DHCP Leases** page contains is contained on the **DHCPv6 Leases** page with respect to DHCPv6 leases. The leases table also has two additional fields. **IAID** is each lease's Identity Association ID. An **Identity Association (IA)** is a collection of addresses assigned to a client, and each IA has its own ID—the IAID. **DUID** is the DHCP Unique Identifier, which is a globally unique identifier that each DHCPv6 client and server has for identification purposes.

There is a second table on this page called **Delegated Prefixes**. The purpose of this table is to list all prefixes that have been assigned to clients so that they can act as routers. Once again, the IAID and DUID are present in this table, as well as the start and end time of the delegation, and the state of the delegation. Note that a client must request a delegation from pfSense before it appears in this table.

VLAN configuration

The networks we have contemplated so far have been relatively simple networks with two interfaces (WAN and LAN). As our networks get larger, we have two primary concerns. The first is the increase in broadcast traffic (packets received by every node on the network). The second is the need to segregate network traffic based on management and/or security concerns.

One way of solving these issues is to divide our networks into different segments. For example, in a corporate network, we may have different subnets for the engineering department, the sales department, and so on.

The problem with this approach is that it does not scale well in the traditional networking paradigm. Each subnet requires a separate physical interface, and there is a limit to how many physical interfaces we can place in a single router.

A better solution is to decouple the physical organization of our network from the logical organization of it. Virtual LANs accomplish this objective. By attaching a special header to an Ethernet frame (known as an 802.1Q tag, named after the IEEE standard that defines VLANs), we can accomplish two feats we could not otherwise do: single interfaces can now support multiple networks, and networks can now span multiple interfaces (less common, but possible).

In addition, VLANs provide some advantages over traditional networks. With VLANs, if a user moves from one location to another, the user's computer's network settings do not have to be reconfigured—the user just needs to connect to a switch port that supports the VLAN of which the user is a member. Conversely, if the user changes their job function, they do not need to move—they only need to join a different VLAN that contains the resources they need to access. Moreover, since broadcast traffic is confined to a single VLAN, it is significantly reduced, cutting down on unnecessary network traffic and improving security, since it is less likely a user can eavesdrop on network traffic not intended for that user.

Since this book is aimed at those whose knowledge of networking and pfSense is at a beginner's level, our discussion of VLANs will not go into the depth that it might otherwise. In particular, we will only discuss how to configure pfSense for use with VLANs, and we will not discuss how to configure a managed switch, which is a necessary step in setting up VLANs. Instead, consult the documentation provided with your switch for more information.

As with DHCP, will we cover the two methods of adding VLANs: at the console and within the web GUI.

VLAN configuration at the console

VLAN configuration can be done at the console; in fact, it can even be done on the initial setup, although many of the more esoteric features of VLANs (such as QinQ tagging) are not available from the console menu. Another disadvantage is that there does not seem to be a way of renaming the optional interfaces, although you could do so from the web GUI later.

To begin VLAN configuration from the console, use the **Assign Interfaces** option in the console (it should be option 1). A list of available interfaces will be provided by pfSense, including the interface device name, the MAC address, link status (up or down), and a description of the interface. Execute the following steps for configuring VLAN at the console:

```
Enter the parent interface name for the new VLAN (or nothing if finished): em2
Enter the VLAN tag (1-4094): 3


VLAN Capable interfaces:

em0      08:00:27:32:4b:fc   (up)
em1      08:00:27:ce:ff:d1   (up)
em2      08:00:27:eb:36:c2   (up)

Enter the parent interface name for the new VLAN (or nothing if finished):


VLAN interfaces:

em2_vlan2       VLAN tag 2, parent interface em2
em2_vlan3       VLAN tag 3, parent interface em2

If you do not know the names of your interfaces, you may choose to use
auto-detection. In that case, disconnect all interfaces now before
hitting 'a' to initiate auto detection.

Enter the WAN interface name or 'a' for auto-detection
(em0 em1 em2 em2_vlan2 em2_vlan3 or a): █
```

VLAN configuration at the console

1. When you select the **Assign Interfaces** option, the first prompt will be, **Do you want to set up VLANs now [y|n]?**
2. At this prompt, type **y** and press *Enter* to begin VLAN configuration.
3. A confirmation prompt is presented next: **WARNING: All existing VLANs will be cleared if you proceed! Do you want to proceed [y|n]?**
4. Type **y** and press *Enter* to proceed.
5. Next, pfSense will provide a list of VLAN-capable interfaces and another prompt: **Enter the parent interface name for the new VLAN** (or nothing if finished).

6. Enter the parent interface name (the device name in the table) and press *Enter*. The next prompt is for the VLAN tag: **Enter the VLAN tag (1-4094)**.

7. Enter a VLAN tag other than 1 and press *Enter*.

8. After you enter the VLAN tag, you will be returned to the *Enter* the parent interface prompt, where you can repeat the process for as many VLANs you wish to set up, and then enter nothing when finished. When you are finished creating VLANs, you will be prompted to assign interfaces, starting with the WAN interface. If you have at least one interface that has not been partitioned into VLANs, you should probably assign one of these interfaces to the WAN. If you do assign a VLAN to the WAN, you will want to make sure the WAN is on a separate switch, for the reasons outlined in the previous section.

9. The next prompt will be for the LAN interface, and you can assign a VLAN to the LAN, although you should be aware of any security issues this creates. Enter the LAN interface and press *Enter*.

10. Once you have assigned the WAN and LAN interfaces, you can assign optional interfaces (OPT1, OPT2, and so on) to the newly-created VLANs. The convention for VLAN interface names is `parent_interface.vlan_number`. For example, if the VLAN20 parent interface is `m3`, the interface name for VLAN20 would be `em3.20`.

11. When you are done assigning interfaces, press *Enter* at the prompt and you will be presented with a list of interfaces and their assignments.

12. After the list, you will see a confirmation prompt: **Do you want to proceed [y|n]?**

13. Type **y** and press *Enter*. pfSense will write and reload the configuration. Interface assignment is now complete.

14. You still need to assign an IP address to the VLANs, which you can do by selecting the second option from the console menu, selecting the number corresponding to the desired VLAN interface, and typing in the IPv4 and/or IPv6 addresses, following the procedure outlined in `Chapter 2`, *Installing pfSense*. You can also configure the DHCP server to work with VLANs using this menu option. Repeat this step for every VLAN you wish to configure.

If you have followed all of these steps, the pfSense portion of VLAN setup will be almost complete. You must still add firewall rules to give the VLANs access to other networks and configure one or more managed switches for the VLANs to work.

VLAN configuration in the web GUI

VLAN configuration can also be done within the web GUI, along with any other tasks related to the setup of VLANs (for example, DHCP and rule creation):

1. Log in to pfSense with the web browser of your choice and navigate to **Interfaces | (assign)**.
2. Click on the **VLANs** tab and you will see a table with any previously created VLANs. Click on the **+ Add** button to add a new VLAN.
3. On the **VLAN Configuration** page, the first setting is the **Parent Interface** drop-down box. Select the interface you want to be the parent interface of your VLANs. Next is the **VLAN Tag** edit box. Valid values for this field are 1 to 4094; you shouldn't use 1, but you can use any other values up to and including 4094. Some low-end managed switches may have problems with larger numbers, so you may want to use low numbers (2 to 8) if you have one of these.
4. The **VLAN Priority** edit box was added with pfSense 2.3. This allows you to utilize the 802.1Q priority code point (PCP) field. This is a 3-bit field that makes reference to the IEEE 802.1p class of service. 802.1p defines how traffic should be treated based on the value of this field. Although the values of the field range from 0 to 7, a value of 1 causes traffic to have the lowest priority, while 7 causes traffic to have the highest priority. A value of 0 causes traffic to receive best effort treatment. As you can see, if you know what type of traffic is going to be prevalent on the VLANs you are creating, you can set the VLAN Priority value accordingly. Otherwise, you can set this value to 0.
5. The last field, **Description**, allows you to enter a non-parsed description of the VLAN. When you are done making changes, click on the **Save** button at the bottom.

In the first series of steps, we have only created the VLANs and have not assigned them to interfaces, so in the next step, we must return to the **Interface assignments** tab. There will be a table on which all interface assignments up to this point will be shown, and you can add VLAN assignments by selecting one of the VLAN interfaces created in the previous step from the drop-down box in the last row (the one labeled Available network ports:) and clicking on the **Add** button. Repeat this process for as many VLANs as you created in the previous step:

1. Once interface assignment is complete, the next step is to configure each of the VLANs.
2. They will be given generic default names (OPT1, OPT2, and so on); click on the first VLAN in the **Interface** column. This will load the **Interface Configuration** page.

3. In the **General** configuration section, check the **Enable** check box. In the **Description** field, you can rename the interface.

4. In the **IPv4 Configuration Type** drop-down box, you will likely want to choose **Static IPv4**. If your VLAN is going to support IPv6, you will likely want to choose **Static IPv6** in the **IPv6 Configuration Type** drop-down box. Depending on whether you selected IPv4, IPv6, or both, you will have to enter IPv4 and/or IPv6 addresses in the sections below the **General configuration** section. Note that you must enter both the IP address of the interface and the CIDR.

5. For IPv4 Upstream Gateway and IPv6 Upstream Gateway, you can leave these drop-down boxes set to None.

The rest of the fields you can likely leave unchanged, but if you are having problems with dropped frames, you may want to enter a larger value in the MTU field.

When you are done making changes, click on the **Save** button at the bottom of the page. Once you have clicked on the **Save** button, you must click on the **Apply Changes** button at the top of the page for the changes to take effect. Repeat the interface configuration as many times as needed. You can reach the configuration page for each VLAN by accessing it from the drop-down menu at the top of the page, or by navigating to **Interfaces | (assign)** once again and clicking on the appropriate VLAN in the **Interface** column.

One of the bugs affecting the pfSense implementation of VLANs is that DHCP6c packets (packets from the DHCPv6 client daemon) were not being tagged with VLAN priority. This bug has been fixed with version 2.4.3.

QinQ and link aggregation

Two features present in the current implementation of VLANs in pfSense that will not be discussed in depth but are worth mentioning are **QinQ** and **LAGG (Link Aggregation)**. QinQ allows you to nest VLAN tags inside each other, thus increasing the possible number of VLANs on your network beyond the 4,093 VLANs that would be possible if no nesting was allowed. **LAGG**, or link aggregation, allows you to combine multiple ports in parallel, thus increasing total throughput and/or providing redundancy. Each of these features has a separate tab on the **VLAN** page.

Remaining considerations

Once you have configured VLANs within pfSense, there are two more steps you must complete before VLANs are fully functional:

- If you do not have floating rules allowing outbound traffic from all interfaces, then you must add rules for each VLAN interface to allow outbound traffic from them; otherwise, all outbound traffic will be blocked by default. pfSense creates two **Allow LAN to any** rules for the LAN interface when it is created (one for IPv4 and one for IPv6). To see these rules, navigate to **Firewall** | **Rules** within the web GUI, and click on the **LAN** tab. You can copy these rules by clicking on the **Copy** icon in the column for the rules (it looks like two sheets of paper on top of each other) and changing the **Interface** (in the drop-down box) from LAN to the VLAN interface name. You might also want to change the **Description** accordingly. There will be a more detailed treatment of firewall rules in Chapter 6, *Firewall and NAT*.

- You must configure one or more managed switches for use with your VLAN. It is not the objective of this book to explain how to accomplish this. There are many manufacturers and models of managed switches (Cisco is currently considered the industry standard-bearer, but there are many others), and all of them have their own specific directions on how they must be configured. To get you started, however, here are some factors to consider:

  - The switch must be a managed switch. Unmanaged switches are essentially dumb devices that simply allow traffic to pass between ports. Managed switches support advanced features such as VLANs.

  - You will have to designate at least one port as a trunk port (these are ports that provide a connection between the managed switch and other switches and routers), and one or more ports as switch ports (these ports are assigned to the VLANs).

  - The trunk ports will be designated as tagged ports (traffic leaving them will have 802.1q tags attached to them), while the switch ports will be designated as untagged ports (traffic leaving them will be stripped of their 802.1q tags).

Summary

In this chapter, we covered a lot of the configuration options that most pfSense users will want to use at some point. We briefly discussed IPv6 addressing, and how it is different compared to IPv4 addressing, because IPv6 addressing is a topic that will recur often as we delve further into pfSense. We covered some additional setup options not discussed in `Chapter 2`, *Installing pfSense*, and also discussed how to enable SSH login, which is useful if you are not at the console but still want to use the console menu or other console commands. We covered how to add interfaces and how to enable DHCP and DHCPv6 servers on those interfaces. Finally, we briefly discussed how to set up a VLAN in pfSense.

In the next chapter, we will cover one of the services that many pfSense users who are utilizing pfSense in a SOHO environment may want to make use of: captive portal.

Questions

1. Abbreviate 2001:00ba:0000:0000:0000:0000:3257:0652 by eliminating the leading zeroes and using double colon notation.
2. (a) Identify the three primary types of IPv6 addresses. (b) What prefix is used for IPv6 site-local addresses?
3. What method can we use to remotely log in to a pfSense system without using a password?
4. What option can we use if we have a device (for example, a file server) that must have the same IP address at all times?
5. What is the minimum requirement for the DHCP range?
6. If I enable a DHCP relay, can I enable the DHCPv6 server on any interface?
7. Identify two different methods we can use to create VLANs.
8. What is the tag used to identify VLAN traffic called?
9. (a) What is the range of valid values for a VLAN tag? (b) Can we have a greater number of VLANs on our network than this range provides, and if so, how?
10. What type of switch do we need to implement VLANs on our network?

Further reading

- If you want to learn more about DHCP, you might consider reading the RFCs that define DHCP. The relevant RFC for standard DHCP is `https://tools.ietf.org/html/rfc2131` and the relevant RFC for DHCPv6 is `https://tools.ietf.org/html/3315`.
- Microsoft (2011). Networking Fundamentals, Exam 98-366. United States of America: John Wiley and Sons, Inc. This exam guide has an excellent overview of both IPv6 and DHCP.
- University of California's VLAN Information (`https://web.archive.org/web/20140312173147/http://net21.ucdavis.edu/newvlan.htm`). This contains an overview of VLANs, presented with the beginner in mind. It is archived from the original.

4
Captive Portal

If you are setting up a network in an environment where customers are going to have access to your wireless network, there is a good chance you are going to want to set up a captive portal for that network. A captive portal is a web page that is displayed when users access a network on which a captive portal has been enabled. Such a web page typically contains, at a minimum, the network terms of service, and getting past the captive portal may require acceptance of the terms of service, authentication, payment, or a combination of all three.

This chapter covers the basics of captive portal, and how to implement a captive portal in pfSense. The different methods of authentication will be covered, and we will also discuss how to troubleshoot captive portal issues.

Completing this chapter should provide the reader with an understanding of the following topics:

- Captive portal basics
- Captive portal best practices
- Enabling a captive portal
- Captive portal examples
- Troubleshooting captive portals

Technical requirements

All of the requirements for Chapter 2, *Installing pfSense*, are identical for this chapter in that you need a PC capable of running pfSense or the ability to run pfSense in a virtual machine. To implement a captive portal, it will be helpful to have a wireless access point.

Sample captive portal pages can be found at: https://github.com/dzient/learn_pfsense/tree/master/ch4.

Captive portal basics

When a captive portal is enabled on a network, users attempting to access the network from a desktop/laptop computer or mobile device are first directed to a web page. Although captive portals can be enabled on wired networks, more typically they are used as gatekeepers on wireless networks.

Captive portal pages are displayed after a user connects to a network protected by a captive portal. The user then will try to access a URL. If the URL request comes from an unknown client, the network operating system—in this case, pfSense/FreeBSD—will recognize that users must pass through the captive portal before they have full access to the network.

The user will be redirected to a web page or splash screen. They may simply have to click on a button to indicate their agreement with the network's terms of service or an **End User License Agreement** (**EULA**), or they may have to provide login credentials. Either way, once the user is authenticated, they will have access to the network.

The page you use for your captive portal must, at a minimum, allow the user to authenticate to the extent you require. There are many different examples of captive portal pages on the internet, and you should be able to find one you can use as a template. Ideally, you will want to customize your captive portal page to make it easy to use and perhaps even to advertise your business (at the very least, you will probably want to put your company's logo on the page) if you are implementing a captive portal for customers.

Implementing a captive portal on a publicly accessible network has several advantages:

- Captive portals help us to separate guest traffic, which has considerable security benefits. They help keep guests away from confidential company data, and can be an integral part of your network access-control policy.
- The terms of service (or EULA) can incorporate the right of the company to collect user data. Captive portal data can be collected based on time, date, and user, and such information can be used as you, or your company, requires. Such data can be channeled in a positive way, such as using the data to create a better user experience, or in a negative way, such as identifying users that are over-utilizing bandwidth and restricting their access.
- A captive portal landing page can be a useful means of marketing your product. Portals can also display exclusive deals and links to your company's social media accounts.

- Some users may abuse a public wireless network by downloading music, videos, other large files, or otherwise hogging bandwidth. Having a captive portal makes it easy to limit the speed at which files are downloaded and the amount of data that can be downloaded, and traffic-shaping can be used to limit how much bandwidth a single user can consume.
- It potentially protects you from legal action being taken against you. Having users agree to an EULA will (hopefully) make them understand that the network may not be secure, and it should also provide a shield from liability if an end user is the victim of a perpetrator of illegal activity on your network.

There are, however, a number of issues with networks that use captive portals, which you should consider:

- For a long time, the possibility of a third-party intercepting network traffic has been a concern. HTTPS is a protocol designed to prevent traffic-interception and alteration by nefarious third parties. But a captive portal works by intercepting and altering the connection between the end user and the network. This is not a problem with HTTP traffic, but sites secured with HTTPS will detect someone intercepting the connection, and will generate an untrusted connection warning. This captive portal can generate false positives when accessing sites that use HTTPS. Such false positives tend to train captive portal users to ignore these warnings, which, of course, is very bad, because they may then ignore an actual man-in-the-middle attack.
- Another issue is that captive portals use a web page for authentication, which makes them unsuitable for use with devices that do not have web browsers. This can cause confusion with users of such devices. Even when the device has a web browser, often the captive portal page will not show until the user accesses a web browser.
- Networks using captive portals can cause issues for browsers that use caches. For example, a user that connects to a network using a captive portal in which URLs are redirected to an authentication page may find that their browser continues to redirect to that page even after they disconnect from the captive portal network. In some cases, the only way to resolve the issue is to clear the browser cache.
- Finally, the argument can be made that captive portals are not user friendly—they force the end user to jump through hoops to connect to the network in the first place, and then often the user can be forced to jump through those hoops again if there is a time limit or data limit placed on the captive portal. Many businesses have turned off captive portals for exactly this reason.

In many cases, however, using a captive portal is the best possible option, especially if you need to have a form of user authentication for a public network, or if you need to bill customers for using your network, since captive portals provide a convenient way of determining how much data specific users are using. If you implement a captive portal, you can mitigate the effects of some of these issues by following best practices for captive portal implementation, which will also be covered in this chapter.

Captive portal best practices

Especially if you are implementing a captive portal on a Wi-Fi network, you should give some consideration to the overall user experience before you plow ahead and set it up. We need to consider the following:

- Is the network easy to connect to, and does it provide an adequate signal?
- Does the captive portal login page contain all the relevant information? Is it user-friendly?
- Have you addressed security concerns?

The network should be as easy to connect to as possible. It might be helpful to consider this issue from the perspective of the customer. You may want to set up several access points to ensure good coverage. If you do this, be sure to make sure overlapping access points are not on the same or adjacent channels, to minimize interference. Consider setting the channels as far apart as possible, for example, one access point on channel 1, another on channel 4, and a third on channel 7.

In addition, try to avoid access points that use the 2.4 GHz band (primarily 802.11 b and g access points), as many devices, such as microwave ovens, use these frequencies, and the band is full of interference. As an alternative, try to use devices that use the 5 GHz and other bands (for example, 802.11 n and ac).

If you are implementing a captive portal as part of your business, consider that the captive portal login page is part of your branding and design it accordingly. The captive portal page should have your company's logo, and it should clearly identify the company. Take care to personalize your captive portal page. You can use the captive portal page as an opportunity to display advertisements, but they should be relevant to your customers. Asking the customer for personal information up front (for example, asking them for email addresses) and displaying lengthy terms of service should be avoided where possible.

Finally, security concerns should be addressed. This can usually be done by keeping the captive portal on a separate network, and making sure sensitive company data is on a separate network or networks that are not accessible from the captive portal. There is always the possibility of someone trying to bypass the security restrictions of a captive portal to try to access your internal networks; depending on how sensitive your company's data is, it may be something you want to be constantly on guard against. Keeping track of captive portal activity by reviewing the relevant log files can help pinpoint areas of concern.

Enabling a captive portal

To get started implementing a captive portal on your network, perform the following steps:

1. Navigate to **Services** | **Captive Portal**. This page displays a table with all of the defined captive portal zones. There is a green **+ Add** button down and to the right of the table; pressing this button allows you to add a zone.
2. When you add a zone, you are initially directed to the **Add Zone** page. Here you are required to enter the **Zone Name**, which can only contain letters, digits, and underscores. You can also enter a brief (non-parsed) description in the **Description** field. Enter this information and press the **Continue** button.
3. Now we will be directed to the **Configuration** page, where we are presented with a warning that contains the following information:
   - Make sure you enable the DHCP server on the captive portal interface
   - Make sure the maximum DHCP lease time is longer than the captive portal hard timeout
   - Make sure the DNS forwarder or DNS resolver is enabled, or DNS lookups will not work for unauthenticated clients
4. To begin configuration, check the **Enable Captive Portal** checkbox. Once this box is checked, the other options will appear on the page.
5. Consider the options that must be changed in order for the captive portal to work. You must select at least one interface on which the captive portal will be enabled, and you can do this in the **Interfaces list** box. In most scenarios where you are setting up a captive portal, you probably want to have a separate interface or interfaces for captive portal users.

6. Scroll down to the **Authentication** section. Here you must select an authentication method: **No Authentication**, **Local User Manager/Vouchers**, or **RADIUS Authentication**:

   - If **No Authentication** is selected, the captive portal user will not be prompted for a username and password or a voucher code—usually, at most, they will be required to accept the network's terms of service.
   - **Local User Manager/Vouchers** covers the cases in which pfSense will handle authentication. Either the user will be prompted for a username/password combination for a user who was previously entered into the pfSense user manager, or the user will be prompted for a voucher code that was generated by pfSense.
   - In the case of **RADIUS Authentication**, the authentication will be done by an external RADIUS server. This will be covered in detail in a subsection, but we will note that, if you choose this option, at a minimum, you will have to enter the RADIUS protocol and the IP address of the primary RADIUS server.

7. The next section is **HTML Page Contents**. You will probably find it necessary to replace the portal page and contents page, and to upload a portal page that is appropriate for the type of authentication you selected. If you are don't require authentication, all you need is a form with a **Submit** button and a hidden field with the `redirurl` name and the `$PORTAL_REDIRURL$` value. If you require authentication, then you need to have either `auth_user` and `auth_pass` or `auth_voucher` (or both if you support both username/password login and vouchers).

8. The pages you uploaded may contain images, and as you probably guessed, you're going to need a means of uploading these images. This is what the **File Manager** tab is for. Any files you upload via this tab with the filename prefix of captiveportal, will be made available in the root directory of the captive portal server. This is useful if you have files that you want to reference in your portal page (for example, a company logo). In addition, you can upload PHP files for execution. The total size limit for all files uploaded via this tab is 1 MB:

   - To add a file, click on the **+ Add** button, which is below the **Installed Files** table and to the right. This loads a separate page where you can upload the file.
   - Click on the **Browse** button to launch a file dialog box.
   - Select a file, click on the **Open** button in the file dialog box, and then click on the **Upload** button.

The preceding guide should be enough to get a captive portal running on your network. There are, however, many other settings for captive portal configuration. Most of them can be kept at their default settings most of the time, but in certain circumstances, they can be altered to ensure the captive portal runs smoothly.

- On the main captive portal configuration page, under the **Interfaces list** box, is the **Maximum concurrent connections** edit box. This setting controls not how many users can be logged into the captive portal, but how many concurrent connections are allowed per IP address.
- The next two settings are **Idle Timeout (Minutes)** and **Hard Timeout (Minutes)**. **Idle Timeout (Minutes)** controls how long it takes before an idle client is disconnected, while **Hard Timeout (Minutes)** controls how long it takes before a client is disconnected even if they are active. Both settings are optional and leaving them blank disables them.
- The next setting is **Traffic quota (Megabytes)**. As the name implies, this sets a limit on the amount of data a captive portal user can use, inclusive of uploads and downloads. After they have reached this limit, they will be disconnected. They can, however, log back in immediately.
- The next setting is the **Pass-through credits per MAC address** edit box. Entering a number here allows a client to pass through the captive portal this number of times without being directed to the captive portal page. Once this number is exceeded, the user is directed to the captive portal login page again. As the name implies, this is done on a per-MAC address basis.
- There is also a **Waiting period to restore pass-through credits (Hours)**. If pass-through credits are enabled, and this parameter is set to a value greater than zero, pass-through credits will be restored to their original count after this number of hours.
- The **Reset waiting period** checkbox, if checked, will result in a waiting period on login attempts being imposed on clients whose pass-through credits have been exhausted. If not checked, such users will be allowed to log in again immediately. The **Logout popup window** checkbox, if checked, will display a pop-up logout page when the users initially pass through the captive portal. This can be used to allow users to explicitly log out, but it also can be used if you want to display a page informing the user that they have successfully passed through the captive portal.

- There are three options covering URL redirects. You can specify a URL on another server by entering it in the **Pre-authentication redirect URL** edit box. After accessing this page, the user will be redirected to the login page. Normally, after login, the user will be able to access the URL they tried to access before logging in, but if you set **After authentication Redirection URL**, you can redirect them to a different page. If you want users whose MAC addresses were blocked to be informed of this, you can set the **Blocked MAC address redirect URL**.

- The next option, **Disable Concurrent user logins**, will, if enabled, cause only the most recent user login to be active. Devices currently logged in with the same username will be disconnected.

- If you check the **Disable MAC filtering** checkbox, the captive portal will not check to confirm that a user's MAC address remains the same during their session. This can be helpful in cases where pfSense cannot confirm the user's MAC address (for example, in cases where the user is separated from the pfSense system by several routers). The downside of this option is that, when MAC filtering is disabled, RADIUS MAC authentication is not possible.

- The **Enable Pass-through MAC** automatic additions option, if checked, will result in a MAC pass-through entry being added for every user who successfully authenticates (or, in cases where authentication is not required, every user who successfully passes through the captive portal). Users of the authenticated MAC address will not have to log in again, unless the MAC pass-through entry is removed from the table on the **MAC** tab.

- The **Enable Pass-through MAC automatic addition with username** option takes effect only if it is checked and the **Enable Pass-through MAC automatic additions** option is also checked. If both are checked, the username used during authentication will be saved.

- The **Enable per-user bandwidth restriction** option, if checked, allows you to restrict each user who logs in to a specified bandwidth. If you enable this option, you need to specify a **Default download** and **Default upload** in the next two edit boxes. RADIUS can override these default settings.

Authentication options

If you choose **No Authentication** as your authentication option, you have covered as much as is needed to get your captive portal up and running. Just upload a form that contains a **Submit** button and a hidden field with the `redirurl` name and the `$PORTAL_REDIRURL$` value, and you will be set. If you require some form of authentication, however, this section will show you how to add it.

Local User Manager/Vouchers

The second option, as the label implies, allows for two different forms of authentication: one that uses pfSense's built-in user manager, and one that uses a voucher ticket system. We will first consider authentication through the user manager.

Local user manager

Utilizing the user manager requires you to add one or more users and grant them the appropriate permissions:

- If you want to utilize the user manager, navigate to **Services** | **User Manager**. You will then need to add as many users as you need to for captive portal access.
- It might also be a good idea to set up a separate group for captive portal users, and you can do that by clicking on the **Groups** tab. Once there, you can click on the **+Add** button on the right side of the page below the table to add a group.
- There is a single section on this page titled **Group Properties**, and in this section, you need to enter a **Group Name.** You can also enter a description in the **Description** field.
- In the **Group membership** list boxes, you can add other groups to which you want members of the new group to belong.
- Once you are done, press the **Save** button.
- We still haven't assigned captive portal privileges to the newly created group, so, once you are redirected to the table, find the group in the table and, under the **Actions** column, click on the **Edit** group icon (the pencil). Once again, the **Group Properties** section is there, but underneath it is a section called **Assigned Privileges** where, as you probably guessed, you can assign privileges to the group. Clicking on the **Add** button will enable you to add privileges.
- This will load a page with a list box with many options; for this group we want to select **User – Services: Captive Portal** login. Select this and click on the **Save** button at the bottom of the page.

- This will take you back to the previous page, so you need to click on the **Save** button on that page, which will return you to the main **Groups** page. We have created a group with captive portal login privileges.

- You need to go back to the **Users** tab and add users to the group that you created in the previous step by pressing the **+Add** button, adding information for each user, pressing the **Save** button, and repeating the process for as many users as you need to add. At a minimum, you need to enter a username and password for each user, and make the user a member of the new group. There are also options to create a user certificate, add an SSH key (so the user can connect to pfSense via SSH without entering a username/password combination), and a field for an IPsec pre-shared key.

- Now that we have created some captive portal user accounts, we can return to the captive portal configuration. Note that following the radio buttons where we select the authentication mention, if **Local User Manager/Vouchers** is selected, there is an **Allow only users with "Captive Portal login" privilege** set checkbox. Although this checkbox is selected by default, when we click on the **Local User Manager/Vouchers** radio button, we can uncheck it, thus eliminating the need to create a group with this privilege added to it.

Voucher authentication

If you need to authenticate users, but do not want to use the user manager, you may want to use vouchers instead. Vouchers are alphanumeric codes that provide access for a specified period of time and typically can only be used once:

- Start the voucher configuration by clicking on the **Vouchers** tab under **Captive Portal**. This page has two sections: **Voucher Rolls**, which shows any existing vouchers, and **Create, Generate and Activate Rolls with Vouchers**. The **Enable** checkbox, when checked, begins the process of creating vouchers.

- The next two fields are for the **Voucher Public Key** and the **Voucher Private Key**. Here, you should paste an RSA public key and RSA private key (64 bits or smaller).

- The next field is **Character set**; this defines the characters contained in the generated tickets. In most cases, you can keep the default value.

- The next three fields must add up to one bit less than the RSA public/private key and therefore will be considered together:
    - The **# of Roll bits** field reserves a range in each voucher to store the roll number to which it belongs.
    - The **# of Ticket bits** field reserves a range in each voucher to store the ticket number to which it belongs.
    - The **# of Checksum bits** field reserves a range in each voucher to store a checksum over the roll number and ticket number. The sum of the roll, ticket, and checksum bits must be one bit less bit than the RSA public/private key.

- The **Magic number** field defines a magic number to be stored in each voucher, which is only stored if there are bits left over in the roll, ticket, and checksum bits. The **Invalid voucher message** and **Expired voucher message** fields define messages to display when the voucher is invalid and expired, respectively.

- The **Voucher Database Synchronization** section of the page allows you to enter the master voucher database ID, sync port, and username/password combination. If this node is the master voucher database node, or if it will be the only node using vouchers, you can leave these fields blank. Press the **Save** button at the bottom of the page when you are done.

- When the **Voucher** page reloads, there will be a new section at the top of the page called **Voucher Rolls**. You can generate new voucher rolls by pressing the **+Add** button below the table on the right side. There are fields for the **Roll #** (the number found on top of the generated vouchers), the **Minutes per ticket** (the time in minutes a user is allowed access), and **Count** (the number of vouchers generated). There is also a **Comment** field where you can enter a non-parsed comment. When you have filled out these fields, press the **Save** button.

- When you return to the main **Voucher** page, the newly created voucher roll will be listed in the table at the top. Under the **Action** column, you can click on the **Export vouchers** icon (the sheet) to download the voucher roll as a `.csv` file. The file contains a series of vouchers that can be used for captive portal authentication. In order to accept captive portal login via vouchers, your portal login page must include the following field: `<input name="auth_voucher" type="text">`.

RADIUS authentication

Remote Authentication Dial-In User Service (RADIUS) provides a means of centralized authentication, authorization, and accounting for network users. To use RADIUS to authenticate captive portal users, you must have a RADIUS server. It is outside the scope of this book to explain how to configure a RADIUS server in depth, but the excellent GPL-licensed FreeRADIUS is available as a third-party package, and we will cover RADIUS captive portal configuration as one of the examples later in this chapter. Here, we will mention some of the more important RADIUS options on the **Captive Portal Configuration** page:

- The first option is RADIUS protocol. pfSense supports several protocols for sending and receiving data from the RADIUS server. **Password Authentication Protocol (PAP)**, **Challenge Handshake Authentication Protocol (CHAP)**, **MS-CHAPv1**, and **MS-CHAPv2** are all supported.
- You can supply a **Primary Authentication Source** and **Secondary Authentication Source**, each of these having a **Primary RADIUS Server** and **Secondary RADIUS Server**. You can supply an IP address, port, and shared secret for each. Entering an IP address for each RADIUS server used is required. If the RADIUS port field is left blank, pfSense will use the default RADIUS port. Entering a RADIUS shared secret is not required, but it is recommended.
- The next section is **Accounting**. Enabling the sending of RADIUS accounting packets to the primary RADIUS server (which you can do by checking the **RADIUS** checkbox) enables you to set bandwidth and traffic limits with RADIUS. **Accounting Port** allows you to set the RADIUS accounting port; in most cases, you can use the default of 1813. Finally, **Accounting updates** controls how often updates are sent to RADIUS. **No updates** disables updates completely, while **Stop/Start** and **Stop/Start (FreeRADIUS)** will log accounting start and stop packets (when the client connects/disconnects). **Interim** can be used to log other client activity and to set traffic limits that can be tracked during active sessions.

- There are several options in the **RADIUS Options** section, which will now be considered:
    - If the **Reauthenticate connected users every minute** option is enabled, pfSense will send access-requests to RADIUS for each user every minute. If an access-reject is received for any user on one of these requests, the user is disconnected from the captive portal immediately. There is also an option called **RADIUS MAC Authentication**. Checking this box will cause RADIUS to try to authenticate captive portal users by sending their MAC address as the username and the MAC authentication secret, specified in the next edit box, as the password.
    - The **RADIUS NAS IP attribute** drop-down box should be set to the pfSense interface facing the network on which the captive portal is enabled. This information is sent from pfSense to the RADIUS server, so it will know where to where a user is trying to connect.
    - The **Session Timeout** option, when enabled, will cause clients to be disconnected when the time specified in the **RADIUS Session-Timeout** attribute is reached.
    - The **Traffic quota option**, when enabled, will cause clients to be disconnected when the amount of traffic specified in the `pfSense-Max-Total-Octets` attribute is reached, including both downloads and uploads.
    - The **Per-user bandwidth restrictions**, when enabled, will cause clients' bandwidth to be limited to the values in the `pfSense-Bandwidth-Max-Up` and `pfSense-Bandwidth-Max-Down` (or comparable WISPr) attributes.
    - The **Type** drop-down box allows you to set the type to either the **default** or to a **Cisco** type. The default is for the **Calling-Station-ID** to be set to the client's MAC address and the **Called-Station-ID** to be set to pfSense's WAN IP address. Changing the type to **Cisco** will cause these attributes to be set to the client's IP address and the client's MAC address, respectively.

- There are two more attributes related to accounting. **Accounting style**, if enabled, causes data counts for RADIUS accounting to be taken from the client's perspective, so that **Acct-Input-Octets** represent download and **Acct-Output-Octets** represent upload. **Idle time accounting** causes time spent idle to be included in the total session time, even if the client is disconnected for exceeding the idle timeout.
- The **NAS Identifier** field allows you to specify a NAS identifier to override the default value.
- The **MAC address** drop-down box allows you to change the MAC address format used in the RADIUS system. **Default** will place a colon every 8 bits; **Single dash** will place a dash in the middle, dividing the address into two 24-bit fields; **IETF** places a dash every 8 bits instead of a colon; **Cisco** places a period (dot) every 16 bits (3 16-bit fields); **Unformatted** results in a single, 48-bit address in hexadecimal format with no separators.

Additional captive portal options

There are a few more options on the page and on the remaining tabs, the most important of which is **HTML Page Contents**. We will cover the remaining options in this section.

- **HTTPS Options** initially has a single option, the **Enable HTTPS login** checkbox, which when checked, will cause the captive portal username and password, over an HTTPS connection, to take advantage of the SSL encryption such a connection provides.
    - If this box is checked, you must provide the **HTTPS server name** and the **SSL Certificate**. The server name should match the **Common Name** (**CN**) in your certificate.
    - By default, when HTTPS login is enabled, clients can connect to the captive portal via HTTPS. You can prevent this by checking the **Disable HTTPS Forwards** checkbox, in which case attempts to connect to port `443` sites will not be forwarded to the captive portal. Users will then have to attempt a connection to port `80` to get forwarded to the captive portal.

- The final section, **HTML Page Contents**, is where you can upload the captive portal pages. A minimal knowledge of HTML or PHP is required to create these pages, and if you don't want to create your own, you should be able to find sample captive portal pages that you can use (some may require some slight modification for your needs). The pages you can upload are the **Portal page contents** (the actual captive portal login page), **Auth error page** contents (the page to display when an authentication error occurs), and **Logout page** contents (the page to display on authentication success when the logout popup is enabled, and which may or may not contain an option to log out of the captive portal). When you have uploaded these pages, you will be done with the configuration of this captive portal zone, and you can press the **Save** button at the bottom of the page.

- There are several other options worth mentioning. The **MACs** tab allows you to control access to the captive portal based on MAC addresses. Clicking the **+Add** button on this page allows you to add a MAC address. Once you do this, you will be at the **Edit MAC Address Rules** page. Here you can specify a **MAC address** (the button to the right of this option allows you to copy your MAC). The **Action** drop-down box allows you to choose what to do with traffic from this MAC address (the options are **Pass** and **Block**). You can also specify **Bandwidth up** and **Bandwidth down** limitations for the MAC address (in Kbit/s), as well as a non-parsed description in the **Description** field.

- The **Allowed IP Addresses** tab allows you to control captive portal access by IP address. Clicking on the **+Add** button on this page takes you to the **Edit Captive Portal IP Rule** page. At a minimum, you must enter the IP address and the CIDR of the address. You can also specify the direction of the access. From allows access from the client IP through the captive portal, to allows access from all the clients behind the portal to the IP. The **Both** option allows traffic in both directions. As with MAC addresses, you can specify **Bandwidth up** and **Bandwidth down** for the specified IP address.

- The **Allowed Hostnames** tab allows you to control captive portal access based on hostname. Again, the **+Add** button on this tab allows you to add entries. You need to enter a hostname in the **Hostname** field, and, as with **Allowed IP Addresses**, you can control the direction of the access, as well as **Bandwidth up** and **Bandwidth down**. You may also enter a non-parsed description in the **Description** field.

Captive portal examples

To illustrate pfSense's captive portal capabilities in action, we will provide some practical examples of captive portal implementation. We will begin with the most common form of captive portal used by most businesses: a captive portal with no authentication.

Example #1 – no authentication

In this example, a business wants to provide wireless internet access to its customers, but it wants to present a page with the EULA, which the user must accept before being granted access. It also wants to segregate captive portal traffic from the rest of the network, so a separate interface must be set up first:

1. To set up the guest network interface, navigate to **Interfaces | Assignments**. You need to have at least one interface in your pfSense system that has not yet been assigned. There are two ways you can go about creating the interface for the guest network:

    - You can select the unassigned interface in the last drop-down box on the page and click on the **Add** button. Then follow the instructions in the section on adding interfaces in Chapter 3, *Configuring pfSense*. Name this interface something that will make its function easy to remember, for example, GUEST.

    - You can set up your guest network as a VLAN. This has the advantage of allowing you to set up more networks later on with the same parent interface. To do so, click on the **VLANs** tab, and click on the **Add** button on that tab. Follow the instructions in the VLANs section of Chapter 3, *Configuring pfSense*. Make sure the unassigned interface is the parent interface. In addition, you will need hardware that is compatible with VLANs in order for this option to work. If you are setting up a wireless network, this means acquiring a wireless access point that supports VLANs.

2. Once you have configured the GUEST interface, you must enable the DHCP server on it so captive portal users will have an IP address assigned to them automatically. How to enable DHCP on an interface is described in the section on *Adding a DHCP server* in Chapter 3, *Configuring pfSense*.

3. Now that the preconditions for setting up a captive portal are out of the way, we can navigate to **Services** | **Captive Portal** and begin setting it up. Click on the **Add** button to add a new captive portal, enter a **Zone name** and **Zone description** into the appropriate fields, and click on the **Save and Continue** button.

4. Check the **Enable Captive Portal** checkbox, which will cause the captive portal options to appear. In the **Captive Portal Configuration** section, you must at least select an interface in the **Interfaces list** box. In this case, you should select the interface created in step 1 (GUEST). Note that you may select more than one interface.

5. You may skip past the other options in this section, as it is not necessary to set them; you should, however, at least give them a look to see which ones you might want to set in order to better manage captive portal usage. In particular, you might consider setting **Idle Timeout** (the amount of time users may stay idle before being disconnected) and **Traffic quota** (the total amount of data users can upload and download before being disconnected).

6. Scroll down to the **Authentication** section and make sure **No Authentication** is selected as the authentication method.

7. Scroll down to the **HTML Page Contents** section and add a page for **Portal page contents**, **Auth error page contents**, and **Logout page contents** (remember, the logout page displays upon proper authentication if the logout popup is enabled). The most important of these pages is **Portal page contents**. Since we are not doing any authentication, the form need only have the following fields:

   - `<form method="post" action="$PORTAL_ACTION$">`
   - `<input name="redirurl" type="hidden" value="$PORTAL_REDIRURL$">`
   - `<input name="zone" type="hidden" value="$PORTAL_ZONE$">`
   - There must also be an `<input>` tag with the type set to `submit` (this will be the button the user clicks on to go through the portal).

8. When you are done, click on the **Save** button. The captive portal should now be enabled on the GUEST network.

Example #2 – authentication with vouchers

Vouchers are useful in a number of scenarios where you need to provide users with temporary access to your network, but also want to have some form of authentication. With vouchers, you can limit their access (vouchers can be set up with a time limit, and there are a number of other ways you can control a user's access); you can also track their usage by keeping track of which voucher codes are given to users.

Setting up voucher authentication is only slightly different from setting up a captive portal with no authentication:

1. As in the previous example, if you want to keep captive portal traffic completely separate from the rest of your network, you will have to add an interface.
2. You must enable the DHCP server on the captive portal interface.
3. Navigate to **Services | Captive Portal**, click on the **Add** button to add a new captive portal, enter a **Zone name** and **Zone description**, and click on the **Save and Continue** button.
4. When the page reloads, check the **Enable Captive Portal** checkbox. Make sure the captive portal interface is selected in the **Interfaces list** box.
5. Scroll down to the **Authentication** section and select **Local User Manager/Vouchers**.
6. Scroll down to **HTML Page Contents**, and upload pages for **Portal page contents**, **Auth error page contents**, and **Logout page contents**. The auth error page and logout page need not be any different from the pages that would be used if you selected **No Authentication**. The portal page, however, must contain a field for inputting the voucher code. You might consider adding username and password fields as well, so you can use the same page for authentication via the local user manager. At a minimum, the following fields must exist in the portal login page for voucher authentication to work (note that the only field that has to be added to our no authentication portal page is the voucher input field):
   - `<form method="post" action="$PORTAL_ACTION$">`
   - `<input name="redirurl" type="hidden" value="$PORTAL_REDIRURL$">`
   - `<input name="zone" type="hidden" value="$PORTAL_ZONE$">`
   - `<input name = "auth_voucher" type="text">`
   - An input tag with the type set to `submit`
7. Scroll to the bottom of the page and click on the **Save** button.

8. We have configured the captive portal to work with vouchers, but we still need to generate the voucher codes. To do this, on the main **Captive Portal** page, click on the **Edit** button for the captive portal you just created and, when the page loads, click on the **Voucher** tab.

9. On the **Voucher** tab, click on the **Add** button.

10. Enter the parameters for the voucher roll. Press the **Save** button when you are done.
    - In the **Roll** # edit box, enter an integer from 0 to 65,535 for the roll number.
    - In the **Minutes per ticket** edit box, enter the time in minutes that a user is allowed access.
    - The **Count** is the number of vouchers (from 1 to 1,023) that will be generated.
    - You may also enter a brief, non-parsed **Comment** in the final edit box.

11. All that remains is to export the voucher roll. In the **Voucher Rolls** section of the **Voucher** tab, there is a column called **Actions**; under that column, there will be an **Export** icon (a sheet of paper with an X on it). Click on this icon to export the voucher file as a **comma-separated values** (**CSV**) file you can open with a spreadsheet application, such as LibreOffice Calc.

Example #3 – RADIUS authentication

Authenticating through a RADIUS server is more involved than voucher authentication or authenticating through the user manager, as it requires installing and configuring a RADIUS server, but pfSense has streamlined much of the process, so it isn't as difficult as you might think. Configuring a captive portal in this case involves three major steps:

1. Installing and configuring the RADIUS server
2. Completing the prerequisites for setting up a captive portal
3. Configuring the captive portal

Step 1 – RADIUS installation and configuration

1. Navigate to **System** | **Package Manager** and click on the **Available Packages** tab.
2. Scroll down to find the freeradius3 package (a free implementation of the RADIUS protocol) and click on the corresponding **Install** button. This will redirect you to the **Package Installer** tab, where you will be asked to confirm the installation by clicking on the **Confirm** button.
3. A text box will appear, updating you on the status of the installation, which should take no more than a couple of minutes.
4. Once FreeRADIUS is installed, you can begin configuration by navigating to **Services** | **FreeRADIUS**.
5. Click on the **Interfaces** tab, and set up the ports for authentication, accounting, and status information.
   - The **Interface IP Address** can be kept at its default value of `*`.
   - In the **Port** edit box, enter the RADIUS listening port of `1812`.
   - Set the **Interface Type** in the drop-down box to **Authentication**.
   - Leave the **IP Version** at its default value of IPv4.
   - Enter a brief **Description**, if desired (for example, **Authentication port**). Click on the **Save** button.
   - Repeat this process for port `1813`, whose **Interface Type** should be set to **Accounting**, and port `1816`, whose **Interface Type** should be set to **Status**. If there are other ports you wish to configure, you can.
6. Click on the **NAS / Clients** tab, and then click on the **Add** button. Now client configuration can begin.
   - Set **Client IP Address** to the IP of the pfSense firewall. You can set this to the loopback address (`127.0.0.1`) for the sake of simplicity. Note that the client is the captive portal, not the end user.
   - **Client IP Version** can be kept at its default value of **IPv4**.
   - You can enter a **Client Shortname** (for example, `Captive-portal`).
   - In **Client Shared Secret**, you should enter a password that will authenticate the captive portal client. You will need this password when you are configuring the captive portal.
   - The remaining fields can remain unchanged, although you may want to enter a description in the **Description** field.
   - Click on the **Save** button when you are done.

7. You need to add one or more users to the configuration, which begins by clicking on the **Users** tab and then clicking on the **Add** button.
   - Enter a username and password in the appropriate fields.
   - **Password Encryption** can be kept at the default value of `Cleartext-Password`, unless you have a need to use MD5 encryption.
   - The remaining fields can be kept at their default values. Click on the **Save** button when done.
   - Repeat this procedure for as many users as you need to add.

Step 2 – captive portal prerequisites

This step covers everything that needs to be done before a captive portal can be enabled on an interface:

1. As with all other forms of captive portal configuration, it is best if a separate interface is used for the portal.
2. The DHCP server must be enabled on the captive portal interface.

Step 3 – captive portal configuration

These steps cover the configuration of the captive portal through a RADIUS server:

1. Navigate to **Services | Captive Portal**, and click on the **Add** button to add a new captive portal.
2. Check on the **Enable Captive Portal** checkbox, which will cause the other captive portal options to appear.
3. Select the appropriate interface in the **Interface** list box.
4. Scroll down to the **Authentication** section, and select **RADIUS Authentication** for the **Authentication Method**.
5. The **RADIUS protocol** can be kept as **PAP**, unless you changed the password authentication in the **RADIUS configuration** to **MD5-Password**, in which case you should select **CHAP-MD5**.
6. For **Primary RADIUS server**, enter the IP address (`127.0.0.1`), RADIUS port (`1812`), and **RADIUS shared secret** (whatever you entered for **Client Shared Secret** during RADIUS configuration).

7. Scroll down to **Accounting**. You don't need to set up accounting, but it will make your life easier when troubleshooting. Check the **RADIUS** checkbox to enable the sending of accounting packets to the RADIUS server. The **Accounting Port** can be left at its default value of 1813. Set **Accounting updates** to **Stop/Start**.

8. Set the **RADIUS NAS IP Attribute** to the IP address of the interface on which the captive portal is running.

9. If desired, you can enable **RADIUS MAC Authentication** by checking the appropriate checkbox. If this is enabled, the RADIUS server will use the user's MAC address as their username and the value entered in the **MAC authentication secret** edit box as the password (in such cases, the actual username entered by the user will be disregarded). This is a convenient option if you don't want to configure separate user accounts, but instead want to have a single captive portal password (the **MAC authentication secret**).

10. In the **HTML Page Contents** section, make sure the appropriate pages are uploaded. In particular, the **Portal page contents** page should have fields for the username and password.

11. Click on the **Save** button when you are done.

You have now completed the captive portal configuration through a RADIUS server. Keep in mind that this example only covers some very basic RADIUS options; we did not cover such RADIUS features as support for SQL databases and the **Lightweight Directory Access Protocol (LDAP)**.

Troubleshooting captive portals

pfSense's captive portal service has many options, which means that there are many more things that can go wrong with captive portal access. We can divide these issues into two general categories:

- Authentication issues (client cannot authenticate, even with seemingly valid credentials)
- Client can establish a captive portal connection, but some other aspect of the service is not working (for example, DNS is not functioning or websites are blocked)

We will first consider authentication issues. The authentication options are **Local User Manager/Vouchers** and **RADIUS Authentication**. If you are using the local user manager, you should confirm that you have created the user accounts correctly and, if **Allow only users/groups with "Captive portal login" privilege set** is checked, you should confirm that the users have this privilege. You can, of course, disable this option and see whether the users can connect to troubleshoot the issue. If you are using vouchers to authenticate, you should confirm that your captive portal login page has `<input name="auth_voucher" type="text">` for entering the voucher.

One possible issue that might arise is that you are trying to use MAC addresses for authentication, but the captive portal service cannot confirm that the MAC address is correct. This could happen if there is a router between the captive portal client and pfSense, and this issue could occur both in cases where a RADIUS server is being used for authentication, and without a RADIUS server. For troubleshooting, you might try allowing users access by IP address and see whether this works. If it does, there's a good chance pfSense is unable to confirm the MAC address.

One other possibility is that the user is trying to access the captive portal page through HTTPS, but your captive portal zone is only configured for HTTP access. In this case, the solution is for the user to try again with HTTP at the beginning of the URL.

One problem that has been reported is that sometimes, when using a captive portal on a VLAN, the captive portal page will not load. This apparently happens when the parent interface of the VLAN is also being used as a separate interface on pfSense. To prevent this problem, when a parent interface is partitioned into VLANs (VLAN1, VLAN2, and so on), the parent interface (for example, OPT1) should not be used separately; only the VLANs should be used.

If a RADIUS server is being used for authentication, the problem could be either a client or server issue. The RADIUS server may be misconfigured, or it may be down. If you have confirmed that the RADIUS server is functioning properly, the problem may be an incorrect configuration of pfSense. Log files can be helpful in further pinpointing the exact problem. Navigate to **Status** | **System Logs** and click on the **Captive Portal Auth** tab. If pfSense cannot connect to the RADIUS server at all, you should check the IP address/port settings for the RADIUS servers, as well as the shared secret.

The second category of issues is when the user is able to pass through the captive portal, but there are other issues. For example, the user may be having DNS issues. Once again, a good indication that a problem is related to DNS is when you can ping the IP address of a site, but you cannot ping the hostname. DNS is likely not functioning if pinging a valid hostname (for example, `https://www.google.com/`) returns the following result:

```
ping: unknown host google.com
```

If you are running the command prompt under Windows, the response might look like this:

```
Ping request could not find host google.com. Please check the name and try
again.
```

If it looks like DNS resolution is the problem, you should check to make sure either DNS forwarder or DNS resolver is running, but not both. If you have confirmed that one of these is running and you are still having problems, the issue may be a DNS server that is down or is not configured properly.

If the user cannot access certain websites, the problem may be that the firewall or proxy server has blocked access to the site. You should navigate to **Firewall** | **Rules** and check to see whether there are any rules for the captive portal interface that might block access. Proxy servers usually have the capability to block websites, so if you are running one, you will want to check the settings for the proxy server. We will cover both firewall rules and proxy servers in greater depth in future chapters.

 Having problems with pfSense's captive portal on iOS devices (for example, an iPad)? This could be due to a problem with the Safari browser. To fix it, disable URL redirection, clear Safari's caches, disable Autofill, and try again.

Summary

We began this chapter by discussing some of the advantages and disadvantages of captive portals. There are some obvious and not-so-obvious security issues related to captive portals, but by following best practices, such as putting captive portal traffic onto a separate interface and auditing captive portal activity, we can minimize the downside of captive portals. We then covered the many options for captive portal configuration in pfSense–namely, the different authentication options. We then discussed examples using these different forms of authentication, and showed that the most difficult of all of these methods—authentication through a RADIUS server—is not all that difficult.

In the next chapter, we will consider other services that you may want to implement on your pfSense system, such as DNS, DDNS, NTP, and SNMP.

Questions

1. Why is the 2.4 GHz band a poor choice for a captive portal's wireless access point?
2. Identify the three authentication choices available with pfSense's captive portal.
3. If we do not want to allow users to use a captive portal with more than one device, what option should we enable?
4. Of the three different HTML pages that can be uploaded, which one is absolutely essential for the captive portal to function?
5. Identify one of the two authentication options we could use if we want to provide temporary network access through the captive portal with some form of authentication, but we do not want to set up separate accounts.
6. Which authentication option should we use if we want to have separate accounts for users but want the authentication done by a separate server?
7. What service must be enabled on the captive portal interface before a captive portal is enabled?
8. Is the RADIUS client the end user? If no, who is the RADIUS client?

Further reading

- An overview of captive portals from Linksys: `https://www.linksys.com/us/r/resource-center/captive-portal/`
- Secplicity – Security Simplified. 2016-08-26. Provides a good overview of the techniques used by attackers on networks secured by captive portals: `https://www.secplicity.org/2016/08/26/lessons-defcon-2016-bypassing-captive-portals/`
- Electronic Frontier Foundation. 2017-08-07. The article discusses some of the security concerns of captive portals and best practices for securing them: `https://www.eff.org/deeplinks/2017/08/how-captive-portals-interfere-wireless-security-and-privacy`

Additional pfSense Services

5

In the previous two chapters, we covered the services and features of pfSense that are essential in most network scenarios. It is difficult to imagine a network of any size not implementing a DHCP server, and captive portals are extremely useful in setting up a public Wi-Fi network. The services that have been omitted until this chapter are those that you may not have occasion to implement on your network, yet they are all vital in their own way.

In this chapter, we will cover the **Domain Name System (DNS)** and discuss the two different ways to implement it in pfSense. We will also provide a preview of Chapter 6, *Firewall and NAT*, and demonstrate how to use firewall rules to prevent users from bypassing your DNS settings. We will also cover **Dynamic DNS (DDNS)**, why it is useful, and how to implement it. Finally, we will cover two services that are not configured as often, but are still significant: **Network Time Protocol (NTP)** and **Simple Network Management Protocol (SNMP)**.

This chapter should provide you with an understanding of the following topics:

- Introduction to DNS
- Configuring DNS
- Configuring DDNS
- **Network Time Protocol (NTP)**
- **Simple Network Management Protocol (SNMP)**

Technical requirements

To follow along with the examples in this chapter, you will need a pfSense system acting as a firewall with at least one node connected to it on the LAN side. To follow along with the DDNS examples, it will be helpful to have a DDNS domain. You can obtain free DDNS domains from such providers as No-IP and Duck DNS. If you want to try some of the more esoteric NTP options, you may want to obtain a GPS or PPS device and try to use those for synchronization. If you want to try configuring pfSense to act as an SNMP server, you'll need at least one client device to confirm that it works.

Introduction to DNS

DNS is a hierarchical, decentralized system for mapping internet names to resources, most notably to IP addresses. It does this by designating authoritative name servers for each domain. Authoritative name servers can delegate authority over subdomains to other name servers. Thus, DNS provides both a form of decentralization and fault-tolerance.

From the earliest days of the internet, the idea of mapping easily-remembered names to less easily-remembered numbers (such as IP addresses). ARPANET used a text file called `HOSTS.TXT` (`/etc/hosts` on UNIX-based systems) that mapped hostnames to their numerical addresses. At the time, addresses were added manually.

Even when the list was relatively small, this manual system was cumbersome and prone to error. By the early 1980s, however, maintaining a single, centralized list became unmanageable, and the growing networks required an automated method of maintaining a list that mapped names to addresses. DNS became that method.

The domain name space is a tree-like structure. At the top is the root zone; the root-zone DNS servers are the authoritative servers for top-level domains (for example, `.com`, `.edu`, `.net`, and `.uk`). Every DNS query either starts with a query to a root-zone server or uses information originally obtained from one.

The following table lists some of the top-level domains:

Top-level domain	Description
`.com`	Reserved for commercial organizations
`.edu`	Reserved for educational organizations
`.gov`	U.S. governmental organizations
`.net`	Network providers and centers
`.org`	Not-for-profit organizations
`.mil`	U.S. military

| `.arpa` | Used for technical infrastructure purposes (for example, reverse-DNS lookups) |
| `.uk`, `.de`, `.fr`, and so on. | Country-specific domains |

Although the assignment of domain names is supposed to generally conform to the structure shown in the preceding table, the assignment of names is not as tightly controlled as you might think. For example, it is possible for a business to have a `.org` or `.net` domain, and some non-profits have `.com` domains. As an example of how domains may be used for purposes other than their originally intended one, consider `.tv`. The `.tv` domain is the country-specific domain of the island nation of Tuvalu, but `.tv` domains are sought after (and therefore economically valuable) because TV is an abbreviation for television. It is said that nearly 10% of the revenue of the government of Tuvalu comes from royalties on `.tv` addresses.

Lower-level domains are controlled by the owners of those domains and are largely open for use however those domain owners see fit. However, the top-level domains tend to be tightly controlled by the **Internet Assigned Numbers Authority (IANA)**, the subsidiary of the **Internet Corporation for Assigned Names and Numbers (ICANN)** to which the management of root zones was delegated.

DNS solves the problem of name resolution by having specific servers that act as name servers. These servers run DNS server software and have the responsibility of receiving, processing, and replying to hosts that need to resolve hostnames to IP addresses. Because the namespace is extremely large, however, there is a good chance that the first DNS server that receives a query will not have the record requested. In such cases, the DNS server will ask another DNS server whether it has a record for the host name.

DNS queries can be either iterative or recursive. In the case of a recursive query, the client asks the DNS server for either the answer to the query or an error message that the information it is looking for cannot be found anywhere. It is the responsibility of the DNS server to do what is necessary to get the job done: to query other DNS servers until it gets the answer, or until it fails to get the answer.

When a client makes an iterative query, the client is essentially asking the DNS server for an answer to the query if it has the answer. If it does not have the answer, the DNS server provides a referral, which is another DNS server that might have the answer (this is typically an authoritative server at a lower level in the hierarchy of servers).

Although the most common type of a DNS database entry is an A record, which maps a hostname to an IP address, there are other types of records (these are specified by RFC 1035, except where otherwise noted):

- **Start of Authority (SOA)**: This is a record of information containing data on DNS zone transfers and other DNS records.
- **Name Server (NS)**: This stores information that identifies the authoritative name servers in the domain store information for the domain zone.
- **Canonical Name (CNAME)**: This stores additional hostnames or aliases for hosts in the domain. When a client performs a DNS lookup on a non-canonical name, such as an alias, the DNS server will look up the canonical name and continue the search with the canonical name.
- **Pointer (PTR)**: A pointer to the canonical name. Unlike a lookup involving a CNAME, DNS processing stops and just the CNAME is returned. It is most often used in reverse-DNS lookups (in which the client tries to find the hostname, given the IP address), but it is also used for other purposes, such as DNS-SD.
- **IPv6address (AAAA)**: Stores information for IPv6 (128-bit) addresses. Specified by RFC 3596.
- **IPv4 address (A)**: As mentioned before, stores information for IPv4 addresses, and is most often used to map hostnames to IP addresses.
- **Mail Exchange (MX)**: Stores information about where mail for the domain is to be delivered. Specified by RFC 1035 and RFC 7505.

Although DNS has served the purpose for which it was created very well, it is not without issues. The first problem is security issues. DNS was first developed in the 1980s, when the internet was not open to the general public. The rapid expansion of the internet in the 1990s changed the security requirements for DNS; in particular, there was a greater need to protect the integrity of DNS data.

One security vulnerability is DNS cache-poisoning (also called DNS-spoofing). If a DNS server does not have a record mapping a hostname to the IP address, it will request the record from another DNS server. This occurs recursively until the record is found. When the server gets a reply, it will often cache the reply for increased performance. If the reply comes from a nefarious source, however, the record may contain false information (mapping the hostname to the wrong IP address), and if the DNS server stores this false record in its cache, then the cache is poisoned. The usual objective is to redirect traffic to a node under the control of the attacker.

DNS cache poisoning has taken several forms over the years. One form was the unrelated data attack. This method entailed the attacker making a DNS query for a nonexistent hostname within a domain controlled by the attacker. The request would be a recursive query, thus ensuring that the DNS server would make additional queries by itself. Eventually, the DNS server would make a query to the authoritative DNS server for the domain. Since the domain is under the control of the attacker, so is the authoritative DNS server. The attacker will answer the query, and the answer can contain unrelated information for other domains. This bogus information would thus poison the DNS server's cache.

The solution to this form of attack was to prohibit anything not related to the original query from being cached. However, this did not eliminate another form of cache poisoning: the related data attack. It was similar to the unrelated data attack in that it started with the attacker making a DNS query for a nonexistent domain within a domain under their control. The remote DNS server's query would eventually reach the attacker's DNS server. The data returned by the attacker has to be related to the query, but there are several relevant records that aren't related to the mapping of hostnames to IP addresses, for example, NS, CNAME, and MX. The attacker can insert bogus data in those records, and thus poison the remote DNS server's cache.

The solution to this form of attack is for the remote DNS server to look through these records, and discard all data not related to the domain for which the attacker's DNS server is responsible. Still, in spite of the fact that many of these forms of attacks have been rendered obsolete, DNS-spoofing and cache-poisoning remain a threat.

The solution to such attacks is to make sure DNS responses come from an authoritative source. One way to accomplish this is to use **Domain Name System Security Extensions (DNSSEC)**, a suite of specifications for securing DNS records. The main mechanism for doing this is by digitally signing DNS records using public-key cryptography. This records are verified using a chain of trust that is recursively verified by all DNS servers up to the root server.

DNS also raises privacy issues. Even when DNS records cannot easily be spoofed or modified, a person with access to the DNS server or who is able to intercept the traffic between the client and the DNS server can obtain the client's IP address, which often identifies the user. This information can then be used to track the user and the websites and domains they visit.

There are different ways to address these privacy issues. One is to use a proxy; instead of connecting directly to a site, the end user connects to a proxy, which then acts as an intermediary, connecting to the site and sending data to and from the end user. Examples of proxies include **The Onion Router** (**Tor**), which directs traffic through a vast, volunteer overlay network of thousands of relays and is designed to conceal a user's location and activity. Another example of a proxy is a **virtual private network** (**VPN**), which involves setting up an encrypted tunnel to a server, which serves as a proxy for the end user. Of course, using a proxy involves an increase in latency (the time it takes to receive and send data); proxies sometimes cache site data as well, so the data you receive may not be up to date.

Another possible solution is to connect to an intermediate DNS server configured with minimal logging, which can be used instead of DNS servers whose privacy policy is either unknown or is known to be untrustworthy. Such servers are likely to become more commonplace in the future.

 In 2018, Cloudflare launched a privacy-first consumer DNS service, with DNS servers at `1.1.1.1` and `1.0.0.1`.

Configuring DNS

You may never have the occasion to set up your own DNS server, but there are compelling reasons to do so. Having your own DNS server can reduce administrative overhead and improve the speed of DNS queries, especially as your network grows. Moreover, the ease with which a DNS server can be set up with pfSense makes it that much more appealing.

It should be noted that pfSense has two separate services for DNS. Prior to version 2.2, DNS services were configurable via **Services** | **DNS Forwarder**, which invokes the `dnsmasq` daemon. For version 2.2 and later, **Unbound** is the default DNS resolver, and it is configurable by navigating to **Services** | **DNS Resolver**. New installs of version 2.2 or greater have **DNS Resolver** enabled by default, while upgrades from earlier versions will have **DNS Forwarder** enabled by default. You can still use **DNS Forwarder** on newer versions, but if you do, you will have to disable **DNS Resolver** or change the port settings for it. By default, both **DNS Forwarder** and **DNS Resolver** are configured to bind to port `53`, and both services cannot bind to the same port.

DNS Resolver

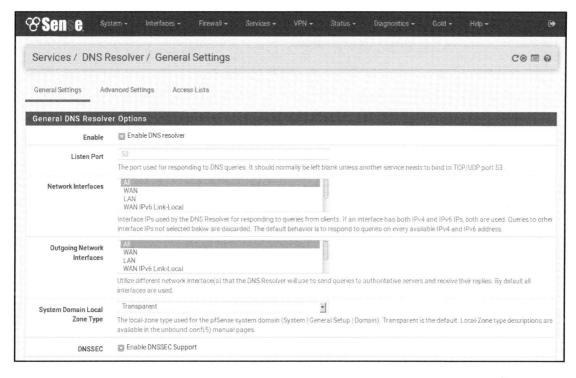

pfSense's DNS Resolver

Since **DNS Resolver** is the default resolver in the current version of pfSense, we will begin by looking at the options available for it. The first tab is labeled **General Settings**, and the first section on the page is **General DNS Resolver Options**. The first option is **Enable**, which enables unbound, and is checked by default. The next option is **Listen Port**, which allows you to set the port used for responding to DNS queries. The default port is port 53 (DNS traditionally uses port 53 and the **User Datagram Protocol** (**UDP**), although DNS also uses TCP for responses larger than a datagram, including DNSSEC and some IPv6 lookups, so take this into account when creating firewall rules for DNS).

The **Enable SSL/TLS Service** checkbox, if checked, will allow the DNS resolver to respond to DNS over TLS queries, thus making clients less vulnerable to DNS-spoofing. The **SSL/TLS Certificate** drop-down box allows you to select the certificate to be used in such queries. The default port for DNS over TLS is 853, but you can change this by entering a different port number in the **SSL/TLS Listen Port** edit box.

The **Network Interfaces** list box allows you to select which interface IPs are used by unbound to respond to queries from clients. Queries to interfaces that are not selected are discarded. If unbound is enabled, however, you must select either **All** or **localhost** for this option. The **Outgoing Network Interfaces** list box allows you to choose which network interfaces the DNS Resolver may use to send queries to authoritative servers and receive their replies.

When there is no domain match from local data, **System Domain Local Zone Type** determines how the DNS Resolver handles the query. There are several options available in this drop-down box:

- **Deny**: The **DNS Resolver** will only answer the query if there is a match in the local data. If there is no match, the query will be dropped silently.
- **Refuse**: This option is similar to **Deny**, except that when there is no match from the local data, the rcode REFUSED will be returned, so the client knows the query was refused.
- **Static**: The **DNS Resolver** looks for a match in the local data. If there is no match, it returns nodata or nxdomain, but it will also return the Start of Authority (SOA) for the root domain, provided that such information exists in the local data.
- **Transparent**: The **DNS Resolver** will answer the query from local data if there is a a match. If there is no match in local data, the query will be passed to upstream DNS servers. If there is a match in the local data, but the type of data for which the query is being made does not exist in the local data, the DNS Resolver will return a noerror/nodata message.
- **Type transparent**: This option is similar to **Transparent**, but in cases in which there is a match in the local data but the type of data being asked for does not exist, the **DNS Resolver** will pass the query to upstream DNS servers.
- **Redirect**: The **DNS Resolver** will attempt to answer the query from local data. If there is no local data other than the zone name, the query will be redirected.
- **Inform**: Identical to **Transparent**, except that the client IP address and port number will also be logged.
- **Inform/Deny**: Identical to **Deny**, except that the query will be logged.
- **No default**: Default contents for AS112 zones will not be returned by queries.

The next option, enabled by default, is **Enable DNSSEC Support**. DNSSEC is a means of protecting DNS data from attacks that use forged or manipulated DNS data, such as DNS cache-poisoning. If you enable it and the upstream DNS server to which you will be forwarding DNS requests does not support DNSSEC, however, DNS resolution may not work. The **Enable Forwarding Mode** checkbox allows you to control whether unbound will query root servers directly (if this option is unchecked) or whether queries will be forwarded to the upstream DNS servers. You should only enable this option if the upstream DNS servers are trusted. If you have enabled DNSSEC support, and you consider this to be important, you should also make sure the upstream DNS servers provide DNSSEC support.

The next option is the **Enable DNSSEC Support** checkbox. This option is checked by default. As mentioned earlier in this chapter, DNSSEC provides a means of digitally signing DNS data. Although the roll-out of DNSSEC has been slow (it was first proposed in the late 1990s; initial deployment did not take place until the late 2000s, and even now has not gained universal acceptance), it has become an increasingly popular method of thwarting DNS cache-poisoning. If the upstream DNS server does not support DNSSEC, enabling this option may prevent DNS resolution from working. In general, **Enable DNSSEC Support** should be enabled unless you know the upstream DNS server does not support it. If DNS resolution does not work and you are troubleshooting the problem, you might try disabling this option. **Enable Forward Mode**, if checked, will cause unbound to send queries to upstream DNS servers, rather than querying root servers directly, which is what would happen if this option is unchecked. Leaving this option unchecked is the safer choice if **Enable DNSSEC Support** is checked, as DNSSEC has been deployed at the root level since 2010. If you choose to check both **Enable DNSSEC Support** and **Enable Forwarding Mode**, you will definitely want to make sure the upstream DNS server supports DNSSEC.

The forwarding mode is necessary if you are using a multi-WAN configuration, which does not have default gateway switching.

Register DHCP leases in the DNS Resolver allows you to register DHCP static mappings. This, in turn, enables the resolving of hostnames that have been assigned IP addresses by the DHCP server. **Register DHCP static mappings in the DNS Resolver** is similar to **Register DHCP leases** in the **DNS Resolver**, except the former allows you to register DHCP static mappings instead of DHCP leases. The **Custom Options** button reveals a text box when you click on it. You can enter any additional parameters here.

The next two sections are **Host Overrides** and **Domain Overrides**. **Host Overrides** allows you to configure a specific hostname to resolve differently than it otherwise would with the DNS servers being used by the DNS forwarder. This can be used for split DNS configurations; it also provides one possible way of blocking access to certain sites (although the user could always defeat this measure by simply entering the correct IP address of the target domain). **Domain Overrides** is similar, except that it allows you to specify a different DNS server to use when resolving a specific domain. This can be useful in certain scenarios; for example, if you have a Windows Active Directory configuration and DNS queries for Active Directory, servers must be directed to the Active Directory's DNS server.

There are two sections called **Host Overrides** and **Domain Overrides**. The former is a powerful option as it allows us to force a hostname to resolve differently than it would with the DNS servers that were specified. This can be used in a number of different scenarios, such as split DNS configurations. You can also use it to block access to certain sites, although the end user could circumvent this by entering the IP address of the site. It can also be used in incredibly arbitrary ways (for example, the Bing search engine, `https://www.bing.com/`, could be redirected to `https://www.google.com/`). Clicking on the **+Add** button will bring up a page where you are asked to input the **Host**, the **Domain**, the **IP address** (the address to which traffic to the hostname specified in **Host** will be sent), and a brief **Description**. You may also enter additional hosts and domains. If you want to specify a different DNS server when resolving certain domains, you can use **Domain Overrides**, which will allow you to specify the IP address of a different DNS server. This is useful in a number of cases: for example, to specify Active Directory DNS servers in Windows Active Directory setups.

The next tab is **Advanced Settings**. We will not cover all the settings that are configurable in this section, but here are some of the more interesting settings:

- **Prefetch DNS Key Support**: Enabling this option causes DNSKEYs to be fetched earlier in the validation process, thus lowering the latency of requests (but increasing CPU usage).
- **Message Cache Size**: This controls the size of the message cache, which stores DNS response codes and validation statuses. The default size is 4 MB.

- **Experimental Bit 0x20 Support**: The small bit size (16 bits) of a DNS transaction ID makes it a frequent target for forgery, which creates a security risk. One of the ways to improve the security of DNS transactions is to randomize the 0x20 bit in an ASCII letter of a question name. For example, the `www.mydomain.com` and `WWW.MYDOMAIN.COM` names will be treated the same by a requester, but could be treated as unequal by a responder. It can thus serve as a sort of covert encryption channel and make DNS transactions more secure.

The last tab on the **DNS Resolver** page is called **Access Lists**. As the name implies, this tab gives you the ability to either allow or deny (and the denial can be either universal or only for nonlocal data, as we will see) access to your DNS servers for specified subnets (netblocks). This can be useful if you need to have different policies for different networks, or if you need to grant access to your DNS servers to certain users, such as remote users connecting through VPNs. Click on the **+Add** button to add an access list entry; you can add as many as you wish. When the page loads, the first field on the page will be **Access List**. Here you can specify a (parsed) list name. The second option is **Action**, which is a drop-down box. Here you can specify what will happen to DNS queries originating on the specified netblock. The currently supported options are:

- **Deny**: Stops queries from the defined netblock. Queries are dropped silently.
- **Refuse**: Stops queries from the defined netblock. Instead of dropping the query silently, it sends back a REFUSED DNS rcode.
- **Allow**: Allows queries from hosts within the defined netblock.
- **Allow Snoop**: Similar to Allow, but allows both recursive and non-recursive access from hosts within the defined netblock. This should only be configured for the administrator for such uses as troubleshooting.
- **Deny Nonlocal**: Allows only authoritative local-data queries from hosts within the defined netblock; other queries are dropped silently.
- **Refuse Nonlocal**: Also allows only authoritative local-data queries from hosts within the defined netblock; other queries send back the REFUSED DNS rcode.

The **Description** field allows you to enter a (non-parsed) description. Finally, the **Networks** field is where you enter the netblock (subnet) on which the access list takes effect. You must also select the CIDR of the subnet in the adjacent drop-down box. To the right, you can enter a description of this netblock. You can add the newly defined access list by pressing the green **Add Network** button at the bottom of the page.

DNS Forwarder

Although the DNS Resolver is the default DNS service in pfSense 2.2 and later, you can use DNS Forwarder instead. To do so, navigate to **Services** | **DNS Forwarder** and click on the **Enable DNS forwarder** checkbox (make sure to disable **DNS Resolver** first). Many of the settings for **DNS Forwarder** are identical to the **DNS Resolver** settings. In this section, we will focus on the settings that are unique to **DNS Forwarder**. As with the **DNS Resolver**, you can register DHCP leases and static mappings, but there is also an option called **Resolve DHCP mappings first**. Invoking this option causes the DHCP mappings to be resolved before the names provided in the **Host Overrides** and **Domain Overrides** tables.

Starting with pfSense 2.2, the DNS Resolver is the default DNS service. Although, in many ways, it is more advantageous to use the DNS Resolver because it implements features not available in DNS Forwarder (for example, access lists), you can still use the DNS Forwarder. To do this, first disable the DNS Resolver, then navigate to **Services** | **DNS Forwarder** and enable the DNS Forwarder. Although the DNS Forwarder lacks many of the features of the DNS Resolver, there is considerable overlap between the two, and thus our focus will be on features that the DNS Resolver does not have. You can register DHCP leases and DHCP static mappings with DNS Forwader, just as you can with the DNS Resolver, but DNS Forwarder also has a unique option called **Resolve DHCP mappings first**, which allows you to resolve DHCP mappings before names in the **Host Overrides** and **Domain Overrides** tables (**Host Overrides** and **Domain Overrides** are examples of features available in both the DNS Resolver and DNS Forwarder).

The DNS Query Forwarding section has several unique options. The Query DNS servers sequentially checkbox, as the name implies, causes the DNS servers specified on the **General Setup** page to be queried sequentially instead of being queried at the same time. The **Require domain** checkbox will drop DNS queries from upstream servers if they do not contain a domain (in other words, queries for plain names). The Do not forward private reverse lookups option, if enabled, results in the DNS Forwarder not forwarding reverse lookups for RFC 1918 private addresses (`10.0.0.0` addresses, `172.16.0.0` to `172.31.0.0` addresses, and `192.168.0.0` addresses).

The **Strict interface binding** checkbox causes the DNS Forwarder to only bind to the IP addresses of interfaces selected in the **Interfaces listbox**. If this option is not enabled, DNS Forwarder will bind to all interfaces. Some of the settings available in the DNS Resolver are also available in the DNS Forwarder, such as the ability to set the port for resolving DNS queries, and the ability to bind only to selected interfaces. One significant limitation of the DNS Forwarder is that Strict Interface Binding does not work with IPv6 addresses. As with the DNS Resolver, the DNS Forwarder allows you to add Host Overrides and Domain Overrides, and there is a field for Custom Options as well.

DNS firewall rules

After you have been diligent enough to configure pfSense to act as a DNS server, it would be a shame if end users on your network could circumvent pfSense and specify whatever DNS server they want. Yet that's exactly what most modern OSes allow the end user to do. The following screenshot shows part of the IPv4 configuration page in a recent version of Mint Linux:

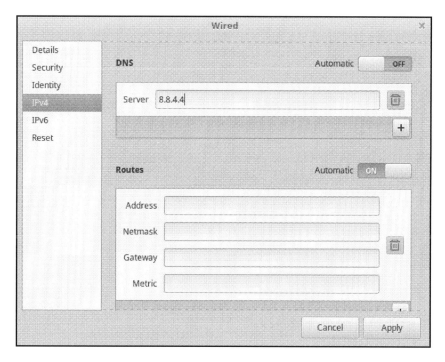

Circumventing the network DNS policy by changing the DNS server in Mint Linux

As you can see, the end user has disabled automatic DNS configuration and specified one of the Google DNS servers instead. Thus, even if we have set up pfSense to act as the DNS server for the local network, the user's computer will bypass pfSense and go directly to 8.8.4.4. Other than the fact that the user is subverting the policy we were trying to enforce, this is bad for a number of reasons:

- Every time the user accesses a site that requires a new DNS lookup, their computer will only cache the results on his computer. If the user had used pfSense as his DNS server, the results of the lookup would be cached on the pfSense system, and therefore would be available to everyone else on the local network.
- The user could specify a DNS server whose security has been compromised, and their computer would now be vulnerable to DNS cache poisoning and other attacks.

Fortunately, there are ways of preventing this sort of end user behavior. Although we have not covered firewall rules yet, it might prove useful to demonstrate how such rules can be used to block users from manually specifying a DNS server.

We know that DNS uses port 53 to communicate, so rules blocking or allowing port 53 traffic is what we need. Specifically, we need the following:

- A rule allowing port 53 traffic on the LAN network whose destination is a LAN node.
- A rule blocking all other port 53 traffic on the LAN network.

We begin by creating the rule allowing port 53 traffic to a LAN node. Using the top menu in the web GUI, navigate to **Firewall** | **Rules** and click on the **LAN** tab. There should already be at least two rules there: default **Allow LAN to any rules** for IPv4 and IPv6, respectively. Since firewall rules are applied from top to bottom with the first rule encountered that applies to the traffic being applied, we want to create a rule above those rules. Otherwise, pfSense will apply one of the **Allow LAN to any rules** first to the DNS traffic, which will defeat the purpose of our rule. Therefore, we click on the green **+Add** button with an up arrow next to the word **Add** to create a rule at the top of the list.

We want this rule to allow traffic, so we leave the **Action** set to **Pass**. We know that DNS traffic uses the UDP protocol, so we set **Protocol** to **UDP**. Scrolling down, we leave the **Source** set to **Any**, but we want to change the **Destination** to **LAN address**.

We want to change the **Destination port range** to port 53, and we can do that either by selecting it in the **From** drop-down box, or by just typing 53 into the first **Custom** edit box. You can enter a brief description in the **Description** edit box (for example, Allow DNS to LAN nodes) and then click on the **Save** button, which will return us to the main **Firewall** page and the rules table for LAN.

We still need a rule to block all other DNS traffic. Actually, what we will be doing is creating a rule that blocks all DNS traffic on the LAN network and placing it after the rule we just created so that all DNS traffic on the LAN network whose destination is not a LAN address will be blocked. It will be easiest to modify the rule we just created, so navigate to the rule in the table and, in the **Actions** column, click on the icon that looks like two sheets of paper to copy the rule. This will create a duplicate of the rule, which we can now modify. Change **Action** to either **Block** or **Reject**, and change **Destination** to any. You probably also want to change the **Description** (for example, Block all DNS). That is all you need to do, then click on **Save**.

When you return to the main **Firewall** page, make sure that the rule for allowing DNS traffic to a LAN node comes before the block DNS rule. If the order is incorrect, you can drag and drop the rules until they are in the correct order. When you are done, click on the green **Apply Changes** button at the top right of the page.

You probably want to confirm that the rules we added do what they are supposed to do, so go ahead and use nslookup to try to look up a domain name using a different server. The nslookup utility is available on Linux, Windows, and macOS, and by specifying a domain name as the first parameter and a DNS server as the second parameter, you can bypass the default DNS server, for example:

```
nslookup packtpub.com 8.8.4.4
```

The preceding command will do a DNS lookup for packtpub using one of the Google DNS servers. If the rules we created work, this should fail, while invoking the same command when omitting the second parameter (so nslookup will use the default DNS server) should work.

These rules can be fairly effective in preventing the end user from bypassing the pfSense DNS server, but there are at least two major flaws:

- The rules only apply to the LAN network. On a larger network, there will be several network segments. We want a means of applying these rules to more than one network.

- The end user can still defeat the rules we created by connecting to a VPN.

We will revisit these issues in `Chapter 6`, *Firewall and NAT*.

DDNS

Although DNS changes circulate through networks relatively quickly, the fact that it is not fully automated, and owing to the distributed nature of DNS, means that it may take several hours to distribute a DNS change. While this is enough for a service that only changes its IP address rarely, it can be an issue if your IP address changes more often. For instance, your public IP address will likely change more frequently if you are running a server on an ISP that assigns IP addresses via DHCP. This is where DDNS comes in handy, which is a way of rapidly updating DNS information.

DNS changes take place relatively quickly, and the amount of time it takes for changes to propagate to all DNS servers has improved drastically. Whereas in the past it may have taken days, now a DNS change might take effect in as little as an hour. Still, due to the number of DNS servers and the fact that the process of updating DNS records is not fully automated, in many cases, it might take several hours for a DNS change to take effect. This may be a problem if the IP address associated with a domain name changes frequently. Consider, for example, a situation in which you are running a server (assuming your ISP allows this), and your ISP assigns your public IP address via DHCP. Perhaps your ISP does not give you the option of paying for a static public IP address, or perhaps you decided the cost of such an address was prohibitive. Whatever the case may be, your IP address is likely to change more frequently than it would otherwise, making traditional DNS undesirable. What you need is a means of rapidly (and if possible, automatically) updating DNS information. DDNS provides us with such a means.

DDNS actually refers to two separate services. The first involves using a client to push the DNS change out to a remote DNS server. The second involves updating traditional DNS records without manually editing them (this mechanism is specified by the IETF's RFC 2136). pfSense provides you with the ability to configure clients for use with both services, and we will cover both of them.

Updating DDNS

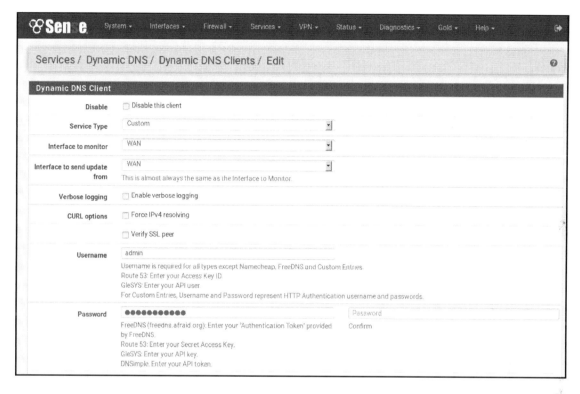

Dynamic DNS configuration

DDNS updating without RFC 2136 can be configured by navigating to **Services** | **Dynamic DNS** and clicking on the **Dynamic DNS** tab (the first tab). This tab will show you a table with all the DDNS clients that have been added. To utilize DDNS, you must first find someone that provides DDNS services. Your ISP may provide DDNS services; if not, there are several organizations that provide DDNS services for a variety of costs (some provide them for free). Cost, ease of use, and the existence of additional security features (such as invisible domains) are all factors you might consider when choosing a service.

The more commonly used form of DDNS is non-RFC 2136 DDNS updating. This can be configured by first navigating to **Services** | **Dynamic DNS**. The **Dynamic DNS Clients** tab should be selected by default. If there are already DDNS clients, they will appear in the table on this tab. To get started with DDNS, you first need to find a DDNS service provider. This could be your ISP (if they provide such services) or another party. Costs range from free to nominal to fairly expensive. When choosing a DDNS service provider, you may want to consider such factors as cost, usability, and the existence of added features (such as the number of configurable domains and security features, such as invisible domains).

Once you have chosen a DDNS service, you can begin the configuration process from your DDNS service's website. First, you will need to create at least one (sub)domain. Once you have created a domain, you need to find out the username and password (if any) that are required for the service, as well as the update URL. You should be able to find this information on the service's website.

Once you have this information, you can go back to the **Dynamic DNS** page in the pfSense web GUI, make sure you have selected the **Dynamic DNS** tab, and click on the green **+Add** button to add a DNS client. This will launch the client configuration page.

The first option is the **Disable this client** checkbox. This allows you to enter the client information without activating DDNS. The **Service Type** drop-down box allows you to select your service from a number of options; many DDNS service providers are listed here (in some cases, there are multiple listings for the same provider). Select your provider here; if there is more than one listing for your provider, check your provider's website for guidance on which option to choose. If your provider is not listed, you can select **Custom**.

Note that if you select **Custom**, several options will appear below the **Service Type** drop-down box that would not appear otherwise. The **Enable verbose logging** checkbox, if checked, provides more detailed logging information. Normally, if both IPv4 and IPv6 addresses are enabled, IPv6 addresses will be preferred, but if you want IPv4 resolution instead, you can check the **Force IPv4 resolving** checkbox. Finally, **Verify SSL peer** will cause libcurl to verify peer certificates, thus providing you with the greatest possible level of security on SSL/TLS connections between pfSense and the DDNS provider.

If you do not select **Custom**, the next option will be the **Interface to monitor** drop-down box. In virtually all cases, this should be set to **WAN**. In the **Hostname** edit box, you need to enter the fully qualified hostname of the hostname you added on your service provider's website. The **MX** edit box allows you to add an IP address of a mail server. Not all services allow you to set up a separate mail server, but if yours does, this is where you would specify it.

The **Enable Wildcard** checkbox, if checked, causes anything typed before your domain name to resolve to your domain name: for example, if your domain name is `mydomain.duckdns.org`, `www.` `mydomain.duckdns.org` will resolve to `mydomain.duckdns.org`. **Enable verbose logging** provides for a more verbose level of logging, which can be helpful in troubleshooting.

Finally, the **Username** and **Password** fields are where you enter the username/password combination you got from your DDNS provider's website. You may be able to leave these fields empty; in other cases, you may have to enter an API user/key combination or some other key or token. Finally, in the **Description** field, you can enter a brief description. Press the **Save** button at the bottom of the page to save the client information. This should return you to the page with the DDNS client table, and the entry you just made should be in the table.

Once you have entered the DNS client information, you still need a means of sending out DNS changes to your DDNS provider. This often comes in the form of updater software that must be run on one of your computers. Once the software is installed, the parameters that you must enter may include such things as:

- The domain you want to update
- A token or some other kind of identifier
- The refresh interval (5 minutes, 10 minutes, and so on)

The software may also provide a means of forcing an update, so that when your WAN address changes, you don't have to wait for the automatic update. Your DDNS provider will have more detailed information on how to install and configure your updater software.

RFC 2136 updating

The other form of DDNS supported by pfSense is RFC 2136 updating. This form of DDNS is more like traditional DNS, and is the standardized method of dynamically updating DNS records. It offers the following advantages over the DDNS method described in the previous section:

- **More secure**: RFC 2136 uses the **Transaction Signature** (**TSIG**), which uses shared secret keys and one-way hashing in order to provide a cryptographically-secure means of authenticating DNS updates.

- **Good for enterprises**: RFC 2136 is supported by many enterprise-level applications, including such directory services as LDAP and Windows' Active Directory. It is also supported by BIND servers and Windows Server DNS servers.
- **Standardized**: While the DDNS services described in the last section often must be configured in different ways depending on which provider you use, all systems that utilize RFC 2136 follow the same standard, thus configuration is somewhat easier.

The second tab on the **Dynamic DNS** page is **RFC 2136 Clients**, which is also the other form of DDNS supported by the current version of pfSense. It offers all of the advantages of the more commonly-used form of DDNS updating, plus the following:

- It provides greater security through the use of a **Transaction Signature (TSIG)**. This provides cryptographic security via shared secret keys.
- It is supported by BIND and such directory services as LDAP, and thus is more appropriate in an enterprise-level setting. If you are a Windows user, consider the fact that it supports Windows Server DNS servers and Active Directory.
- All systems that use RFC 2136 must conform to the standard outlined in the RFC 2136 document. Because all services using RFC 2136 follow this standard, configuration is easier.

There are also some disadvantages to using RFC 2136. Wildcarding is not supported by this standard. Also, there does not seem to be a means of forcing updates, so it may take somewhat longer for updates to take effect.

You can get started with the RFC 2136 configuration by navigating to **Services** | **Dynamic DNS** and clicking on the **RFC 2136** tab. You will see an RFC 2136 client table, which is similar to the table on the **Dynamic DNS** tab. Click on the green **+Add** button to the lower-right of the table to add a client.

While the DDNS client configuration page had a **Disable** checkbox, the RFC client configuration page starts off with an **Enable** checkbox that you must check for this client to be enabled. The next option is the **Interface** drop-down box. The selected interface should almost always be **WAN**. Next is **Hostname**, in which you must enter the fully qualified domain name of the host to be updated. Below that is **TTL**, or Time to Live, which controls how long the DNS record to be updated should be cached by caching nameservers. You will likely want to make this a relatively small number (smaller than the traditional 86,400 seconds), as this parameter controls how long a DNS server could be showing the old value after an update.

The next value is **Key Name**, which is whatever name you gave the key when you created it on your DNS server. Usually it is identical to the fully qualified domain name. The **Key Type** value must match the type of the key specified in **Key Name**; usually you can specify **Host** as the option. The **Key** field should be the secret key generated when you created the specified key.

In the **Server** field, you must specify the IP address of the DNS server the client will be updating. The next option is the **Use TCP instead of UDP** checkbox. DNS uses TCP for zone transfers and for queries larger than 512 bytes, and UDP for name queries, so in most cases, you should leave this unchecked. If you are updating a zone record, however, you will want to check this box. You should probably check this box, especially if you are using DNSSEC and/or IPv6.

The **Use public IP** checkbox will attempt to use the public IP address to fetch if the DNS server's IP address is private. The **Record Type** option allows you to specify whether the client should update A records (for IPv4), AAAA records (for IPv6), or both. Finally, in **Description**, you can enter a brief (non-parsed) description of this entry. Click on the **Save** button to save the entry, and you should be returned to the client table with the new entry in the table.

Checking IP services

If your firewall is behind an upstream NAT device, it may be necessary for the DDNS client to use a custom IP address to determine the public IP address of the firewall. The following diagram illustrates the problem:

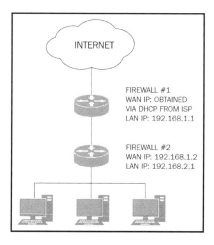

Network with two firewalls–the final destination of traffic for our domain is behind Firewall #2

Assume that NAT redirects all queries to our DDNS domain to a node behind Firewall #2. If we perform our DDNS updates the usual way, with updater software running on one of the nodes behind Firewall #2, it will report the WAN IP of Firewall #2 (192.168.1.2), not our public IP address, which is the WAN IP of Firewall #1.

The solution is to have an external site do the updating for us, taking advantage of the fact that an external server knows where to send a reply to query, and therefore knows our public IP address. Fortunately, since version 2.3.3, pfSense supports such services.

To begin checking the IP services configuration, click on the **Check IP Services** tab. Click on the green **+Add** button to add a new service. On the **Check IP Service** configuration page, the **Enable** button enables the service being configured. The **Name** field contains the name of the service. The **URL** field is where you enter the full URL to the check IP service page. You must also enter a username and password combination in the appropriate fields. Checking the **Verify SSL Peer** checkbox should be checked if the service has a self-signed SSL certificate or one in which the CA is not trusted by pfSense. Finally, you may enter a non-parsed description in the **Description** field. Click on the **Save** button when you are done.

Troubleshooting DDNS

If you tried to implement DDNS but it is not working, there are several potential causes. If you are using DDNS via a DDNS provider, you should confirm that you set up the domain correctly and also confirm that your provider's service works with pfSense. Once you have done that, you should go through the client configuration step by step. Many DDNS providers have instructions for different routers, including pfSense routers, and if such instructions are available, you should follow them. Also, make sure you have installed and configured your provider's updater software correctly. If you have gone through all of these steps and DDNS is still not working, you may want to contact your provider's technical support, if such support is available.

If you are trying to implement RFC 2136 DDNS, the process involves setting up the initial records on the DNS server, generating the keys, and configuring the client under pfSense. You need to make sure both the server and client configuration were done correctly. Some possible sources of problems include:

- The TTL setting is too long, which could result in cached nameservers not updating quickly enough

- Not setting the client up to update IPv6 (AAAA) records in an environment where IPv6 is being used–check the **Record Type** setting
- Trying to update a zone record without checking the **Use TCP instead of UDP** checkbox

Another point that seems fairly obvious but is worth mentioning is that you need to check DDNS functionality from the other side of the firewall. This is especially true if you have services that rely on NAT port-forwarding. In most cases, NAT is configured to forward traffic to certain ports only if they come in on one of the WAN interfaces. Since internal traffic does not come in on a WAN interface, NAT will not be invoked, and no port-forwarding will take place.

NTP

NTP is an application-layer protocol that controls the synchronization of various devices over the internet to within a few milliseconds of **Coordinated Universal Time** (**UTC**). NTP is hierarchical, with servers organized into different strata. At stratum 0 are high-precision time devices such as atomic clocks. At stratum 1 are computers that are synchronized within a few microseconds to their directly connected stratum 0 devices. At stratum 2 are computers that are directly connected to stratum 1 computers, and so on. Synchronization is achieved by adjusting the system time based on an offset. The offset is calculated by taking an average of the differences of the timestamps on request and response packets between the client and the server. The clock frequency is then adjusted to reduce the offset gradually, and the newly adjusted clock provides timestamps for the next request and response packets, creating a feedback loop known as clock discipline.

The purpose of the **Network Time Protocol** (**NTP**) is to control the synchronization of internet-connected devices to UTC. If it is functioning properly, devices will be synchronized to within a few milliseconds of UTC. NTP is an application-level protocol. NTP is a hierarchical system with different strata of NTP servers. The highest strata (stratum 0) consists of high-precision devices. Stratum 1 devices should be synchronized within microseconds of stratum 0 devices. Stratum 2 devices are directly connected to stratum 1 devices. This continues through successively lower levels, with each level slightly less precise than the others. As you might have guessed, any time data is requested, it must take into account the fact that responses are not instantaneous; there is a latency that must be taken into account.

Therefore, there is a synchronization process that applies an offset to the system time. The offset is calculated by making a series of requests to the NTP server. The average of the differences of the timestamps between request and response packets becomes the offset. The clock frequency is adjusted gradually to rescue this offset. Then the process is repeated, with the newly adjusted clock providing a set of timestamps to calculate the new offset. This creates a feedback loop that is known as clock discipline.

NTP is often overlooked, mainly because it does its job and in pfSense, it requires minimal configuration. You may recall that in the **Setup Wizard**, you were asked to specify a time server, but a default time server was provided. Many users will give no further thought to NTP configuration. You may, however, have reason to deviate from the default settings:

- Your pfSense system may be involved in validating certificates as part of a PKI infrastructure, in which case time synchronization is essential.
- You may be running pfSense on an embedded system that does not have a battery to preserve the time and date settings.
- Even if you don't fall into either of these categories, maintaining the proper time is still important, since it determines the timestamp on logs.

pfSense's NTP service provides synchronization via a conventional NTP server, as well as from **Global Positioning System** (**GPS**) devices and **Pulse Per Second** (**PPS**) devices. We will cover all of these methods in the next section.

Configuring NTP

To begin NTP configuration, navigate to **Services** | **NTP**, as shown in the following screenshot. The **NTP** page has three tabs and the first (and default) tab is **Settings**. The first option on this page is the **Interfaces** list box, in which you can select the interfaces on which the NTP service will listen. The default setting is to listen on all interfaces, but since the NTP server is probably upstream, you can select **WAN** as the only interface on which to listen (or multiple WAN interfaces, if you have them).

The next option is **Time Servers**. The time server you specified when you initially configured the system will be listed here, but you can also specify additional servers by clicking on the **Add** button. You need to specify the hostname. You can optionally check either the **Prefer** or **No Select** option. **Prefer** indicates that the NTP services should favor this server over all others. **No Select** indicates that NTP should not use this server for time, but it will collect and display stats from the server. You can check more than one **Prefer** checkbox, but when you save the settings, only the first **Prefer** checkbox on the list that you checked will remain checked.

The **Orphan Mode** option allows pfSense to use the system clock when no other clocks are available. The number entered in this edit box specifies the stratum reported during orphan mode. You might recall that stratum indicates how close the computer is to a high-precision time device; higher numbers indicate that the device is further away from such a device and thus has a lower priority. Whatever number you set here, it should be high enough to ensure that all other servers are preferred over this server. The default is 12.

The **NTP Graphs** checkbox, if enabled, generates **round-robin database** (RRD) graphs of NTP data. You can view these graphs by navigating to **Status | RRD Graphs** and clicking on the **NTP** tab. The next two subsections involve logging options. **Log peer messages**, if enabled, logs messages between the NTP client and server, while **Log system messages** logs other messages generated by the NTP service. **Log reference clock statistics** logs statistics generated by reference clocks, which are generally radio-time code receivers synchronized to standard time (for example, a GPS or PPS device). **Log clock discipline statistics** logs statistics related to the clock synchronization process, while **Log NTP peer statistics** logs statistics related to NTP client/server communication.

The next subsection is **Access Restrictions**, and it contains a number of important options. The first option is **Enable Kiss-o'death packets**. When checked, this enables the client to receive kiss-of-death packets, which are packets sent by the NTP server to tell the client to stop sending packets that violate server access controls. This, in turn, will cause the client to stop sending data to the server. The next option is **Deny state modifications by ntpq and ntpdc**. The ntpdc daemon queries the ntpd daemon about its current state and then requests changes to that state. If this option is checked (the default), ntpdc's change requests will be denied. The next two options are inverses of each other: **Disable ntpq and ntpdc queries** and **Disable all except ntpq and ntpdc queries**. **Deny packets that attempt a peer association**, if checked, will block any peer associations that are not explicitly configured. Finally, **Deny mode 6 control message/trap service**, if enabled, will decline to provide a mode-6 control-message trap service to hosts. This service is a subsystem of mode 6, which is intended for use for remote event-logging.

The final option on this page is **Leap seconds**. **Leap seconds** have been implemented to keep UTC close to mean solar time, and are added to UTC on an average of 1 per 18 months. This option allows the NTP service to advertise an upcoming leap second addition or subtraction. You must add a leap-second configuration routine in order to do this; it can be pasted into an available edit box or uploaded in a file. Configuring this option is only important if your NTP server is a strata 1 server, in which case it likely has other NTP servers making queries to it. When you are done configuring these options, you can press the **Save** button at the bottom of the page.

If configuring all these options doesn't provide enough accuracy for you, you can always connect either a GPS or a PPS device to the serial port and use it as a reference clock. Also, if the GPS device supports PPS, it may be used as a PPS clock reference. Using a USB GPS is not recommended owing to USB bus-timing issues; however, a USB GPS device may work.

You can configure a GPS device by clicking on the **GPS** tab. The first option is the **GPS Type** drop-down box, which lets you select a predefined configuration. If your GPS type is listed in the box, you should select that type. If it is not listed, you should select **Generic**. Selecting **Default** is not recommended.

The next option is the **NMEA Sentences** list box. NMEA defines an electrical and data specification for communication between marine electronics; GPS is but one of the types of devices that utilize it. There are different NMEA sentence types, and they are listed in this list box. If you know what sentence type your device uses, you can select it here; otherwise, you can leave it set to **All**.

The **Fudge Time 1** edit box allows you to specify a GPS PPS signal offset, while **Fudge Time 2** allows you to specify the GPS time offset. The **Stratum** edit box allows you to set the GPS clock stratum. Normally you would probably want to set it to **0** (and that is the default value), but you can change it here if you want ntpd to prefer a different clock.

There are several flags you can set. Prefer this clock, as the name implies, causes the GPS clock to be preferred over all other clocks. If you went to the trouble of setting up a GPS clock, you probably want to use it, but if you don't, you can check the **Do not use this clock, display for reference only** checkbox. The **Enable PPS signal processing** checkbox, if enabled, treats the GPS as a PPS device. By default, PPS processing occurs on the rising edge of the pulse, but checking **Enable falling edge PPS signal processing** will cause processing to occur on the falling edge. The **Enable kernel PPS clock discipline** checkbox, if checked, will result in NTP using the **ppsu** driver, which reduces the incidental jitter sometimes associated with PPS clocks. Normally, the GPS will send location data to ntpd, but if you check the **Obscure location in timestamp** checkbox, it won't. Finally, if you need to fine-tune the GPS time offset (**Fudge Time 2**), you may want to check the **Log the sub-second fraction of the received timestamp** checkbox.

In the **Clock ID** edit box, you can enter a GPS clock ID. If the **Advanced** button in the **GPS Initialization** subsection is clicked, you will see the GPS initialization commands, and you will also be able to edit them. Finally, **NMEA Checksum** allows you to calculate an NMEA checksum by entering an NMEA command string and pressing the **Calculate** button. The result will appear in the box to the right of the **Calculate** button. When you are done making changes, press the **Save** button at the bottom of the page.

If you have a serial PPS device, such as a radio that receives WWV (time) signals, you can configure it by clicking on the **PPS** tab. The first option on this page is the **Fudge Time** edit box, which is used to specify the PPS signal offset. In the **Stratum** edit box, you can enter the PPS clock stratum. As with GPS devices, you probably want to leave it at **0** (the default), but you can change it here.

The first two flags, **Enable falling edge PPS signal processing** and **Enable kernel PPS clock discipline**, are identical to the flags available on the **GPS** tab. The only unique flag on this tab is the **Record a timestamp once for each second** option, which is useful in constructing frequency-deviation plots.

The last option is the **Clock ID** edit box, which is identical to the **same** option on the **GPS** tab and simply allows you to change the PPS clock ID. When you are done making changes, click on the **Save** button at the bottom of the page.

Troubleshooting NTP

NTP is a fairly straightforward protocol, and unless you are using some of the more esoteric NTP options, there is little that can go wrong; however, if it does break, it can create problems with other services–for example, the aforementioned certificate validation. Therefore, you shouldn't overlook the possibility of an NTP failure.

Checking to make sure the preferred NTP server is up is always a good idea, and you can do that with the `ntpq -p` command. You can do this by typing the following at the console shell (or just navigate to **Diagnostics** | **Command Prompt** and type this in under **Execute Shell command**):

```
ntpq -p HOSTNAME
```

Where **HOSTNAME** is the hostname of the site whose NTP server we wish to query. If **HOSTNAME** is omitted, the local NTP server is queried. Running this query will result in output something like this:

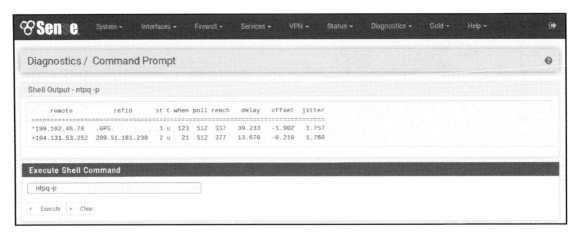

Checking to see whether the preferred NTP server is running

As you can see, running this command produces a wealth of information about the local NTP server. remote is the IP address of the remote NTP server, while refid is the IP address of the time source to which remote is synced. st is the stratum of the remote NTP server, and t is its type (in this case, u for unicast). when is the number of seconds elapsed since the remote NTP server was polled, while poll is the polling interval (both these fields are in seconds).

reach is an 8-bit left-shifting register, which indicates success or failure within connecting with the NTP server. A 1 indicates success, while 0 indicates failure. The register is presented in octal format. The octal value of 377 is 11111111 in binary, indicating here that the last 8 attempts to connect to the NTP server were all successful.

delay is the time delay in milliseconds to connect to the NTP server, while offset is the offset between local and remote time. Finally, jitter is the observed jitter of time with the remote server.

If you are trying to set up a GPS or PPS device as a reference clock, this can create a host of potential causes. One possibility is to try temporarily disabling these devices (with the Do not use this clock option) and see whether it solves your NTP problems. If it does, then you know you have to revisit your GPS and PPS settings. If you are using a GPS device, it is possible that you selected the wrong GPS type or wrong option for NMEA sentences. It is also possible that your GPS device is not supported by your version of pfSense. If so, you may still be able to get it to work by manually entering the GPS initialization commands.

PPS devices are a bit more straightforward, but you may want to try checking the Enable PPS clock discipline checkbox and see whether it resolves your problem. You may also want to try changing signal processing from the rising edge of the pulse to the falling edge.

SNMP

SNMP is another application-layer protocol supported by pfSense. SNMP collects and organizes information about managed devices, and is often used to monitor network devices. SNMP-managed networks consist of managed devices, software running on the managed devices (known as agents), and software running on the manager, known as a the **network management station** (**NMS**). Management data is organized hierarchically in structures known as **management information bases** (**MIBs**).

Enabling SNMP in pfSense will allow it to act as a network-management station, and this will enable you to monitor network traffic and flows, pfSense queues, as well as system information (for example, CPU, memory, and disk usage). It is also capable of running traps on managed devices that are triggered by certain events. SNMP is implemented under pfSense with the bsnmpd service.

It contains the most basic MIBs available, but it can be extended by loadable modules:

SNMP configuration in pfSense

To activate the SNMP daemon, navigate to **Services** | **SNMP** and check the **Enable** checkbox under the **SNMP Daemon** section. You can run SNMP without changing any of the defaults, but you should review the options before continuing.

The second section is **SNMP Daemon Settings**, and the first option under it is the **Polling Port** edit box. The default port is 161 (the standard port for SNMP), but you can change it if necessary. You can enter an optional **System Location** and **System Contact** in the next two edit boxes. In the **Read Community String** edit box, you can enter a passphrase that will be required by all hosts querying the SNMP daemon. You should enter a strong passphrase here.

The next section is **SNMP Traps Enable**, under which there is an **Enable** checkbox for enabling traps. Checking this box reveals the **SNMP Trap Settings** section with several trap options. In the **Trap server** edit box, you should enter the hostname or IP address of the trap server. In the **Trap Server Port**, you can enter the port where the traps will be received. The default is 162, but if your SNMP trap receiver is on a different port, you can change it here. The **SNMP Trap String** field is a string that will be sent along with any generated trap.

Under the **SNMP Modules** section, you can choose which modules to run. The choices are as follows:

- **MIBII**: This provides information provided in the management information base tree (defined by RFC 1213), which covers networking information and networking interfaces. This module will allow you to query network interface information.
- **Netgraph**: This module provides some netgraph-related information. Netgraph is a graph-based kernel networking subsystem that is part of FreeBSD.
- **PF**: This provides information about pfSense, including the rules, states, interface information, and tables.
- **Host Resources**: A module that provides additional information from the MIB tree (for example, system uptime and the amount of physical memory).
- **UCD**: A module that implements parts of the UCD-SNMP-MIB toolkit. It allows you to get memory, load average, and CPU usage, among other things.
- **Regex**: A module that produces counters from logs or other text files.

The last section on the page, **Interface Binding**, has only one option, the **Interface Binding** drop-down box, which determines the interfaces on which the SNMP daemon is listening. The default is **All**, but you can select a single interface on which to listen (or **localhost**). Selecting multiple interfaces without using the **All** option is not supported. When you are done making changes, click on the **Save** button at the bottom of the page.

Troubleshooting SNMP

If you are having problems with SNMP, you should first confirm that SNMP is running on pfSense. You can do this by navigating to **Status** | **Services** and looking for **bsnmpd** (the SNMP daemon) in the table. If it is not running even though you enabled it, there may be a resource-allocation issue.

If not, the most common problem with SNMP is that the agents are unable to communicate with **bsnmpd**. This could happen for a variety of reasons. There may be no connectivity between the agent and **bsnmpd**; it is unlikely, but it is still a possibility that should be considered before moving on to other possible causes. It is possible that access to the SNMP ports is being blocked by pfSense or another network device; check your firewall settings to see whether this is the case.

Once you have determined that a node has connectivity with the pfSense node running **bsnmpd**, you should make sure the agent software is running on the node. If the agent software is running, make sure the agent is sending the correct community string; without it, **bsnmpd** will reject any attempts to connect to it. Keep in mind that community strings are case-sensitive.

Once you have determined that a node has connectivity with the pfSense node running **bsnmpd**, you should make sure the agent software is running on the node. If the agent software is running, make sure the agent is sending the correct community string; without it, **bsnmpd** will reject any attempts to connect to it. Keep in mind that community strings are case-sensitive.

If none of these works, you may consider other possibilities, such as the following:

- **Wrong version of SNMP**: The SNMP daemon on pfSense runs version 3; the agent may be using an earlier version.
- **Incorrect Object Identifier**: In a custom probe, the **Object Identifier (OID)** used by the agent may be wrong.
- **Software bug in the agent**: This is not likely if the software is relatively stable, but is still a possibility.

In many cases, once the obvious possibilities have been exhausted, the process of troubleshooting an SNMP node is dependent on the platform you are using (Windows, Linux, macOS, and so on) and the software you are using. As a result, consulting any troubleshooting resources the software provider has made available is an important step in resolving the problem.

Summary

In this chapter, we introduced the **Domain Name System** (**DNS**), which is the internet's method of mapping hostnames to IP addresses; showed how it works, and briefly mentioned the security and privacy issues it raises. pfSense is capable of acting as a DNS server, and we discussed how to configure a DNS server, and how to minimize the risk of end users circumventing the network's DNS policy. However, sometimes we need to have a form of DNS that updates faster than traditional DNS, and thus we showed you how to configure DDNS in pfSense. Finally, we introduced two services that pfSense is also capable of providing: NTP and SNMP.

In the next chapter, we will introduce something we briefly mentioned in this and previous chapters, but did not fully elaborate on: firewall rules and **Network Address Translation** (**NAT**).

Questions

1. (a) What type of DNS record maps hostnames to IPv4 addresses? (b) What type of DNS record maps hostnames to IPv6 addresses? (c) What type of record is used in reverse-DNS lookups?
2. (a) What can happen if a DNS record contains false information? (b) What is a method we can use to prevent that from happening?
3. (a) Name the two services available in pfSense for DNS. (b) What is the default service in the current version?
4. (a) What port does DNS use? (b) What protocol does DNS use?
5. What option on the DNS Resolver allows us to configure the service to resolve specific hostnames differently?
6. What are the two forms of DDNS supported by pfSense?
7. Under what circumstances might you want to configure pfSense's NTP service?
8. What command-line utility can be used to make sure the preferred NTP service is running?
9. (a) In SNMP, what software is running on the managed devices? (b) What is the manager known as?
10. If the SNMP daemon is running, what is the likely cause of an SNMP failure?

Further reading

- Kabelová, Alena and Libor Dostálek, Libor. DNS in Action. Birmingham, UK and Mumbai, India: Packt Publishing, 2006.
- Understanding DNS – Beginner's Guide to DNS. Steve's Internet Guide's DNS tutorial: http://www.steves-internet-guide.com/dns-guide-beginners/
- RFC 1034 – Domain Names – Concepts and Facilities. This is an introduction to DNS: https://www.ietf.org/rfc/rfc1034.txt
- RFC 1035 – Domain Names – Implementation and Specification. The official DNS specification: https://www.ietf.org/rfc/rfc1035.txt
- RFC 5905 – Network Time Protocol Version 4 Protocol and Algorithms Specification. The RFC for NTP: https://tools.ietf.org/html/rfc5905
- What Is NTP? A more concise overview of NTP than you will find in RFC 5905: http://www.ntp.org/ntpfaq/NTP-s-def.htm
- RFC 1157 – A Simple Network Management Protocol. The SNMP specification: https://tools.ietf.org/html/rfc1157
- SNMP Basics: What is SNMP and How Do I Use It? This is a good overview of SNMP: https://www.networkmanagementsoftware.com/snmp-tutorial/

6
Firewall and NAT

Regardless of your deployment scenario, there is a good chance you will want to utilize pfSense to filter network traffic, as having control over traffic entering and leaving our networks is one of the main functions of a pfSense firewall. The primary mechanism that we employ for filtering traffic is the creation of firewall rules, and we will detail the process in this chapter. We will also introduce some real-world examples of using pfSense to selectively block traffic, or to allow certain traffic only during certain hours via scheduling.

Another component that we sometimes use in filtering traffic is **Network Address Translation (NAT)**. NAT played an important role in forestalling IPv4 address exhaustion, as it enabled a network to have one IP address for the public internet and many private addresses, with NAT directing traffic in both directions to the correct destination. Although NAT is likely to diminish in importance with the continuing migration to IPv6, it is nonetheless likely to be a component of our networks in the near future, and will be covered in this chapter.

The following topics will be covered in this chapter:

- Firewall fundamentals
- Firewall best practices
- Creating firewall rules
- Scheduling
- Aliases and virtual IPs
- **Network Address Translation (NAT)**
- Troubleshooting

Technical requirements

There are no additional technical requirements for this chapter beyond what was required for previous chapters. To implement the examples contained in this chapter, you will need a working pfSense firewall in either a real or virtual environment.

Firewall fundamentals

On a fundamental level, the purpose of a network firewall is to act as a packet filter. A firewall is placed on the boundary between trusted (internal) networks and untrusted (external) networks. When packets coming from the external network to the internal network do not match the packet filter's set of rules (ruleset), the packets are either silently discarded (in other words, dropped) or an **Internet Control Message Protocol** (**ICMP**) message is returned to the sender (in which case we say the packet was rejected). If the packets match the ruleset, they are allowed through the firewall (in which case we say the packet passes through).

As you might have deduced, a good default firewall policy is to block all traffic not explicitly allowed. This is generally the policy that pfSense follows. In addition, the following two rules are in place when pfSense is initially installed and configured:

- On the WAN interface, the RFC 1918 (private) and bogon (currently unassigned) networks are blocked by default, which makes sense, because we don't want private addresses to be the source or destination of packets sent over the public internet. It is not allowed, and routers on the public internet wouldn't know what to do with them anyway. The same goes for currently unassigned networks. Bogon networks cannot be the source of legitimate traffic; they may very well be the source of an attack, and we can eliminate the possibility of such an attack by blocking them.
- On the LAN interface, there are two default rules: an **Allow LAN to any rule** for IPv4 traffic, and an **Allow LAN to any rule** for IPv6. These rules exist to make pfSense as plug-and-play as possible; without them, the LAN network would be blocked from accessing the WAN side of the network (thus, it would likely be blocked from accessing the internet). Note that these default rules are only automatically created on the LAN interface; if we add other interfaces in order to create more private networks, we will have to generate these rules ourselves, or create floating rules that apply to multiple interfaces.

pfSense has three options for firewall rules: pass, which allows traffic that matches the rule; block, which will silently drop traffic that matches the rule, and reject, which will also drop the traffic, but will send back a port unreachable message to the sender. In floating rules, there is also a match option, which allows us to divert traffic into queues, assuming that we have created such queues.

Early network firewalls were stateless–in other words, they treated each packet as a separate entity. Such firewalls did not know whether a packet was part of an existing connection, was trying to establish a new connection, or was a stray packet. By the 1990s, however, firewall developers realized that much overhead could be eliminated if firewalls kept track of the state of network connections–the IP addresses, the ports, and the sequence numbers of the packets. If packets were part of an already-established connection, they would be allowed through the firewall without having to be re-evaluated. Firewalls that keep track of network connections are called stateful firewalls.

pfSense is a stateful firewall. Thus, traffic that is part of an existing connection is allowed through. This is done through a mechanism known as stateful packet inspection.

The protocol used in a connection was not mentioned as one of the attributes of a connection that the firewall tracks. As a result, traffic that matches the IP address and port of the initial connection is allowed through even if it doesn't match the protocol of the initial connection. This allows, for example, the passage of ICMP control packets on a TCP or UDP connection.

While stateful firewalls greatly reduce the amount of work a firewall must do, they come with a downside. These connections, or states, have to be kept track of, which is done by creating entries in a table called a state table. In pfSense, each table entry uses up about 1 K of RAM. We can set the firewall's maximum number of connections and maximum number of state table entries by navigating to **System** | **Advanced** and clicking on the **Firewall and NAT** tab. The **Firewall Maximum States** and **Firewall Maximum Table Entries** parameters are the relevant settings. The former parameter controls the maximum number of connections, whereas the latter controls the maximum number of entries, which can be greater than the number of connections–the use of a proxy server, for example, will not create an additional connection, but it will take up another entry in the table. You will want to make sure that **Firewall Maximum Table Entries** is set low enough that the state table does not use up all available memory.

The fact that the state table has a finite maximum size sets up a potential attack vector. If the number of connections reaches the number specified in **Firewall Maximum States**, unpredictable things may happen if any additional connections are attempted. Connections may be dropped in order to ensure that the number of connections does not exceed the allowed maximum, or new connections may not be possible. Attackers, realizing this, may flood your firewall with fake connection attempts, thereby preventing legitimate traffic from reaching your site. This is called a **denial-of-service (DoS)** attack:

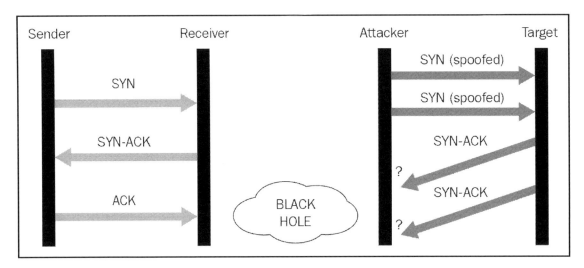

One particular form of a DoS attack is known as a SYN flood attack. A SYN flood attack exploits a weakness in the TCP three-way handshake. The TCP three-way handshake entails the following:

1. The client sends a SYN (synchronization) packet, along with a randomly-chosen initial sequence number.
2. The server sends back an acknowledgment that it received the SYN packet (a SYN-ACK packet), along with the client's sequence number plus 1, and its own randomly-chosen initial sequence number.

3. The client sends back an acknowledgment that it received the SYN-ACK packet (an ACK packet), along with the server's sequence number plus 1.

Note that the client and server have their own sequence numbers, and when data is sent to either the client or the server, the other side will increment this number by 1 and send it. This ensures the proper ordering of the packets. The SYN, SYN-ACK, ACK sequence ensures that each side is ready to send and receive data. All three steps must be completed before a connection is established.

With the SYN flood attack, the attacker sends out SYN packets, but never ACK packets, even if the SYN-ACK packet is received. If the firewall creates an entry in the state table as soon as the SYN packet is received, that is one less entry that could be used by a legitimate connection. Enough SYN packets could cause all state table entries to be used up and prevent legitimate traffic from getting through.

There are a number of different ways to mitigate such attacks. One is to try to block the source of the attack from connecting to your network. This might work, but the attacker might spoof its IP address, thwarting your attempts to block them. Another way is to set up the state table so that entries are not created until the final ACK packet is received.

Another security problem with stateful firewalls is that an attacker might establish a legitimate connection and then trick a host behind the firewall into doing its bidding and establishing connections. In this case, the return traffic is the security vulnerability. The only way to defeat these exploits is to audit software running on your network. Also, protocol dissectors in stateful firewalls have had known security issues, highlighting the importance of keeping your firewall software up to date.

There are essentially two types of filtering with firewalls. Ingress filtering involves filtering traffic coming into our networks, while egress filtering involves filtering traffic going either from our internal networks to the public internet, or from one network segment to another internal network segment. Ingress filtering is by far the more common form of firewall filtering, and it is easy to see why. We would tend to assume that most attacks would be coming from public, untrusted networks, and would thus want to filter traffic accordingly.

There are, however, several reasons why egress filtering is also a good idea. One reason is that in the case of a network operated by a company for business reasons, egress filtering can help cut down on network abuse by employees. Egress filtering can limit access to non-work-related applications. Egress filtering combined with content filtering can be used to block employee access to non-work-related websites, thereby cutting down on net abuse and improving worker productivity.

Along with network abuse, there is the issue of bandwidth abuse, which can be costly to a company. Assume that one-third of bandwidth is used by employees for non-business-related purposes. By employing egress filtering, you can potentially cut bandwidth usage by a third and possibly even downgrade to a lower tier of service while still having the same amount of bandwidth you had for business-related purposes before you employed egress filtering.

Another reason for egress filtering is to eliminate liability to third parties should our networks become compromised. Despite our best efforts, it is possible that malware may find its way onto our local networks. If you do not employ egress filtering, it will be possible for this malware to either phone home or to attack external networks. The goal of malware could be to send data back to a network controlled by the attacker; it may also want to turn your computers into bots that then launch attacks on other networks. In either case, a lack of egress filtering will allow the malware to achieve its objectives and potentially leave you liable for damage done to external networks. Harm can come to other networks in the form of **distributed denial-of-service** (**DDoS**) attacks, or spam or phishing campaigns. This can become especially problematic if you have several connections to the internet. If you are running a DNS server on your network, someone might use it to host the zone data for a malicious domain. In short, you could unwittingly be an accomplice to criminal activities, which is definitely something we want to avoid doing.

Once a network is compromised, usually all egress filtering will do is minimize damage. Sometimes, however, egress filtering can prevent a network from being compromised. And in some cases, it can stop malware in its tracks. Often, malware needs outbound network access to work at all. Consider the case of the **Code Red** worm. This worm exploited a vulnerability in Microsoft's **Internet Information Services** (**IIS**) web server, whereby a string overflowing a buffer could contain arbitrary code that would then be executed by IIS. The worm placed its payload in the overflow. Code Red was set up to look for other IIS servers during the first 19 days of the month; if it found other IIS servers, it would spread itself to them (assuming they hadn't already patched the vulnerability). On the 20th day of the month, the worm would launch DoS attacks on certain IP addresses; these attacks would continue for a week. The worm would remain dormant for the rest of the month, and every month the cycle would repeat.

By using egress filtering, we would block Code Red, even if it had already infected our system. Without outbound access, it would be unable to infect other IIS servers, and it would be unable to use our network as a springboard for launching DoS attacks (and so we would not be implicated in such attacks). While we may not always be this fortunate, this example illustrates that egress filtering can be a valuable tool.

Finally, egress filtering can help detect misconfigured network devices. A good example is an SNMP-enabled device trying to connect to a non-existent SNMP server. The traffic is unnecessary, and egress filtering can help us detect it so that we can configure these devices correctly.

Firewall best practices

The fundamental principles discussed in the previous section should help us in developing a set of best practices for creating firewall rules. Some of these will seem obvious, while others will be less so:

- The principle of least privilege should apply to our firewall rules; many firewall rules are too permissive. When possible, avoid creating firewall rules that have any in the destination, or at least limit the port range. Take advantage of the fact that pfSense blocks all network traffic by default.
- Periodically check your firewall rules, and delete rules that are no longer relevant. For example, a subnet may have a printer that is shared with other subnets. A rule is created to grant access to the printer on those subnets. If the printer is subsequently decommissioned or moved, the firewall rules should be changed accordingly. In corporate environments, obtaining information necessary to know what rules need to be deleted or changed may be difficult, as it might require interdepartmental communication. Still, it is a good idea to be proactive about such matters, as it helps keep your network as secure as possible.
- Firewall rules should be documented. This obviously becomes more important in corporate scenarios, but even in less formal settings, it is an important practice. Even if you know why a rule was implemented, others may not, and proper documentation will potentially make network management and troubleshooting much easier.
- Firewall rules should be automated, whenever possible. Human error is often the cause of firewalls not performing as they should, and when possible, this element should be minimized.
- Firewall rules should be backed up on a regular basis. In pfSense, you can perform a backup of just the firewall rules separately (we will cover how to back up and restore your pfSense system in the appendix). In a corporate environment (and this is good practice even in a home or SOHO environment), such backups should be maintained off-site. Backups can be invaluable in the case of a crash or other mishap.

- Create your rules in a manner that is consistent with your company's written security policy, if your company has one. Once you are done, you should review the rules to make sure they are consistent with said policy.
- Eliminate redundant and/or unnecessary firewall rules. Keep the ruleset as simple and concise as you can.
- Audit your rules on a regular basis.
- Keep track of when pfSense is updated, and patch the firewall with the latest updates in as timely a manner as possible.
- Limit the number of applications running on the firewall so that the firewall can consume the lion's share of CPU cycles, and network throughput should improve. Any application that can be moved onto a dedicated system should be.
- A corollary to the previous point is that the firewall rules should be organized for maximum efficiency. That means having as few evaluations as possible. Always place more specific rules first; this will minimize the number of packets later rules must evaluate.
- As new exploits are being discovered all the time, it is a good idea to routinely test your firewall. In some cases, this may take the form of a penetration test (or pen test), which is an authorized simulated attack on a computer system performed to evaluate security. Penetration tests may be done in isolation or as part of a more comprehensive security audit. In many cases, the penetration test may be performed by a third party rather than the company's network admins. In any case, it is good practice to test the firewall, and this means all interfaces.
- Speaking of security audits, if your company is required to comply with the **Payment Card Industry Data Security Standard (PCI DSS)**, you should review your firewall policy to make sure it meets the requirements of this standard. It is outside scope of this section to provide a comprehensive overview of PCI DSS, but it's worth mentioning that version 1.1.6 of the standard requires a complete firewall review every six months. The latest revision of the standard is version 3.2.1, released in May 2018.
- You should enable logging–at least if you are going to review the logs. If not, they are a waste of CPU and disk usage.
- Logging is generally a good idea, but hackers who have compromised the security of your firewall may delete or alter the logs to cover their tracks. Therefore, it might be a good idea to run a remote syslog server.
- If you have remote users, require that they run software to secure their computers. At a minimum, you probably want to require them to run a personal firewall.

Some of these bullet points may seem excessive if you are a home or SOHO user. In such cases, you should view most of these as just suggestions. But even in such cases, deleting outdated rules and documenting firewall rules are good practices on all networks.

Best practices for ingress filtering

By now, we should be able to articulate some best practices for ingress filtering. The default behavior of pfSense is to block all ports, and we want to take advantage of that. Inevitably, we are going to have to open some ports, but even then we want our rules to be as restrictive as possible. The best practices for ingress filtering, at least according to the IETF, are outlined in the following documents:

- Defeating DoS attacks, in particular, ones that employ IP spoofing: `https://tools.ietf.org/html/bcp38`.
- Different strategies for ensuring that packets come from the origin they claim to come from, with particular attention to multi-homed networks (networks that have multiple points of access to the public internet): `https://tools.ietf.org/html/bcp84`.

These documents are not particularly long, but here are the most relevant points contained in them:

- Traffic that employs IP-spoofing should be blocked, and only packets that have valid source addresses should be allowed. That means, at a minimum, packets with known fallacious addresses (for example, all private addresses, such as `1.2.3.4` and `0.0.0.1`) should be rejected.
- If we allow remote-access users, automatic filtering should be employed on those users. If a user is connecting through an ISP, then only the IP address assigned by that ISP should be allowed.
- DHCP and BOOTP both involve communicating with clients who have not yet been assigned an IP address and who do not know the IP addresses of the server from which they want to receive an IP address. Therefore, they use `0.0.0.0` as the source address, and the broadcast address (`255.255.255.255`) as the destination address. Therefore, if DHCP and/or BOOTP is being used, those addresses must be allowed.

- BCP84 is targeting ISPs and system admins running edge routers, and discusses was for using **reverse path-forwarding** (**RPF**) to defeat DDoS attacks. Basically, it is proposed that if a packet doesn't come from the best path between the source and the destination (a possible sign the source is being spoofed), the packet should be rejected.

Here are some additional best practices for ingress filtering:

- Block TCP packets in which the SYN and the FIN flag are both set to 1. These flags should never be set to 1 on the same packet, and if they are, there's a good chance the packet is part of a SYN flood attack.
- Block legacy ports not being used–for example, Telnet (23) and NetBIOS (135 to 139).
- Block **Trivial File Transfer Protocol** (**TFTP**) on port 69.

Best practices for egress filtering

As with everything else related to firewall rules, best practices are going to be handled differently for the home/SOHO user than they would for admins on a corporate network. The home/SOHO user can get started by compiling a list of services that require outbound access (for example, DNS, SNMP, and HTTP/HTTPS). The network admin likely will want to consult the company's security policy. They may also want to consult with whoever is in charge of network security, and possibly other stakeholders.

You should also use egress filtering to prevent IP spoofing; this potentially stops a lot of malware. Basically, you want to do the following:

- All packets that have private IP addresses as their destination should be dropped.
- All packets that do not have valid private addresses as their source should be dropped. For example, if you only have one internal interface with a subnet of 192.168.1.0/24 and there is a packet with a source address of 192.168.2.1, this packet should be dropped.

Creating firewall rules

Creating a firewall rule in pfSense is easy, even if getting it to do exactly what you want isn't. To begin, navigate to **Firewall | Rules**. The **Rules** page has several tabs:

- Each subnet gets its own tab. Thus, every non-VLAN interface gets a separate tab, and every VLAN gets a separate tab.
- The leftmost tab is **Floating**, which is devoted to floating rules–rules that can apply to more than one interface and that can apply to traffic in both directions.
- If you have configured VPNs, each different VPN protocol gets its own tab (for example, IPsec and OpenVPN):

Creating a rule involves the following steps:

1. Once you have navigated to **Firewall | Rules**, click on the tab for the subnet for which you want to create the rule.
2. Click on one of the **Add** buttons to add a new rule. One button has an up arrow and the other has a down arrow. The **Add** button with the up arrow adds a rule to the top of the list, while the one with the down arrow adds a rule to the bottom of the list. Rules are evaluated on a top-down basis, so where you place it on the list is crucial. You can always, however, move the rule to its correct location after the fact.
3. Once the **Edit** page loads, you can start configuring the firewall rule. The first section of the page is **Edit Firewall Rule**.
    - The first setting is the **Action** drop-down box. This determines what happens to packets that match the rule. The options are:
        - **Pass**: Let the traffic pass
        - **Block**: Drop the packet silently
        - **Reject**: Drop the packet, but send back either a TCP RST error, or an ICMP port unreachable error (TCP RST, or reset, is for TCP packets; ICMP is for UDP packets)
4. Whether or not you use **Block** or **Reject** will likely depend on your own circumstances. **Reject** allows the end user to know right away that access to the resource is not allowed, while with **Block**, the user's connection will eventually time out. If the user is attacking our network, **Block** can be a useful way of confounding the attacker, since they won't be able to tell whether there is a network error, the resource doesn't exist, or access to the resource is being blocked.

5. The next setting is the **Disabled** checkbox, which allows us to disable the rule. This is useful if we want to temporarily disable the rule for testing. This setting allows us to do just that without deleting the rule from our ruleset.

6. Let's look at the **Interface** drop-down box, which controls which interface packets must come from to match the rule. Note that we can set this to any interface, regardless of which tab we were on when we clicked on **Add**.

7. The **Address Family** drop-down box allows you to select the version of **Internet Protocol** (**IP**) to which the rule applies. The choices are **IPv4**, **IPv6**, or both (**IPv4+IPv6**).

8. The last option in this section is the **Protocol** drop-down box. This controls what protocol the packets must use in order for there to be a match. In most cases, we will be using either **TCP** (the default) or **UDP**, but there are many choices here.

9. The next section is **Source**, which is the source the packet must have to be a match. Typically we leave the **Source** drop-down set to the default of any. There is also an **Invert match** checkbox, which enables us to invert the meaning of the source selected. For example, if we select **LAN** as the source, and we check the **Invert match** checkbox, the source for the rule will be all packets that do not have LAN as their source. Clicking on the **Display Advanced** button will cause the **Source Port Range** options to appear.

10. The next section is **Destination**, which is the destination the packet must have to be a match. This is the setting we are more likely to change. As with **Source**, there is an **Invert match** checkbox, so that the match will be on the opposite of what we set here. The **Destination** port range allows us to set a port range or a single port.

11. In the **Extra Options** section, there are several options:
    - If the **Log** checkbox is checked, pfSense will log packets that match the rule. Normally, we do not want to log packets just because they match a certain rule, since it will just use up disk space. If we are troubleshooting, however, or if we just need a record of every time the rule is invoked, we can enable this option.
    - We can enter a brief non-parsed description in the **Description** edit box.

- There are several advanced options we can display by clicking on the **Display Advanced** button. We will not discuss all of the options available, but some of the more significant ones deserve a mention:
  - The **Source OS** option allows us to apply the rule only to packets that come from a specific OS. All of the common OS options are available (for example, multiple versions of Windows, Linux, and macOS), along with some less-common ones (for example, BeOS and OS/2).
  - **Max src. states** allows us to limit the number of states per host for a rule. This is potentially useful in blocking DoS attacks.
  - **TCP Flags** allows you to apply the rule only to packets with the specified TCP flags set. We will take advantage of this option later on to create a rule to block SYN flood attacks.
  - The **Schedule** option allows us to invoke the rule only during specific times, defined by a schedule entry. If you have created schedule entries, then they will appear in the drop-down box for Schedule, and you will be able to select the entry.
  - **Gateway** is useful in multi-WAN setups. If you want to send packets that match this rule to a gateway other than the default gateway, and you have more than one WAN interface, you can select the gateway in the drop-down box.
  - The **In/Out** pipe allows you to take packets coming in from one interface (the **In** interface) and send traffic leaving the interface to another interface (the **Out** interface).
  - **Ackqueue/Queue** allows you to pipe traffic into a specific traffic-shaping queue and send ACK traffic into a specific ACK queue. We will discuss traffic-shaping in greater detail in the next chapter.

12. Once you are done configuring your rule, you can click on the blue **Save** button to save the rule. Once the page reloads, click on the **Apply Changes** button to force a reload of the firewall filter rules.

13. The rule has now been added, but are the rules in the right order? If they aren't, you can click on the new rule and drag it into the correct position. After moving the rule, click on the **Save** button at the bottom of the table and then click on the **Apply Changes** button to reload the rules.

The newly-created rule can be found on the table for the subnet to which the rule applies. There are a number of columns on the table, which tell us pertinent information about the rule:

- **States**: This column tells us how many states exist (as well as the total amount of data passing through the firewall) because of traffic allowed by this rule. This can be useful when troubleshooting. If you created a rule that allows traffic to pass (Action=Pass) and the rule has been in effect for a while, yet there are zero states associated with the rule, it's a good sign that the rule has had no effect.
- **Protocol**: Lists both the network-layer protocol and transport-layer protocol to which the rule applies. The network-layer protocol will be either IPv4, IPv6, or both, and the transport-layer protocol will be TCP, UDP, or one of many other supported protocols.
- **Source/Port**: The source of the traffic to which the rule applies.
- **Destination/Port**: The destination of the port to which the rule applies.
- **Gateway**: We are allowed to specify the gateway to which traffic that matches the rule is sent. Otherwise, the system routing tables are used. This column lists the gateway specified; if no gateway was selected, there is an asterisk in this column.
- **Queue**: We are allowed to specify a queue into which traffic that matches this rule will be sent. That queue will be listed here; otherwise, there is an asterisk in this column.
- **Description**: This is the information that was entered into the **Description** edit box when the rule was created/edited.

In the rightmost portion of the column, there are several icons that enable us to perform tasks related to the rules. The icon that looks like an anchor allows us to move checked rules above the rule (there is a checkbox in the leftmost column of each entry). Clicking on this icon with the *Shift* key held down allows us to move checked rules below the rule. Clicking on the icon that looks like a pencil allows us to edit the rule. Clicking on the icon that looks like two pieces of paper on top of each other allows us to copy a rule. This can come in handy when creating a rule that only differs from an existing rule in one or two ways. Clicking on the icon that is a circle with a line through it allows us to disable a rule. The icon then changes into a box with a checkmark in it; clicking on it re-enables the rule. Finally, clicking on the icon that looks like a trash can allows us to delete the rule.

Floating rules

The leftmost tab on the **Rules** page is **Floating**. From this tab, you can create rules that are different from the rules described previously in several ways:

- Whereas rules applying to a single subnet can only be applied to traffic leaving the subnet/interface, floating rules can apply to traffic entering or leaving a subnet. It can also apply to traffic going in either direction.
- Floating rules can apply to more than one interface.
- As with other rules, there is an **Action** drop-down box, and the **Pass**, **Block**, and **Reject** options are supported. There is a fourth option, however, called **Match**. If **Match** is selected and traffic matches the rule, the pass/block status of the traffic will not be affected, but the rule will be invoked. This is useful in traffic-shaping scenarios, as it allows us to divert the traffic into different queues, including ones we created when setting up traffic-shaping.

To begin creating **Floating** rules, we first click on the **Rules** page and then click on one of the **Add** buttons. You will notice that the options are similar to those we saw before, when creating non-floating rules, with some significant differences:

- As mentioned earlier, the **Action** drop-down box has an option called **Match**.
- There is an option called **Quick**. This checkbox, if checked, will cause the rule to be evaluated before the per-subnet/per-interface rules. The default behavior (when this option is not checked) is to evaluate the floating rules last.
- More than one interface can be selected in the **Interface** list box.
- With the **Direction** drop-down box, you can choose to apply the rule to traffic coming into the interface (in), traffic leaving the interface (out), or both.

The **Quick** option is a powerful one, and potentially useful. A floating rule without **Quick** enabled is enforced only if none of the rules on the subnet/interface tabs and (since rules are evaluated on a top-down basis) only if none of the rules above it on the **Floating** tab match the traffic first. Thus, if we need to enforce a rule before all other rules, we can use the **Quick** option. Floating rules without **Quick** enabled, however, are an effective way of enforcing default behavior on multiple interfaces.

 If **Quick** is enabled, the fast-forward icon (two adjacent green sideways triangles) will appear on the left hand side of a rule's entry in the **Floating Rules** table.

Because this can seem confusing at first, it should be mentioned that non-floating rules are always enforced on traffic that is inbound to an interface. Thus, if we want to create a floating rule that behaves the same as non-floating rules, we would set **Direction** to **in**. If you need to filter outbound traffic or traffic in both directions, then select the **out** or **any** option.

Example rules

To demonstrate the pfSense rules in action, we will walk through the process of creating three example rules: two standard rules and one floating rule.

Example #1 – rule to block a website

For this rule, let's assume that we have decided that employees spend too much time on the popular Apple blog `appleinsider.com` and have decided to block it. We perform a DNS lookup and find out that the IP address for this site is `207.58.150.178`.

 Note that we selected a website that uses a single IP address. Trying to block a website that uses multiple IP addresses can be more challenging; one way is to use aliases, discussed in the next section.

We begin by navigating to **Firewall** | **Rules** and clicking on the appropriate tab (for example, LAN). We then click on one of the **Add** buttons to add a rule. When the page loads, set the **Action** to **Block**; all other options in the **Edit Firewall Rule** section can remain the same. In the **Destination** section, select **Single host or alias** in the drop-down box and then enter `207.58.150.178` in the adjacent edit box. You can enter a brief description in the **Description** edit box (for example, `Block Apple Insider rule`) and then click on **Save** when done. When the page reloads, click on the **Apply Changes** button.

The final step is to make sure the rule is placed in the appropriate place; in particular, it should be placed with any **Allow LAN to any** rules, or it will never be reached. One this is done, if the rule order has been changed, click on the **Save** button below the table, then click on the **Apply Changes** button, and the rule should take effect. Users on the LAN net should now be blocked from accessing `appleinsider.com`. To confirm that this is the case, try accessing the site while the rule is enabled, then disable the rule and see what happens. Be sure to clear your browser cache beforehand to make sure you aren't accessing a cached version of the site.

Example #2 – universal allow any rule

As we mentioned previously in this chapter, pfSense creates two default **Allow LAN to any** rules that provide outbound access for the LAN interface. If we subsequently create other subnets or interfaces, however, we must create our own **Allow** rules for these interfaces. We can make life easier, though, by creating a floating **Allow** rule that works on multiple interfaces. Here, we will show you how.

Once you navigate to **Firewall | Rules**, click on the **Floating** tab. On that tab, click on one of the **Add** buttons. When the page loads, keep the **Action** at the default of **Pass**. In the **Interface list** box, select all the interfaces for which you want this rule to apply (usually it would be all non-WAN interfaces). For **Address Family**, select **IPv4+IPv6**. For the **Protocol**, select **any**. The **Source** and **Destination** can be kept as their default values of any. Enter a brief description in the **Description** edit box, and click on the **Save** button. As with the other rule, make sure that the rules are in the correct order. If any rules are moved, click on the **Save** button and then click on the **Apply Changes** button.

Since eliminating redundant rules is part of the firewall rules best practices, you should next go back to the LAN tab and disable the two **Allow LAN to any** rules. Before that, you should make sure the **Anti-Lockout Rule** is enabled (this setting can be found at **System | Advanced** on the **Admin Access** tab). Otherwise, if the floating rule wasn't set up correctly, you could end up being locked out of pfSense. Once the rule takes effect, users of all interfaces should have outbound access if the per-subnet/per-interface rules do not prevent such access. One test you can do to confirm that floating rules take effect last by default is to try to access `appleinsider.com` with the **Quick** option for this rule disabled (access should be blocked), and then try to access it with the **Quick** option enabled (access should be allowed, because now our floating **Allow** rule takes precedence).

Example #3 – rule to prevent SYN flood attacks

At the beginning of this chapter, we discussed SYN flood attacks. We also mentioned that the SYN and FIN flags should never both be set on the same TCP packet. If they are, there's a good possibility that the packets are part of a SYN flood attack. In any case, it's not a valid packet and can be dropped safely.

Fortunately, pfSense gives us the means to block such packets. To do this, navigate to **Firewall | Rules** and on the **WAN** tab, click on the **Add** button with the up arrow (we want this rule to appear at the beginning of the list). Once the **Edit** page loads, change the **Action** to **Block**, and the **Address Family** to **IPv4+IPv6**. The other fields in the top section can be kept at their default values.

The **Source** and **Destination** can also be kept at their default values of **Any**. We don't care what the source of the traffic is, and we don't particularly care what the destination within our network is, either.

Scroll down to **Extra Options** and click on the **Display Advanced** button. Once you do this, scroll down to **TCP Flags**. We want to block packets that have the SYN and FIN flags set, so check the **SYN** and **FIN** columns in the set row. This should enable us to match the relevant packets. Once you are done, scroll down to the bottom of the page, click on the **Save** button, and then click on **Apply Changes** when the page reloads. The rule should be at the top of the table. If not, you should move it to the top.

You may have noticed that we created the rule on the WAN interface and not on any of the internal interfaces. This seems reasonable, as we are mainly concerned with SYN flood attacks coming from external networks–not with SYN flood attacks being launched from our networks. The latter case might be a concern, but unless we have reason to believe that it might happen, adding this rule to our internal interfaces will just generate a lot of work for our firewall that it doesn't need to do.

Scheduling

One thing we haven't mentioned so far in our discussion of firewall rules is that sometimes we do not want rules to take effect all the time. They don't have to, though, and that's when scheduling comes in handy. Each schedule can have a single or multiple time ranges, and can be applied to one or more rules.

To begin creating schedules, navigate to **Firewall | Schedules**. The main **Schedules** page will display a table with any previously created schedules. To create a new entry, click on the **Add** button.

The **Edit** page is simple and only has two sections. The first is **Schedule Information**, and in this section you can configure options. In the **Configured Ranges** section, the already-defined ranges for the rule appear.

The first option is **Schedule Name**. Here you enter the name, which can consist only of letters, numbers, and the underscore character. You can also enter a non-parsed description in the **Description** field. In the **Month** drop-down box, you can select the month that will appear in the **Date** section (selecting a month here does not cause the rule to only take effect in a specific month, however). Time ranges can consist of individual dates or days of the week. You can click on an individual date on the calendar to select a specific date, or you can click on a weekday header to select all instances of a weekday.

If you need something more granular than just days of a week or a specific day, you can select a time range in the **Time** section. The allowed fields are **Start Hrs**, **Start Mins**, **Stop Hrs**, and **Stop Mins**, and the time is in 24-hour format. Note that you can only select minutes in 15-minute increments (0, 15, 30, and 45). You can also enter a non-parsed description in the **Time range description** field, and when you are done, you can click on the **Add Time** button. You can also click on **Clear selection** to clear the fields. Once you click on the **Add Time** button, you should see the time range in the **Configured Ranges** section. You can create additional time ranges by selecting additional dates or days of the week and time ranges, and clicking on the **Add Time** button again. Existing ranges can be deleted by clicking on the **Delete** button for an entry. When you are done, click on the **Save** button at the bottom of the page.

Example – blocking a website only during certain hours

For this example, assume that we have decided that our rule blocking `appleinsider.com` was too broad. We want to block the site only during business hours. Furthermore, we want to allow access to the site during the lunch hour (noon to 1 PM).

This can be achieved by altering the rule we created in the previous section, and by using scheduling. Navigate to **Firewall | Schedules** and click on the **Add** button. Enter a **Name** (for example, `WORK_HOURS`) and a **Description**. For **Date**, we are concerned with workdays, so select the **Mon**, **Tue**, **Wed**, **Thu**, and **Fri** columns. For **Time**, enter 9 for **Start Hrs**, 0 for **Start Mins**, 12 for **Stop Hrs**, and 0 for **Stop Hrs**. You can enter a brief **Description** for this time range if you wish. Then click on the **Add Time** button.

Now we need to define a second time range for the afternoon hours. The calendar will be cleared, so you will have to click on the weekday columns again. For **Time**, enter 13 for **Start Hrs**, 0 for **Start Mins**, 17 for **Stop Hrs**. and 0 for **Stop Hrs**. You can enter a brief **Description** if you wish. Then click on the **Add Time** button again. Our schedule entry is now defined, so click on the **Save** button.

We have defined a schedule entry, but it will have no effect until a rule uses it. So navigate to **Firewall | Rules** and click on the tab for the interface onto which the rule blocking `appleinsider.com` was added. Find the rule in the table and click on the rule's edit icon.

On the rule's **Edit** page, scroll down to the **Extra Options** section and click on the **Display Advanced** button. Additional options should appear on the page. Scroll down to the **Schedule** drop-down box and select the newly-created scheduling entry (the name of the entry should appear in the drop-down box). Once you have done this, click on the **Save** button and, when the page reloads, click on **Apply Changes**.

Now, the rule will only apply to business hours, with the exception of the lunch hour. As with the rules that were created in the previous sections, you may want to test the rule to make sure the scheduling is having the intended effect.

 When a Block or Reject rule is in effect, the Schedule column for that rule in the rules table will display a red stop symbol when the rule is active. If a Pass rule is in effect, a green play symbol will be displayed. If the rule is not active, a yellow pause symbol will be shown.

Aliases and virtual IPs

In this section, we will briefly consider two items from the firewall menu: aliases and virtual IPs. Of the two, you are more likely to utilize aliases, so we will look at them first.

Aliases

Aliases allow you to group ports, hosts, or networks into named entities that you can refer to in firewall rules, NAT rules, and in traffic-shaping. Judicious use of aliases will enable you to make changes in IP addresses, ports, and/or networks without making multiple configuration changes.

You cannot use aliases everywhere within the pfSense web GUI, but you will always know when you can: an edit box that is alias-friendly will have a red background. If you start to type the alias name into such a box, the autocomplete functionality built into pfSense will complete the name for you.

To begin creating aliases, navigate to **Firewall | Aliases**. The main **Aliases** page has four separate tabs. There is **IP**, **Ports**, **URLs**, and **All**. Clicking on one of these tabs will show a table with all of the already-created aliases for that category. If you want to create an alias of a certain type, you can click on the appropriate tab and click on the **Add** button under the table.

In reality, however, clicking on the right tab is not necessary, because you can create an alias for any supported type from any tab. This is because you can change the type of the alias being created by changing the value in the **Type** drop-down box on the **Alias Edit** page.

The first section on the **Edit** page is **Properties**; the name of the second section depends on what type you select in the **Type** drop-down box. The first option is **Name**, where you enter the name pfSense will use to identify the alias; as with schedule names, it may only consist of letters, numbers, and the underscore character. You may enter a brief description in the **Description** field. The Type option is where you specify the type of alias. There are several options, some obvious and some less so:

- **Host(s)**: This enables you to enter one or more hosts, which are denoted by either their IP address or hostname. If you specify the hostname, it will be re-re solved and updated on a regular basis. For IP addresses, you can specify an IP range or subnet.
- **Network(s)**: With this option, you can specify a network, by specifying the network prefix and CIDR.
- **Port(s)**: This option allows you to specify one or more ports. You can specify a range of ports by separating the first and last ones with a colon.
- **URL (IPs)**: With this, you can specify one or more URLs that, in turn, point to text lists of IP addresses. You can enter more than one URL. Each file should be limited to 3,000 IP addresses or ranges.
- **URL (Ports)**: Similar to URL (IPs), but allows you to specify lists of ports. Again, each file should have no more than 3,000 entries.
- **URL Table (IPs)**: Similar to URL (IPs), except you can only specify a single URL, but the list pointed to by the URL will be downloaded and refreshed periodically. Longer lists are allowed.

The second section of the page is where you enter information about what the alias stands for–it will be either a hostname (actually, a **Fully Qualified Domain Name (FQDN)**), and IP address/range, a port/range of ports, or a URL. For all types except the two **URL Table** options, multiple entries are allowed, and you add more than one entry by clicking on the green **Add** button at the bottom of the page after you define an entry. When you are done adding entries for the alias, click on the **Save** button, and then when the page reloads, click on the **Apply Changes** button.

There is another method of generating aliases that can be helpful in some cases. Assume you want to block a website that uses multiple IP addresses (such as YouTube). Creating a rule or rules to block such sites can be cumbersome, but if we could create an alias for all IP addresses the site uses, it would be helpful. We can do this somewhat automatically in pfSense.

First, we navigate to **Diagnostics** | **DNS Lookup**. On the **DNS Lookup** page, enter the hostname in the **Hostname** field (for example, `www.youtube.com`) and then click on the **Lookup** button. When the results of the lookup appear, there should be a new button labeled **Add Alias**. Click on the button, and an alias should be created with the same name as the hostname, except that any dots should be converted to underscores (for example, `www_youtube_com`). Navigate back to **Firewall** | **Aliases**, and the new alias should be listed there.

Keep in mind that this method is not necessarily a foolproof method for creating aliases for sites that use multiple IP addresses. Sites such as YouTube are constantly adding to the pool of IP addresses they use, and you will find that if you use an alias created in this way for such a site, it will work immediately after the alias was created, but will soon become outdated–within days, if not hours. There are other ways to block such sites, which we will discuss later in this book.

Example – creating an alias and making a block rule based on the alias

For this example, we will create an alias for YouTube and then use it to create a rule to block YouTube. We begin by navigating to **Diagnostics** | **DNS Lookup**, enter `www.youtube.com` into the **Hostname** field, and then click on the **Lookup** button.

Performing a DNS lookup on YouTube should result in multiple A and AAAA records being returned with valid IP addresses for the site. Click on the **Add** alias button to create an alias. A message should appear on the page to notify us that the alias was created successfully. To confirm that it was created, navigate to **Firewall** | **Aliases** and find the new alias in the table.

Next, navigate to **Firewall** | **Rules**, and click on the tab for the interface on which the `appleinsider.com` rule was created. Find that rule and click on the copy icon for the rule. This will create an identical copy of the rule. Settings for the previously created rule to block a website are mostly right; we just need to change the **Destination**. Keep **Single host or alias** as the setting and replace the IP address for `appleinsider.com` with the newly-created alias.

That is all you have to do, unless you want to change the scheduling option. When you are done making changes, click on the **Save** button and when the page reloads, click on **Apply Changes**. You will likely find that this rule is effective immediately after you create the alias, but will become ineffective as YouTube adds new IP addresses.

Virtual IPs

Virtual IPs (VIPs) are IP addresses that do not correspond to a single physical interface. They are used in multiple scenarios:

- **Network Address Translation (NAT)**
- When fault tolerance is needed, such as failover and CARP setups
- When mobile users need to have a consistent virtual IP address even as their actual (physical) IP address changes.

To begin, navigate to **Firewall** | **Virtual IPs** and click on the **Add** button below the table. There are four options for VIPs: **IP Alias**, **CARP**, **Proxy ARP**, and **Other**. The following caveats need to be specified about these options:

- CARP and IP Alias can be used to bind to and run services; the others cannot.
- All options except for Other generate layer-2 (ARP) traffic.
- All options except Proxy ARP can be used for clustering, but if IP Alias VIPs are used as part of a CARP VIP, they must be in the same subnet as that CARP VIP.
- Although you can generate a VIP that is in a different subnet than the real interface IP, it is recommended that you keep them on the same subnet to avoid potential issues.
- For IP Alias, the subnet mask should match that of the interface IP, or it should be /32. If the IPs are in different subnets than the original IP address, at least one IP Alias VIP needs to have the correct mask for the subnet.
- CARP and IP Alias VIPs respond to ICMP ping attempts; the others do not.
- CARP and IP Alias VIPs must be added individually; the others can be added as part of a subnet.

Setting up a virtual IP is not difficult. To do so, follow these steps:

1. Select one of the four options mentioned previously.
2. Select a physical interface for the VIP, which you can do in the **Interface** drop-down box.
3. For the **Address** type drop-down box, you can select either **Single address** or **Network** (you can only select **Network** with **Proxy ARP** or **Other**).

4. In the **Address(es)** edit box, enter either the VIP or the virtual subnet, as well as the CIDR. There are also several options only available if you selected CARP:

- You must enter a **Virtual IP Password** for CARP VIPs.
- Next is the **VHID** drop-down box. Each VIP to be shared by multiple nodes needs to use a unique **Virtual Host ID (VHID)** group. This VHID must be different from any VHIDs in active use on any directly connected network interface. You can use 1 as your VHID if CARP is not set up and you are not using Cisco's **Virtual Router Redundancy Protocol (VRRP)**. The VHID should automatically increment itself.
- Next is **Advertising Frequency**. This value depends on the node's role. The master's value should be 1, while a backup should be set to 2 or higher.
- Finally, there is the **Skew** drop-down box. This value controls how often the node advertises itself as a member of the redundancy group, measured in seconds. Lower values tend to ensure that backup nodes will become master nodes if the master node fails.

5. You can enter a brief description in the **Description** field.
6. When you are done, click on the **Save** button at the bottom of the page. When the page reloads, click on **Apply Changes**.

NAT

Network Address Translation (NAT), as the name implies, is a means of mapping one address space into another address space. It is often equated with port forwarding, a subcategory of NAT that allows a computer on a public network, such as the internet, to connect to a computer on a private network (for example, our LAN) by remapping the IP address and port. This is the form of NAT that you are most likely to use. But there two are other forms of NAT, which we will cover in this section. Outbound NAT allows traffic from internal networks whose destination is an external network to reach their destination. 1:1 NAT is a form of remapping public IP addresses to private IP addresses in such a way that each public IP address corresponds to one private IP address.

Port-forwarding

Port-forwarding is typically used in scenarios where we have a single public IP address and several resources–in many cases on separate nodes–that must be made accessible to the internet. In such cases, it is useful to map traffic to different nodes based on the port on which the traffic entered the network–hence the term port-forwarding.

Port-forwarding is rarely seen in corporate networks (corporations are more likely to be able to afford separate IP addresses for different services), but are commonly seen in home and SOHO networks. Fortunately, pfSense is designed to work with a variety of networks and supports port-forwarding. However, we must take into account the following:

- Port-forwarding in pfSense is always applied before 1:1 NAT.
- Port-forwarding rules in pfSense are applied before firewall rules.
- Port-forwarding is always a 1:1 proposition. Thus, we can only map a port number to a single node. If we want to have multiple FTP servers, for example, we cannot have them on the same port.
- The creation of a port-forwarding entry does not in itself make the port accessible from the WAN side. pfSense blocks all traffic on all interfaces and all ports by default, and in order for traffic to pass, there must be a corresponding firewall rule. Fortunately, pfSense streamlines the process of creating a matching firewall rule.

Creating a port-forwarding entry is as easy as following these steps:

1. Navigate to **Firewall | NAT**. The **Port Forwarding** tab should be selected by default.
2. There will be a table on this page showing all the current port-forwarding entries. Click on one of the **Add** buttons below the table to add a rule.
3. The first option on the page is **Disable**, which allows you to disable a rule without deleting the rule. As with firewall rules, this is useful when troubleshooting.
4. The **No RDR (NOT)** checkbox, when checked, will cause **Redirect target IP**, **Redirect target port**, and Filter rule association to have no effect. This is a rarely-used option, but can come in handy if you want to exclude a subset of ports from a larger range of ports that is being redirected. It also might be useful if a proxy is running on the port.
5. The **Interface** drop-down box allows you to select the interface to which the rule applies. In most cases, we can leave this at its default value, which is **WAN**. This is because port-forwarding is mainly concerned with traffic originating on the internet.
6. The **Protocol** drop-down box allows you to select the protocol that the traffic must have for the port-forwarding rule to match.
7. **Source** and **Source port range** are hidden because, in most cases, we don't care about the source of the traffic, and, although we can change these values, usually we can leave them set to **Any**.

8. Most of the time, **Destination** can be left set to **WAN address**, since users on the public internet will be targeting your WAN address. This may be different if you have a multi-WAN setup, in which case you may want to change your destination to one of your other WAN interfaces. Destination port range is something you will have to set, however, since this is the port or range of ports you want to forward to one of your network's private IP addresses.

9. The **Redirect target IP** edit box is where you enter the private IP address of the node to which you want to map the port or range of ports. This is usually identical to the port specified in the **Destination port range**, but it doesn't have to be.

10. In the **Description** edit box, you can enter a brief non-parsed description.

11. The **No XMLRPC Sync** option, if enabled, results in the rule not being synced to other CARP members (note that this option does not apply to CARP slaves, who can still have their NAT rules overwritten by CARP master).

12. The **NAT Reflection** drop-down box allows you to select different NAT reflection options:
    - **Use system default** allows you to use the NAT reflection option chosen in **System** | **Advanced** under the **NAT** tab.
    - **Enable (NAT + Proxy)** sets up a proxy daemon which will receive/reflect connections, but it only works with TCP connections and only with ranges up to 500 ports.
    - **Enable (Pure NAT)** creates automatic rules to do redirection without a proxy daemon.
    - **Disable** disables NAT reflection.

13. The **Filter rule association** drop-down box allows you to choose what type of firewall rule is created to correspond to the port-forwarding rule:
    - **Add associated filter rule** causes pfSense to generate a firewall rule that is updated every time the NAT rule is updated.
    - **Add unassociated firewall rule** causes pfSense to generate a firewall rule corresponding to the NAT rule, but it is not updated automatically.
    - **Pass** does not create a new firewall rule, but it allows traffic that matches the NAT rule through the firewall. This might prove confusing if you ever have to troubleshoot firewall issues.
    - **None** causes pfSense to not create any firewall rule, explicit or implicit. Traffic matching the NAT rule will only get through if there is already a firewall rule allowing it to pass.

14. When you are done, you can click on the **Save** button and, when the page reloads, click on the **Apply Changes** button.

NAT reflection is a feature that enables users on the internal network to access a resource (for example, a file server) that exists on the internal network using that resource's public IP address (an alternative to using the private IP address of that resource).

Example – DCC port-forwarding

In this example, we will create a NAT rule to allow DCC ports through the firewall. For the purpose of this exercise, we will assume that the target node is on the LAN subnet, that the LAN uses the `192.168.1.0/24` subnet, and that the target node's IP address is `192.168.1.2`.

Direct Client-to-Client (**DCC**) is an IRC-related subprotocol. It is typically used by IRC users to exchange files, but it can also be used to perform non-relayed chats.

We begin by navigating to **Firewall | NAT** and clicking on one of the **Add** buttons. Keep **Interface** and **WAN** at their default settings. We also do not have to change the default **Source**. Keep **Destination** set to **WAN address**, since that is where the port-forwarding traffic will be entering the network. Set the **Destination port range** to `5000` to `5010`.

Next, set **Redirect target IP** to `192.168.1.2` and set the **Redirect target port** to `5000` (the end port will be calculated automatically). You may also enter a brief description in the **Description** field. Keep the **Filter rule association** set to **Add associated filter rule**, because we will need a firewall rule to let the DCC traffic through the firewall. Finally, click on the **Save** button, and when the page reloads, click on **Apply Changes**.

You'll want to navigate to **Firewall | Rules**. There, you should be able to see the newly-created firewall rule to allow DCC traffic to pass on the **WAN** tab.

Outbound NAT

Outbound NAT deals with traffic from private, internal networks to external networks. Even if you have never configured outbound NAT on your pfSense system, chances are you are already using it. This is because the initial pfSense installation already automatically translates outbound traffic to the WAN IP address. If there are multiple WAN interfaces, traffic leaving any of these WAN interfaces is translated into the WAN IP address of the WAN interface being used:

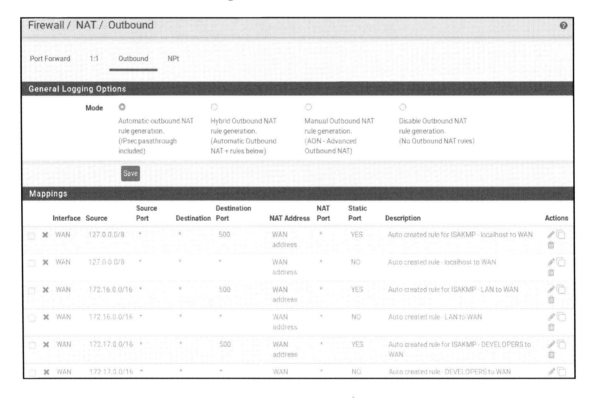

If you navigate to **Firewall | NAT** and click on the **Outbound NAT** tab, and you haven't done any configuration to outbound NAT, you should find that the **Outbound NAT Mode** is set to **Automatic outbound rule generation**. This means that as new subnets/interfaces are added to the system, pfSense automatically generates outbound NAT rules to let traffic pass through to the WAN interface. An easy way to confirm that these rules are necessary is to change this setting to **Disable Outbound NAT** and then click on the **Save** button. Unless you have reconfigured your network so it is no longer dependent on NAT, the internet should be inaccessible from the LAN side of your network. To resolve this, switch back to **Automatic outbound rule generation**.

Note that the outbound NAT rules that handle most of the outbound NAT traffic involve non-static port mappings. This is tremendously helpful. For example, if I request a standard web page, it uses the HTTP protocol, which uses port 80. If outbound NAT used a static mapping for this port, the WAN interface would also use port 80, and anyone else on the network requesting a standard web page would be blocked from receiving one until my request had been fulfilled and the state expired. But by using a non-static mapping, Outbound NAT can re-map this to an arbitrary port–a non-standard port above 49152–so that other users will not be blocked from requesting web pages.

 Note that there are two rules for each interface. The first rule is a non-static rule that is used for most outbound traffic. The second rule is an **Internet Security Association and Key-Management Protocol (ISAKMP)** for IPsec key exchange.

The two other settings for outbound NAT mode are as follows:

- **Hybrid outbound NAT rule-generation**: This will still automatically generate outbound NAT rules for internal subnets/interfaces, but you will also be able to add outbound NAT rules of your own.
- **Manual outbound NAT rule-generation**: This will not automatically create any new rules, but previously created automatic rules will remain. Using this setting might cause some confusion if you add interfaces later on without remembering that you must add outbound NAT rules. The new interfaces will not have internet access until you do.

It is outside the scope of this chapter to provide a detailed discussion of outbound NAT. If you set up a VPN, however, you will likely be utilizing outbound NAT in order to direct traffic to the VPN tunnel. It can also be useful in certain scenarios, such as monitoring network traffic.

For example, if we suspect that users on one particular interface are using too much bandwidth, we could create a virtual IP address for the WAN interface, and then redirect outbound traffic on that interface to the virtual IP by changing the outbound NAT rule for that interface. To the end user, there will be no difference, but it will make it easier to search the logs for outbound traffic from that interface, since we need only search for the newly created virtual IP.

1:1 NAT

1:1 NAT essentially allows us to map one public IP address to one private IP address. As a result, a resource or resources that otherwise would only be available on our private network will now be available via the internet. It works both ways, with incoming traffic from the public IP being mapped to the private IP, and outgoing traffic from the private IP being mapped to the public IP, and in the course of this, outbound NAT settings are overridden.

1:1 NAT configuration can be done by following these steps:

1. Navigate to **Firewall** | **NAT** and click on the 1:1 tab. There you can click on the **Add** button.
2. The **Negate** option allows you to exclude the rule from the NAT. This is useful if you are redirecting a range of addresses and must exclude a subset.
3. **No BINAT**, if enabled, will disable redirection for traffic matching the rule. Again, it is useful if you need to exclude a subset of a range from redirection.
4. The **Interface** option allows you to select the interface to which the rule applies; typically this can be left set to **WAN**.
5. The **External subnet ID** edit box is the place where the external subnet's starting IP address is entered.
6. The **Internal IP** edit box is where the internal subnet is specified. The subnet size for the internal subnet determines how many IPs are mapped. To provide an example, assume we have **External subnet IP** set to 10.1.1.1 (we shouldn't because 10.x.x.x is an internal network, but this is just an example), and **Internal IP** is set to 192.168.1.100/30, with **Network** as the type specified. 30 bits for the network identifier in an IPv4 address leaves 2 bits for the node identifier, or 4 total nodes. Thus, 10.1.1.1 will be mapped to 192.168.1.100, 10.1.1.2 will be mapped to 192.168.1.101, and so on, up to and including 10.1.1.4/192.168.1.103.
7. You can enter a brief description in the **Description** field.

8. The **NAT reflection** drop-down box allows you to access mapped nodes from behind the firewall using the public IP address. There are two options in the drop-down box (**Enable** and **Disable**).

9. Click on the **Save** button when done, and when the page reloads, click on **Apply Changes**.

Troubleshooting

If your firewall rules are not doing what you expect them to do, you will need to troubleshoot them, and odds are that it will happen at some point. The obvious first step is to diagnose the problem. For example, nodes on a particular network may not be able to access the internet. Narrowing the scope of the problem is important. If the problem is limited to a certain interface, or certain application/service or protocol, then it will help us in pinpointing the source of the problem.

It is good practice to start by checking the Floating Rules tab. This is because floating rules can take precedence over rules for an individual interface, and if the problem is a floating rule, we can save time that would have been spent checking (and probably double-checking) an interface's ruleset.

If you are running a proxy setting, you may want to check the settings on the proxy before you check the affected interface's ruleset. This is because a proxy server's allow and deny lists will often take precedence over firewall rule settings.

Finally, if you still haven't found the source of the problem, you will want to check the firewall rules for the affected interfaces. Remember that firewall rules are evaluated from the top down, and make sure that the order of the rules isn't preventing the rule from taking effect. Also, check the allowed and/or blocked protocols for rules. One example of a rule in which protocol is crucial is a rule for a video server. If a rule is designed to allow video-streaming clients to connect to your video server, and the firewall rule for the server only allows TCP traffic to pass through an interface, a video-streaming client that uses UDP will not work.

If you want to find out whether a **Pass** rule is effective, then, as mentioned earlier, you may want to look at the rules table and check the States column. This is the leftmost column, and it tells us the number of current states created and the total amount of data that passed through the firewall as a result of packets matching this firewall rule.

If you hover your mouse over this column, you will see even more information, such as the total number of evaluations, packets, bytes, states, and state creations. If a **Pass** rule has been enabled for some time and no data is passing in connection with the rule, there are two likely possibilities:

- The rule is misconfigured.
- Traffic matches another rule before it gets to this rule. This may be as you intended; if not, you need to rethink your ordering of the rules.

pfSense makes disabling and enabling rules incredibly easy. Therefore, you should take advantage of this when troubleshooting. A good methodology is to disable one or more rules, take note of what happens on the network after they are disabled, and then re-enable the rules one at a time. As you do, you should take note of any changes that occur. This should help isolate the rule (or rules) that are causing the problem.

If this trial-and-error approach does not work, you might consider enabling logging for any rules you suspect may be the cause of the problem. Enabling logging usually is not recommended, as you can easily use up disk space doing this, but often examining the logs for rules can help. One you enable logging, navigate to **Status** | **System Logs** and click on the **Firewall** tab. There are a number of filtering options available (click on the filter icon at the top of the page, and they will appear), and they can be used to help find relevant entries. For example, you can filter the logs by source IP address and destination IP address, by source port and protocol, or destination port and protocol flags.

If the logs don't offer enough information to troubleshoot the problem, you could use **tcpdump**, a command-line utility (which can be run from within the web GUI as well) which is included with pfSense. **tcpdump** is a packet-analyzer that can be used to print the contents of network packets. We will not cover **tcpdump** in depth here, but we will revisit it in Chapter 11, *Troubleshooting*, and if you want to augment your networking credentials, you might consider familiarizing yourself with this powerful utility.

There may be a situation in which you make a change to the firewall rules, and some traffic is getting through the firewall that seems to violate the new rules. If this happens, it is possible that the state-table entries for the connections that violate the rules predate the rule change. If you want the connections to be dropped, you must reset the state table. In order to reset the state table, navigate to **Diagnostics** | **States** and click on the **Reset States** tab. Click on the **Reset** button, which will empty the state table. This will also reset any active connections.

This is different from going to **Status | Filter Reload** and clicking on the **Reload Filter** button, which will simply force a reload of the firewall rules.

Summary

In this chapter, we introduced you to the world of firewall rules and NAT. We briefly discussed some basics of firewalls, including pfSense's default behavior, and also mentioned firewall best practices and why both ingress and egress filtering are a good idea. We walked through the process of creating firewall rules, and also introduced some example rules. Finally, we discussed NAT. The form of NAT you are most likely to use is port-forwarding, but we also briefly discussed Outbound NAT and 1:1 NAT.

You will want to review this chapter if you haven't fully grasped the concepts discussed within it, as the next chapter builds heavily on what was covered here. We will discuss traffic-shaping in the next chapter, which, to a large degree, relies on firewall rules.

Questions

1. Identify the three main options of a firewall rule's **Action** setting and how they differ (assume we are not concerned with floating rules).
2. What do we mean when we say that pfSense is a stateful firewall?
3. What are the two main types of filtering that firewalls perform?
4. Why is it generally considered a bad idea to log packets that match a firewall rule?
5. (a) Identify the main differences between floating rules and other firewall rules. (b) What option can we use if we want to ensure that a floating rule is evaluated before rules for specific subnets/interfaces?
6. If we want traffic entering our network through a specific port to be sent to a node on our internal network, is it enough to create a valid port-forwarding entry for that port and that node? Why or why not?
7. (a) Can we use port-forwarding to map a single port to several different internal nodes? (b) Can we use port-forwarding to map several ports to the same internal node?
8. If we want to map one public IP address to a single private IP address, what feature should we use?

Further reading

- Firewall Rules Overview – a good summary of some of the basics: `https://cloud.google.com/vpc/docs/firewalls`
- Fine-tuning Firewall Rules: 10 Best Practices – reinforces a lot of the ideas mentioned in this chapter and even has a few new ideas: `https://www.esecurityplanet.com/network-security/finetune-and-optimize-firewall-rules.html`
- Network Address Translation (NAT) – an overview of NAT: `http://www.rhyshaden.com/nat.htm`

Traffic Shaping

Regardless of the size or purpose of your network, and regardless of your budget, you will derive benefits from optimizing the performance of your network. You have already taken a step in the right direction by learning about pfSense and, in previous chapters, we discussed some ways to improve performance, such as setting up our own DNS server and optimizing firewall rules. Another way to improve performance is to enable traffic shaping on our network. Without traffic shaping, network traffic is processed on a **first-in, first-out (FIFO)** basis. While, in some cases, this form of traffic management is adequate, it is far from optimal, and can lead to connections becoming saturated, which, in turn, causes buffering and increased latency. Traffic shaping, also known as **quality of service (QoS)**, is a form of bandwidth management in which network traffic is made to conform with a traffic profile. The purpose of this is to improve performance, as well as reduce latency and increase usable bandwidth.

In this chapter, we will first cover some fundamental concepts of traffic shaping. We then will demonstrate how to use pfSense's built-in traffic shaper to optimize network performance. The traffic shaper has its own wizard that makes it easy to set up traffic shaping, but sometimes we need to manually configure traffic shaping and add our own traffic shaping rules, and we will discuss how to do that. Finally, on occasion, the built-in traffic shaper does not meet our requirements, and we will introduce a third-party solution—Snort—that goes beyond what the base pfSense installation can do.

In this chapter, we will cover the following:

- Traffic shaping fundamentals
- Configuring traffic shaping
- Manual rule configuration
- Using Snort for traffic shaping
- Troubleshooting

Technical requirements

As with the previous chapters, you need to have a working pfSense system, in either a real or virtual environment. To work through the examples in this chapter, it will help to have at least one node on the network running at least one application where a low degree of latency is required (such as a VoIP application) and at least one application where latency is less important (such as a peer-to-peer file-sharing application).

Traffic shaping fundamentals

Traffic shaping allows us to manage network traffic in a way that prioritizes some traffic over other traffic in order to conform to specific predefined constraints. These constraints are known as a traffic profile or agreement. For an example of such an agreement, consider looking at your contract with your ISP. Most likely, it contains a **service level agreement** (**SLA**), a **traffic conditioning agreement** (**TCA**), or both. These agreements define what traffic your ISP will accept. If packets are sent from your local network to the ISP that violate these agreements, the ISP may block them from being forwarded upstream, or, at the very least, forwarding may not be guaranteed. As a result, we generally want to make sure that traffic leaving our network is in compliance with these agreements. One of the ways we can do this is with a traffic shaper.

The traffic shaper does its job by examining packets. If packets meet certain criteria, then they are handled differently. Thus, traffic shaping is similar to implementing firewall rules; in fact, we will use firewall rules to implement traffic shaping. When we create a firewall rule, packets that meet the criteria of that rule either pass or are blocked. With traffic shaping, packets that meet the criteria of a traffic shaping rule are placed in a separate queue. A traffic shaping queue is implemented as a FIFO buffer. Priority traffic enters a priority queue, where it is sent immediately. Lower-priority traffic is held back until higher priority traffic passes.

Traffic shaping is always implemented where the flow of data can be controlled, and, in pfSense, traffic can be controlled when packets are leaving the router. Hence, traffic shaping of incoming traffic to the LAN is applied when traffic leaves the LAN interface; traffic shaping of outgoing traffic is applied when traffic leaves the WAN interface, and so on.

Here are some common scenarios in which traffic shaping is used, with a particular emphasis on how it could be used on our networks:

- When low latency is required, it is typically beneficial to use traffic shaping. VoIP traffic is the commonly cited example. If VoIP traffic does not have higher priority, then it can be affected by anything that consumes bandwidth, such as someone downloading a large file. Another example is someone playing an online game, in which they want the response time to be as fast as possible. In other cases, some degree of latency may be tolerable, such as when video streaming through online streaming services is used.

- Traffic shaping can be used to limit the amount of bandwidth used by peer-to-peer applications. One way of accomplishing this is by lowering the priority of traffic entering and leaving certain well-known peer-to-peer ports. Another method is by employing **deep packet inspection** (also known as **Layer 7 inspection**—Layer 7 referring to the OSI model discussed in the first chapter). Neither method is foolproof. A port-based method is easy to implement and will work in many cases. However, users can circumvent such restrictions by using other ports, and it won't work well with applications such as many BitTorrent clients, which seem to use random ports. Layer 7 inspection has the advantage of generally being more effective in actually identifying peer-to-peer traffic. Unfortunately, it is also CPU-intensive and does not help us when traffic is encrypted. Furthermore, small changes to peer-to-peer protocols can thwart deep packet inspection. Complicating matters further is the fact that Layer 7 inspection is no longer supported by the built-in pfSense traffic shaper and requires a third-party add-on.

- Traffic shaping can make asymmetric (unequal upload and download bandwidths) connections work more efficiently. If you are like most broadband customers in North America, you have significantly greater download bandwidth than upload bandwidth. Moreover, your maximum download bandwidth may appear unobtainable in many cases. In the context of a file download using the TCP protocol, this is likely because the download client is sending ACK packets (acknowledging receipt of a packet) back to the file server, but these packets are being sent out in a FIFO queue with all other upstream traffic (such as web page requests). You can use traffic shaping to prioritize ACK packets, putting them in a dedicated queue, and thus get much closer to the maximum download speed.

- As mentioned in the previous chapter, non business-related traffic can be costly to a company. Therefore, if we use traffic shaping to prioritize business-related traffic, we can save money.
- ISPs can use traffic shaping to see what customers are doing, and target services to those customers. This is more difficult to do, however, as customers start encrypting their traffic.
- ISPs can use traffic shaping to ensure a certain quality of service to certain applications and users. This allows certain applications to gain priority, while other applications are free to use remaining bandwidth. This allows them to provide services such as low-latency gaming for an additional fee.
- In some cases, ISPs use traffic shaping to limit bandwidth consumption of certain programs. Often, they target such peer-to-peer applications such as BitTorrent; in other cases, they might target certain video streaming services. Since their connections are often advertised as unlimited connections, such policies have generated some controversy, and there is some debate as to whether this constitutes false advertising. What is clear, however, is that this is yet another example of traffic shaping being used to enforce a specific policy.

Traffic shaping comes into play very heavily in the current debate on **net neutrality**. Advocates of net neutrality argue that internet data should be treated equally. Opponents of net neutrality argue for a two-tier, or multi-tiered, internet. Such opponents argue that there have always been different levels of service, that net neutrality increases the regulatory burden on ISPs, and that overall, customers will benefit from less regulation and greater freedom of choice. Regardless of the outcome of this ongoing debate, net neutrality will likely continue to play a role in public policy regarding the public internet. It should, however, have little impact on private networks, which are the main focus of our discussion.

Queuing disciplines

We would be remiss if our discussion of traffic shaping didn't include a mention of different queuing disciplines. We have already introduced one type of queue: the FIFO queue, also sometimes referred to as a **first come, first served** (**FCFS**) queue. FIFO queues might be described as net neutrality writ small. No packet has priority over others, and there are no different classes of traffic. Packets are treated equally and they are sent out in the same order in which they arrive.

FIFO queues are useful structures. Indeed, even when we implement traffic shaping, the different queues are often themselves FIFO queues; they are easy enough to implement.

But, if we place all incoming and outgoing data into FIFO queues, some users and applications may end up consuming all or most of the bandwidth. Even if they don't consume bandwidth on a constant basis, often their usage will spike at inconvenient times, which will delay important—and often time-sensitive—data. Moreover, if the queue fills, important traffic may be dropped because of less important traffic already in the queue.

If you have a high-bandwidth connection with little congestion, you might get by with FIFO queuing. If not, it is time to start considering the alternatives.

An early improvement over FIFO queuing was fair queuing. With fair queuing, each program process is given its own FIFO queue, which prevents a badly behaving process from using up bandwidth. The earliest versions of fair queuing used round-robin scheduling between a LAN and the internet and was an improvement over FIFO queuing, but work soon began on refining fair queuing. A further improvement was **weighted fair queuing (WFQ)**. This method provided a form of priority management in which packets were classified into high- and low-bandwidth traffic. High-bandwidth traffic is prioritized over low-bandwidth traffic. High-bandwidth traffic gets a share of the connection; this share is proportional and based on assigned weights. Thus, low-bandwidth streams, representing the lion's share of network traffic, will be transmitted in a timely manner. Since WFQ requires an examination of packets, it may not work over encrypted connections.

Next, we will consider the queuing disciplines supported by the current version of pfSense: **priority queuing (PRIQ)**, **class-based queuing (CBQ)**, and the **Hierarchical Fair Service Curve (HFSC)**.

Priority queuing

Priority queuing is much like regular queuing, with the addition of each queue having a priority level. These queues are similar to queues you may have been introduced to in a course on data structures. Items are being pushed into, and pulled out of, the queue. An item pulled out of a queue is always the highest priority item, and the process continues until the queue is empty.

Priority queuing tends to ensure that high-priority traffic is handled. We can even set it up so that high-priority queues get all the bandwidth. For example, imagine a series of queues of different priority in which the highest priority queues start to fill up. When they do, we start to treat certain queues as high-priority queues and halt low-priority queues until the high-priority queues start to empty. This lessens the chance that prioritized traffic will be rejected as a result of a queue reaching its maximum capacity.

The way pfSense implements priority queues is that there are seven levels, with seven being the highest priority. Thus, there is a flat hierarchy of priority levels. pfSense scans each interface, and then queues are scanned for packets in descending order of priority. The highest priority queue is scanned first, followed by the next highest priority queue, until all queues have been scanned. The packet at the head of the highest queue is the packet that gets sent first.

The behavior of a priority queue is set by rules that describe the manner in which packets should be assigned to the queues. Packets can be classified in a number of different ways. They can be classified by protocol or subprotocol type, by the interface they come in on, by the packet size, and by a number of other different criteria.

The main advantage of PRIQ is easy to see. It is easy to configure, easy to understand, and it also guarantees that absolute priority goes to packets that are in the highest priority queue. The primary disadvantage is that priority always goes to the highest priority queue. This may not seem like a problem, but there is no way of circumventing this arrangement, or for moving traffic from a lower to a higher level of priority. As a result, lower priority traffic can be completely starved of bandwidth. Moreover, in pfSense, we only have seven levels of priority. This limits somewhat the granularity of traffic shaping. Hence, we begin our search for a more sophisticated form of queuing.

Class-based queuing

Class-based queuing allows a greater degree of control than PRIQ does. CBQ groups traffic into different classes, and gives each class a percentage of total bandwidth. This grouping of classes has a hierarchy, with classes further being divided into sub-classes. As with PRIQ, we can use many different criteria for classifying traffic. We can classify traffic based on protocol, the application used, the IP address of the source, and so on. CBQ operates at the IP network layer (Layer 3 of the OSI model). In addition, CBQ is in the public domain.

With CBQ, classes are allocated a certain amount of bandwidth. Packets in each class are processed until the bandwidth limit for the class is reached. With this system, even low-priority packets that would be starved of bandwidth in PRIQ receive some bandwidth. The first goal of CBQ is quantitative bandwidth sharing—every class should get some bandwidth. A secondary goal, however, is that when a class is not using all of its bandwidth, allocation of this excess bandwidth should not be arbitrary. On the contrary, the distribution of this bandwidth should follow set guidelines.

To illustrate how PRIQ and CBQ would work in practice, consider a small college that has 1.5 Gbps of download bandwidth and 500 Mbps of upload bandwidth. They also have four networks: one for administration, one for faculty, one for students, and a DMZ for a web server and other resources that need to be made available to the public. It is decided that two-thirds of the download bandwidth and half the upload bandwidth should go to the administration and faculty networks. In addition, 60% of this share of the bandwidth is allotted to the faculty network. Thus, faculty should get 600 Mbps of download bandwidth and 150 Mbps of upload bandwidth, administration should get 400 Mbps of download bandwidth and 100 Mbps of upload bandwidth, with the remainder allocated to the students and the DMZ.

PRIQ does not give us a means of guaranteeing that the administration and faculty receive a fixed share of bandwidth. We could assign higher priority levels to the faculty and administration networks, so that faculty has a higher priority than administration, which, in turn, has a higher priority than students and the DMZ. However, this could result in the students and the DMZ being starved of bandwidth, as a packet from either the faculty or administration networks will always win out over one from the students or DMZ networks.

CBQ solves all of that. Each of the subnets can be assigned a percentage of the total bandwidth. Moreover, we can arrange the classes in a hierarchical manner, with faculty and administration occupying a higher level on the hierarchy of classes, and with the faculty being assigned a greater portion of the shared bandwidth.

Hierarchical Fair Service Curve – HFSC

The third, and easily the most complex, queuing discipline supported by the current version of pfSense is the Hierarchical Fair Service Curve. Think of an HFSC as a form of bandwidth allocation in which certain guarantees are made about latency. An HFSC queue is defined by a nonlinear curve. This curve has two parts. The first, *m1*, determines the amount of bandwidth the queue gets, up to *p* milliseconds. Once *p* milliseconds have elapsed, *m2* determines the behavior of the queue. This second part, *m2*, is the amount of bandwidth guaranteed to the queue.

If we place VoIP traffic in a queue with 25% of the bandwidth, and the download in a queue with 75% of the bandwidth, we will fulfill the requirements for each connection, as we will be able to send a VoIP packet every 30 ms and a download packet every 9 ms. This, however, will result in a high amount of latency for the VoIP connection, which is something we want to avoid.

Now imagine a different service curve, such that the VoIP connection gets the bulk of available bandwidth until 10 ms. We will call this *m1*. For *m1*, the VoIP connection gets 75% of available bandwidth. The result is lower latency for VoIP traffic, but a higher latency for the file download traffic, but this is acceptable, since throughput is more important than latency with respect to file downloads.

The primary disadvantage of HFSC is that, unlike PRIQ and CBQ, which are defined by very simple criteria and, hence, are simple to implement, HFSC queues are inherently more complex because they are defined by nonlinear curves. Moreover, there will be times when HFSC cannot guarantee service to all curves at the same time, and it cannot guarantee service fairly. In spite of this, if we are using services that benefit from decoupling latency from bandwidth, HFSC is a good choice.

Configuring traffic shaping

It is easy to get overwhelmed by the complexity of traffic shaping as a result of the number of options available, as well as the number of shaper rules and queues. You will likely find it easiest to work with the traffic shaping wizard, at least until you understand how traffic shaping works. To access the wizard, navigate to **Firewall** | **Traffic Shaper**, and then click on the **Wizards** tab. In the current version of pfSense, there are two wizards: **Multiple Lan/Wan** and **Dedicated Links**. **Multiple Lan/Wan** is the more commonly used option, and it can be used in a variety of circumstances in which there are one or more LAN-type interfaces, and one or more WAN interfaces. Dedicated Links is for situations in which certain LAN/WAN pairings do not mix with other traffic, such as when users on one subnet have a different internet connection than users on another subnet. This would be the case in a multi-WAN setup in which we have an LAN and a DMZ, with LAN using WAN to connect to the internet and the DMZ using WAN2. Because each LAN-WAN link has its own traffic shaping requirements, we would use the **Dedicated Links** wizard. In most cases, however, you can use the **Multiple Lan/Wan** wizard.

The Multiple Lan/Wan configuration wizard

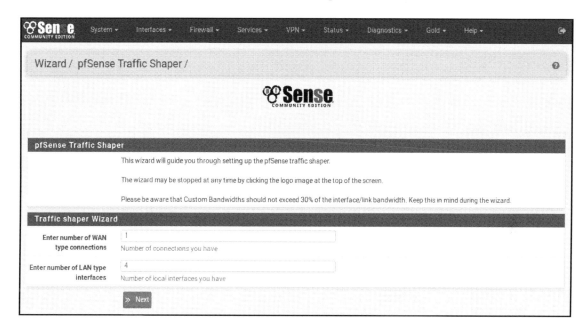

When you launch the **Multiple Lan/Wan** configuration wizard, you will first be asked for the number of WAN-type connections and the number of LAN-type connections. The wizard detects the number of interfaces automatically, so, in most cases, you do not have to change the values in these edit boxes (unless you don't want to apply the traffic shaper to all interfaces), and can click on the **Next** button. The wizard won't let you enter more than the total number of interfaces; if you do, you will get an error message. When you are finished making changes, click on **Next**.

The next page is **Shaper configuration**, and, on this page, you can configure each of the individual interfaces. The page will have different sections, each labeled **Setup connection and scheduler information for interface X** (in this case, X is LAN #1, LAN #2, and so on, or WAN #1, WAN #2, and so on). There are two drop-down boxes for each LAN interface. The first drop-down box is where you select the interface. The second drop-down box is where you select the queuing discipline. **PRIQ** is the default queuing discipline, but you can also select **CBQ** or **HFSC**. In subsequent pages of this wizard, the interfaces will not be specified by name; rather, they will be identified based on the assignments made on this page. For example, if you have an interface called SALES, and you specified it as the LAN #1 connection on this page, then, on subsequent pages, **Connection LAN #1** will always refer to the SALES interface.You will probably want to make note of the assignments you make for your own reference (and possibly for the reference of others).

It will save you time and from having to click on the back button to remind yourself what the assignments are.

The different queuing disciplines were discussed in detail in the previous section, so we will only mention them briefly here:

- **PRIQ**: The simplest (and default) algorithm. Packets are given different priority levels and are placed in different queues based on these levels. This is a good way of ensuring low latency for high-priority traffic, but it is possible that low-priority traffic can be starved of bandwidth.
- **CBQ**: Traffic is organized into classes. Each class is assigned an upper and lower bandwidth bound. Classes can be hierarchical, and there is a mechanism for redistributing excess bandwidth. This queuing discipline tends to ensure that even low-priority traffic gets bandwidth, but latency for high-priority traffic could suffer.
- **HFSC**: Each queue in HFSC has a curve with two portions. The first is a fairness curve, and the second is a service curve. The fairness curve is there to provide a minimum level of latency. There is no guarantee that all goals of HFSC will always be met. Nevertheless, it may be the best option for minimizing latency for high-priority bandwidth, while ensuring that all traffic gets some bandwidth.

The next step is setting up the WAN connections. As with the LAN interfaces, you can select the queuing discipline for each WAN interface (the same three options are present). The wizard will also prompt you for the upload and download bandwidth for each of the WAN interfaces. In order to ensure that the traffic shaper works optimally, try to approximate the actual upload and download speeds as closely as possible.

The next page, **VoIP**, controls the settings for VoIP. By checking the prioritize Voice over IP traffic, you will do just that. To optimize this feature, you need to specify your VoIP provider in the **Provider** drop-down box. The choices are as follows:

- **VoicePulse**: This company offers VoIP services to both residential and business customers. Another service they offer is trunking via the **Session Initiation Protocol** (**SIP**) for VoIP gateways and PBX systems.
- **Asterisk/Vonage**: Asterisk offers a means of setting up a PBX with software that has both an open source component (GNU GPL) and a proprietary one. Asterisk provides you with a way of implementing many features that previously were only available in proprietary PBX systems, for example, voicemail and conference calling. Asterisk also provides support for protocols such as SIP, the Media Gateway Control Protocol, and H.323. Vonage is a well-known VoIP company, offering both residential and business plans, not to mention cloud services targeted at enterprise-level customers.

- **PanasonicTDA**: The Panasonic KX-TDA series of phones work with VoIP and supports both H.323 and SIP trunking.
- **Generic (lowdelay)**: This is the default option. You can select this if your VoIP service doesn't fall into any of the previous categories.

Next is the **Upstream SIP Server** edit box, which allows you to enter the IP address of a remote PBX or SIP server; the traffic shaper will prioritize this server. If you use this option, then the **Provider** field will be ignored. The value entered in this edit box can be an alias.

The remaining edit boxes in this section allow you to enter the upload bandwidth for WAN connections, and the download bandwidth for LAN connections. These edit boxes give you the opportunity to specify the minimum bandwidth that will be reserved for VoIP traffic. The amount of bandwidth required for a VoIP connection will vary based on your provider and the number of VoIP phones and/or devices, so you'll want to do some research before entering this information. When you are finished, click on the **Next** button.

The next page, **Penalty Box**, allows you to limit the bandwidth of a specific IP address. There are two sections on the page: **Penalty Box** and **Penalty Box specific settings**. The first section only has one option: the **Penalize IP or Alias** checkbox. If this is enabled, the priority of the traffic from the IP or alias specified in the **Address** field in **Penalty Box specific settings** will be lowered, or, more specifically, placed into low-priority queues. The wizard also requires that you specify a bandwidth to which the specified host or hosts will be limited. Only values between 2% and 15% are allowed—even though the drop-down box has different options, such as percentage, bits/s, and kilobits/s, if you select anything other than percentage, the entry will not be validated. Instead, when you click on the **Next** button, you will get an **Only percentage bandwidth is allowed** error message on the page.

 Since the pfSense traffic shaper relies heavily on what ports traffic uses in order to classify traffic, a P2P application could still thwart the traffic shaper by using a port used by another protocol. For example, a P2P application could use the SNMP ports (161 and 162), and the traffic shaper would have no way of telling the difference. We must utilize third-party add-ons if we want to stop such activity.

The next section is **Enable/Disable specific P2P protocols**, where you can specify which P2P protocols pfSense will recognize. For each service that you want to be recognized, check the corresponding checkbox. The current version of pfSense lists 21 protocols, including Aimster, BitTorrent, DCC, Gnutella, and Napster. When you are finished, click on **Next**.

The next page of the wizard is **Network Games**. This page allows you to specify settings for network games, and since many games rely on low latency for a good gaming experience, you likely will want to enable **Prioritize network gaming traffic** if you or other network users play online games. The overall gaming experience can be adversely affected by other users downloading large files, or even by other players downloading game patches while playing. Enabling the prioritization of network games raises their priority, ensuring that game traffic will be transferred first and be given a guaranteed share of network bandwidth.

The page has two additional sections. **Enable/Disable specific game consoles and services** allows you to enable the game consoles and services you will be using. PlayStation, Wii, and Xbox are all represented here, along with some popular game services such as BattleNET and Games for Windows Live. The last section of the page is called **Enable/Disable specific games**. A number of popular games are represented on this list, including Call of Duty, Doom 3, Minecraft, Quake, and World of Warcraft. If a game that you play is not on the list, you can choose a game anyway so that you can configure a reference rule later. Click on **Next** when you are done.

The next page of the wizard is called **Raise or lower other Applications**. This page provides a list of applications and services—there are 41 in the current version—for which you can raise or lower the priority level. Each of the applications or services listed has its own drop-down box with three options: **Default priority**, **Higher priority**, and **Lower priority**. If you run any of these applications/services, you can tailor these settings to your specific network requirements. The applications and services that require a higher priority seem to be grouped closer to the top of the page, while the ones whose priority can be lowered are grouped closer to the bottom. If you enabled the **P2P Catch All** option earlier, you will want to specify protocols that you utilize, even if you just select the **Default priority** option, so that they are not penalized by the **P2P Catch All** rule. When you are done here, click on **Next**.

The next page is the final page of the wizard, at which point all rules and queues will have been created, but they will not yet be in use. Clicking on the **Finish** button will cause the new rules to load and be active. It will also redirect you to the **Filter Reload** page, where you will see the process of the rules and queues reloading. Traffic shaping will now be active, but the new rules and queues will only be applied to new connections. If you want the shaper to take effect on all connections, you need to clear the state table, which you can do by navigating to **Diagnostics | States**, clicking on the **Reset States** tab, and then clicking on the **Reset** button found at the bottom of this page.

The Dedicated Links wizard

If we have different traffic patterns for different parts of the network (for example, a multi-WAN setup), we might find that we need to have different traffic shaping configurations for different parts of the network, and for that we have the **Dedicated Links** wizard. To use this wizard, navigate to **Firewall | Traffic Shaper**, and, from the **Wizards** tab, click on the second option. On the first page of the wizard, you will be warned that custom links should not exceed 30% of the interface link/bandwidth, so take this into account. There is also an edit box for entering the number of WAN connections. As with the other wizard, this one will automatically fill in the number of WAN connections. Therefore, unless you want to use this traffic shaper on less than the total number of WAN interfaces, you can leave this value unchanged. Click on the **Next** button when you are done.

On the **Shaper configuration** pages, which are the next few pages of the wizard, you will enter the parameters of each of the connections. There are two boxes for local interface: in the first one, you will enter the interface that will use this connection, and, in the second one, you will specify the queuing discipline (**PRIQ, CBQ, HFSC**). The two **WAN Interface** drop-down boxes are set up the same way—you specify the interface and queuing discipline. The subsequent edit boxes are **Upload** (where you specify upload bandwidth) and **Download** (where you specify download bandwidth). When you are done, click on **Next**. This page will repeat itself for as many WAN connections as you specified on the first page of the wizard.

The remaining pages of the wizard are identical to those for the **Multiple Lan/Wan** wizard, so we will not cover them in detail here, but instead will refer you to the previous subsection. We will note that the **Voice over IP**, **Penalty Box**, **Peer-to-Peer Networking**, **Network Games**, and **Raise or lower other applications** pages all are the same as the corresponding pages in the other wizard. And, as with the **Multiple Lan/Wan** wizard, you will be presented with a final page, and when you click on the **Finish** button on that page, the new rules and queues will be loaded. You can apply these new settings to all connections by using the **Reset States** option in **Diagnostics | States**.

Advanced traffic shaping configuration

If you find that the traffic shaping wizard does not provide enough customization to meet your needs, there are two possibilities. You could use a third-party package, such as Snort, but before you do that, you should determine whether the rules or queues the wizard created can be modified or added to in order to create custom rules that suit your needs. In this section, we will demonstrate how to do this, considering changes to queues first.

Changes to queues

To begin queue configuration, navigate to **Firewall | Traffic Shaper**. You have a choice of clicking on either the **By Interface** or **By Queue** tabs. If you choose the **By Interface** tab, you will see a list of interfaces at the root level, along with a list of queues that are available on each interface (which ones are available will depend on the choices you made in the traffic shaping wizard); if you choose **By Queue**, a different hierarchy will appear, with a list of queues at the root level, and a list of interfaces utilizing a queue will appear when you click on each queue. You can edit queues from either tab and get the same result. If you are creating new queues, you will likely find that the easiest way to add queues is to start on the **By Interface** tab. From there, you can create a queue on a single interface, and then make the queue available on other interfaces by clicking on the **By Queue** tab and using the **Clone Shaper to this Interface** button.

Once you have selected a queue on an interface to edit, several options will appear. The **Enable/Disable** checkbox gives you the ability to disable a queue and any children queues, if the checkbox is unchecked. The **Name** edit box allows you to change the name, and the priority edit box allows you to set a priority level from 0 to 7, with higher-numbered priority levels taking precedence over lower-numbered ones—but this field will be ignored if the queue is an HFSC queue. HFSC queues can be identified by the fact that their configuration pages have a section called **Service Curve (sc)**.

The **Queue Limit** edit box allows you to enter the queue limit. This limit is expressed in terms of total packets. The **Scheduler** options checkboxes allow you to apply additional traffic shaping algorithms to the queue. There is a **Default Queue** checkbox that will make the queue the default queue for the interface selected. There are several other options:

- **Random Early Detection**: With this algorithm, the traffic shaping queue is a buffer that, once full, will drop packets. This is often referred to as tail drop, since packets are dropped from the end of the buffer. This can be a problem, since when the network is congested, all buffers can become full, with many packets being dropped. **Random Early Detection** (RED) attempts to avoid this problem by randomly dropping packets as the buffer starts to fill up.
- **Random Early Detection In and Out**: This is a variation of RED, in which we still use the RED algorithm, but have separate in and out buffers. To make it more effective, the out queue will be more aggressive than the in queue in dropping packets. The idea is that the out queue will be controlled before any in traffic needs to be dropped. This type of queue is sometimes referred to as RED with In and Out, or RIO.

- **Explicit Congestion Notification**: This type of queue takes advantage of an extension to TCP/IP defined in RFC 3168 (2001). This extension provides for end-to-end notification of network congestion.

- **CoDel Active Queue**: This type of queue was developed to address perceived shortcomings in RED/RIO. The latter is based on the assumption that average queue length is a sign of network congestion (the more items in a queue, the more congested it is). CoDel rejects this assumption and uses the minimum amount of delay experience of any packet in the running window in order to measure congestion. CoDel's objective is to minimize the delay and keep the delay below five milliseconds. If the minimum delay rises above five milliseconds, then packets are dropped from the window. This continues until the delay falls below the allowed level. This type of queue assumes that there are good queues and bad queues. Good queues handle bursts of traffic with only minor increases in delay. Bad queues will fill up upon a burst of traffic and stay filled. CoDel ignores the good queues and focuses on lowering the delay on bad queues.

These algorithms are designed to deal with an occurrence of excess buffering of packets, known as bufferbloat. This causes high latency and packet delay variation. Over time, network card manufacturers have incorporated larger buffers into their cards. This has not been as beneficial as you might think. The TCP algorithm uses the number of dropped packets to determine when a connection is saturated. Large buffers just postpone the point at which saturation occurs; it takes several seconds for the buffers to fill and the packets to drop. The buffer thus becomes a bottleneck until TCP adjusts. This illustrates how large buffers can actually cause TCP's congestion avoidance algorithms to work less effectively than they would with small buffers. Appropriate countermeasures must be taken when large buffers are present in order to avoid congestion.

In the **Description** edit box, you can enter a brief, non-parsed description for your own reference.

The preceding options are available for queues that employ **PRIQ** or **CBQ**; however, if **HFSC** was chosen, there are other options available on a section of the page labeled **Service Curve (sc)**. The first option is **Bandwidth**, which simply allows you to set the maximum bandwidth of the queue. The remaining service curve options allow you to configure the service curve.

Each service curve has three parameters: *m1*, *d*, and *m2*. If you followed the discussion of HFSC earlier in this chapter, you should already know what these are. *m1* and *m2* represent two portions of the service curve. d represents the dividing point between *m1* and *m2*. For the first *d* milliseconds, the queue receives the bandwidth defined by *m1*. After that, the queue gets the value defined by *m2*. There are three configurable service curves for each of the queues, which are defined as follows:

- **Max bandwidth for the queue (Upper Limit)**: This curve limits HFSC bandwidth to that which is available upstream
- **Min Bandwidth for the queue (Real Time)**: This service curve guarantees a precise minimum bandwidth, regardless of class hierarchy
- **B/W share of a backlogged queue (Link Share)**: This curve distributes bandwidth according to a class hierarchy

You can click the **Save** button when you are done. You can also choose **Add new queue** (create a brand new queue) or **Delete this queue** (eliminate the current queue).

Limiters

The limiters option in pfSense allows you to set up a series of dummynet pipes. **Dummynet** is a command-line, FreeBSD traffic shaping utility that was designed to simulate different connections. You can do such things as set bandwidth limits and impose scheduling and queue management policies.

You can begin setting up a limiter by navigating to **Firewall** | **Traffic Shaper** and clicking on the Limiters tab. On the left-hand side of the page, there will be a button enabling you to set up a new limiter; you can also edit existing limiters on this page. Keep in mind that it is a good idea to set up both in and out queues, and that any newly created limiters will have no effect until traffic is assigned to it.

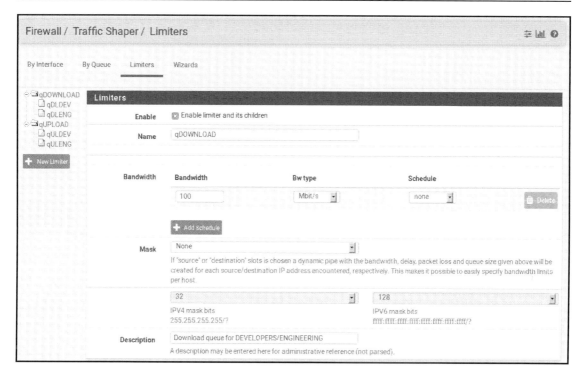

There are two sections on the configuration page for limiters: limiters and advanced options. The first option, the **Enable** checkbox, allows you to enable the limiter and all its children. There is a **Name** edit box where you must edit a name for the limiter.

The next section of the page, **Bandwidth**, is where you enter the upper limit for the bandwidth. The **Schedule** drop-down box allows you to select a time frame in which the bandwidth limit will be imposed, provided that you defined a schedule entry using pfSense's Schedule option. You can have multiple schedule entries by clicking on the **Add Schedule** button, or avoid using schedules entirely by selecting none in the **Schedule** drop-down box.

In the **Mask** drop-down box, you can set up the limiter so that it only applies to either source or destination addresses. Selecting either **Source address** or **Destination address** will cause a dynamic pipe to be created for each IP address encountered, thus making it easy to specify bandwidth limits per host. If you choose a source or destination address as your mask, you must also specify either **IPv4** or **IPv6** in the appropriate drop-down box. You may also enter a description in the **Description** field.

The next section, **Advanced Options**, is mainly useful if you want to simulate certain network connections. I don't foresee them being used that often in real-world scenarios, since they involve deliberately creating a suboptimal data pipe. For example, **Delay (ms)** allows you to specify a delay, and **Packet loss rate** allows you to specify a rate of packet loss expressed as a fraction of 1 (0.1 will drop 1 in 10 packets; 0.01 will drop 1 in 100, and so on). **Queue size (slots)** allows you to specify a number; pfSense will then create a fixed-sized queue accommodating the number of packets specified. **Bucket size (slots)** is the parameter where you can specify the number of slots in the bucket array used for source or destination hashing. When you are done, click on the **Save** button.

The question remains as to what these limiters are good for, anyway. One possibility is that you could use them to set up guaranteed minimum bandwidth queues. You can do this by creating a total of four queues, or two pairs of queues (each pair will have an upload queue and a download queue). The first pair will be for guaranteed minimum bandwidth. For these queues, set the upper bandwidth limit as the amount you want as the guaranteed minimum bandwidth. The pair should have the upper bandwidth limit set to whatever bandwidth is left after you have allocated bandwidth to the first pair. Then, when you configure your traffic shaping rules, make sure that you direct guaranteed service traffic into the first pair of queues, and everything else into the second pair of queues.

Manual rule configuration

Thus far, we have shown how queues can be added and edited, but the queues have no effect unless a firewall rule places packets into one of these queues. We covered these rules in depth in Chapter 6, *Firewall and NAT*.

At one point, pfSense had a separate tab for traffic shaper rules. More recent versions have done away with this tab, and to see the traffic shaper rules, navigate to **Firewall** | **Rules** and click on the **Floating** tab. The traffic shaper rules will be here, and so will any other floating rules you created. You should be able to differentiate traffic shaping rules by their description, by the fact that traffic shaping rules tend to have **Match** designated as their action (as opposed to pass, block, or reject), and by the fact that all traffic shaping rules have a value specified for **Queue**.

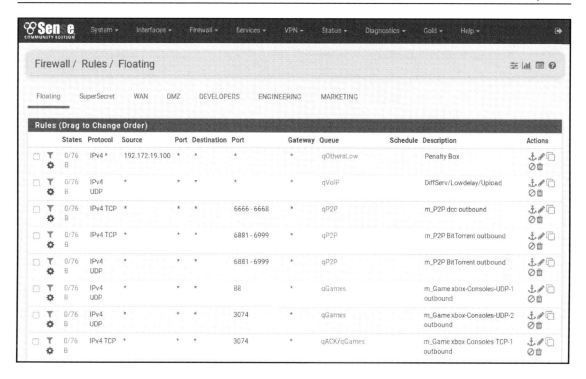

To edit one of these rules, click on the **Edit** icon; to delete a rule, click on the **Delete** icon. You can also change the order of the rules by clicking on them and dragging them to a different position, or by checking the rules and clicking on **Move checked rules** above this one icon (this is often an easier way of moving multiple rules). To add a new rule, click on one of the **Add** buttons, and to create a rule based on an existing rule, click on the **Copy** icon.

Each rule has several matching criteria, ensuring that traffic is fed into the right queue. Separate queues can be created for inbound and outbound traffic. Traffic shaping rules could take advantage of this to feed inbound and outbound traffic into different queues, but most of the rules generated by the pfSense traffic shaping wizard seem to have the same queue for inbound and outbound traffic. These rules utilize the fact that floating rules can apply to traffic in both directions and feed such traffic into the same queue. Since each rule can only feed traffic into a single queue, this saves the wizard from having to create more than one rule for a traffic shaping task.

By clicking on the **Edit** option for a traffic shaping rule, you can alter that rule's settings. You can also see that traffic shaping rules have much in common with other rules, with some significant differences. First, there is the fact mentioned earlier that traffic shaping rules use the **Match** option. In addition, the interface selected is usually the WAN interface. Most of the rules seem to apply to traffic in both directions.

These settings are the same for virtually all traffic shaping rules, but the core of traffic shaping rules are what differentiate the traffic. In most cases, pfSense uses the protocol and port number to filter traffic. TCP is commonly used in traffic shaping rules, but ones that apply to VoIP and gaming services often use UDP.

One example of an automatically generated rule is to send DCC traffic to the P2P queue. **TCP** is selected as the **Protocol**, and the **Destination port range** is set to 6666 to 6668. A user could easily circumvent such a rule by changing the port range (at least when receiving files—sending files over a different port range will require a new NAT entry). However, the auto-generated rules should work pretty well with rules that always use the same ports.

Although they seldom seem to be used by the traffic shaping rules, the TCP flags are another way in which traffic could be matched. The TCP flags indicate various states of a connection. They can be matched based on whether they are set or cleared. We can also leave both the set and cleared check-boxes unchecked if we don't care whether they are set or not.

The last option in **Advanced Options** for **Floating Rules** is **Ackqueue**. This is where matching traffic is assigned to a queue. The first drop-down box is where the queue for ACK traffic is selected. The second one selects the queue for all other traffic. In many cases, **Ackqueue** is left undefined (set to **None**) and Queue is the only selection made. However, it is a good idea to set up a dedicated queue for ACK traffic; this prevents delays caused by the remote end of a connection waiting for ACKs stuck in a queue with non-ACK traffic.

Although it is easy to change traffic shaping rules, it is good practice to make a backup before making any rule changes. This enables you to revert back to your old ruleset in case the changes you made do not have the desired results.

Example #1 – modifying the penalty box

The next two subsections will demonstrate how we can modify and add traffic shaping needs to meet specific requirements not addressed by the traffic shaper wizard. Since modifying an existing rule is somewhat easier than adding new rules, we will walk through the process of modifying a rule first.

As you might recall, the traffic shaper wizard lets us assign a single IP or alias to the low-priority queue. This queue is the qOthersLow queue. Let's assume we want to make the following modifications to the rule:

- The offending traffic has, as its destination, the IP address 10.1.1.1 (a private address, but acceptable as an example).
- The offending traffic has been traced to one or more macOS nodes; so we only want to penalize traffic coming from macOS systems.
- The only traffic from this range of IP addresses that we want to ban is VoIP traffic. Therefore, we will only penalize UDP traffic.

Although the traffic shaper wizard does not give us this level of granularity, we can do this easily by changing the existing penalty box rule. Thus, we begin navigating to **Firewall | Rules**, clicking on the **Floating Rules** tab, and then clicking on the **Edit** icon for the penalty box rule. The necessary changes are relatively easy to make:

1. **Protocol** is currently set to **Any**; we want to change that. Select **UDP** from the drop-down box.
2. In the **Destination** section, select **Single host or alias** in the drop-down box, and then enter 10.1.1.1 in the adjacent text box.
3. The next option is in the **Advanced Options** section. Thus, click on the **Display Advanced** button.
4. The first option is the **Source OS** drop-down box. Select **MacOS**.
5. Click on the **Save** button at the bottom of the page. When the **Floating Rules** table reloads, click on the **Apply Changes** button.

Hence, with little difficulty, we are able to alter the penalty box to meet some very specific requirements. In a real-world scenario, you might want to monitor the network for the next few days to make sure that the rule has the intended effect.

Example #2 – prioritizing EchoLink

In other cases, the traffic shaper wizard does not list the application that we want to put in a priority queue. Fortunately, in such cases, we can create our own rules.

EchoLink is a program that enables amateur radio operators to communicate. It uses UDP on ports 5198 and 5199. It uses TCP on port 6000. If we want to prioritize EchoLink traffic, we will have to create two rules.

1. Navigate to **Firewall | Rules**, click on the **Floating** tab, and click on one of the **Add** buttons.
2. When the **Edit** page for the new rule loads, select **Match** in the **Action** drop-down box.
3. Select **WAN** in the Interface listbox.
4. The **Direction** should already be set to any; you may retain this.
5. In the **Protocol** drop-down box, select **UDP**.
6. The **Destination port range** should be set to 5198 to 5199.
7. Click on the **Show Advanced** button. When the advanced options appear, scroll down to **Ackqueue/Queue**.
8. Select **qOthersHigh** in the **Queue** drop-down box.
9. You may also want to enter a description for self-reference in the **Description** field.
10. Click on the **Save** button when done.
11. To save time, copy this rule. Click on the **Copy** icon on the newly created rule. This will enable us to make a new rule based on this rule.
12. When the **Edit** page loads for the new rule, set the **Protocol** to **TCP**.
13. Change **Destination port range** to 6000 for the new rule. You may also want to enter a brief description.
14. When you are done, click on the **Save** button, and then on the **Apply Changes** button.

I suspect the two ports that use UDP comprise the VoIP component of EchoLink, and the TCP port is used for other purposes, such as downloading directories of users. Therefore, you could just create the first rule and it is likely to have substantially the same effect.

Using Snort for traffic shaping

Layer 7 traffic shaping is no longer part of pfSense's built-in traffic shaping. It is now recommended that you use a third-party solution such as Snort. While configuring Snort can be somewhat complex, if your traffic shaping requirements include some form of Layer 7 traffic shaping, Snort can perform this task.

Installing and configuring Snort

The initial installation of Snort is easy, especially if you have already gone through the process of installing a package. First, navigate to **System | Package Manager** and click on the **Available Packages** tab. Find the entry for Snort in the table, and when you find it, click on the corresponding **Install** button. Click on the **Confirm** button to confirm installation; this will transfer you to the **Package Installer** tab. This page will provide information on the progress of Snort's download and installation. The entire process seldom takes more than a few minutes.

When installation is complete, you should be able to navigate to **Services | Snort** to begin configuration. Click on the **Global Settings** tab first; this covers settings that will apply to all interfaces on which Snort is enabled. Under **Snort Subscriber Rules**, there is an **Enable Snort VRT** option. If you check this box, an edit box will appear. In this box, you can enter a **Snort Oinkmaster Code**. If you haven't already, you should sign up for an account on the official Snort website and obtain an Oinkmaster code. This code will enable you to download rules from the Snort website. Registration is free, and it enables you to download the restricted rules. Subscriptions to the personal and business tiers, however, are not free.

To register at the official Snort website, navigate to `https://www.snort.org/subscribe` and fill out the registration form on that page. The website will send an email confirmation. When you have confirmed your registration, you will be able to log into the official Snort website. Once there, click on your email address in the upper right-hand corner and you will be able to see your account information. There should be a link on the menu on the left-hand side of the page for the Oinkcode. Click on that link to generate the code. Once you have the code, you may enter it in the appropriate box in **Global Settings**.

The settings that you chose will depend on your security requirements. You will likely want to enable the download of **Snort GPLv2 Community rules**, and downloading the **Emerging Threats Open rules** isn't a bad idea either. **Rules Update Settings** is where you can choose when Snort updates the rules. Note that it does not update the rules by default; therefore, you will want to choose a reasonable value for the **Update Interval**. Since Snort does not automatically download the rules, click on the **Updates** tab and click on the **Update Rules** button.

Snort will now be installed and the most basic of configuration is done, but Snort won't do anything until we enable it on one or more interfaces. You can do this by clicking on the **Snort Interfaces** tab and clicking on **Add**. When the page loads, you will be able to check the **Enable Interface** checkbox (under **General Settings**) and then select an interface that has not yet been added to Snort in the **Interface** drop-down box. Most of the traffic that will be of interest to us will be reaching the WAN interface eventually.

Therefore, in most cases, you can just add **WAN** (assuming you don't have a multi-WAN setup). In some cases, however, we may be interested in internal traffic, for example, malware may be running inside our network. We can run Snort on more than one network, but take into account that running Snort on an interface is a resource-intensive matter. Therefore, unless you have a specific need to monitor internal traffic, you probably should only run Snort on WAN.

Once Snort is installed and enabled on the WAN interface, we have a much better chance of, for example, detecting and blocking peer-to-peer traffic. To do this, follow this procedure:

1. Click on the **WAN Settings** tab.
2. Under **Alert Settings**, check the **Block Offenders** checkbox—doing so will block any traffic that generates a Snort alert.
3. Once you have done this, click on the **Save** button.
4. Once the page reloads, click on the **Edit** icon, and then click on the **WAN Categories** tab.
5. Scroll down to the list of rulesets, and click on **emerging-p2p.rules**. Click on any other rulesets you wish, and then scroll down to the bottom and click on Save.
6. By clicking on **WAN Rules** and selecting **emerging-p2p.rules** in the **Category Selection** drop-down box, you should see the newly-added p2p rules.

If you leave this ruleset in place, you are likely to find that Snort is much more effective than the built-in traffic shaper in blocking peer-to-peer traffic.

Troubleshooting

Troubleshooting traffic shaping issues can prove difficult. First, there is the chance that we have made an error in configuring our traffic shaping rules. Second, even if our traffic shaping rules are configured exactly right, they may not have the intended effect. In such cases, it often behooves us to return to the established methodology for troubleshooting IT problems: diagnosing the problem, forming a hypothesis, testing the hypothesis, implementing a solution, verifying system functionality, and documenting the problem and solution. This methodology will be covered in greater depth in Chapter 11, *Diagnostics and Troubleshooting*. There are some common issues, however, that crop up with traffic shaping, and we will cover them here.

Sometimes, we may find it difficult to keep P2P traffic in the P2P queue; this is a direct consequence of pfSense relying on ports to classify traffic. Many P2P applications, however, rely on non-standard or random ports. If you are having trouble with P2P traffic, there are two broad alternatives:

- Use a third-party solution such as Snort. This may be problematic if you simply want to divert P2P traffic into a low-priority queue—Snort makes it much easier to block P2P traffic than to lower its priority.
- You could make the P2P queue the default queue for all traffic. The downside of this, of course, is that you must create rules for all traffic you don't want to have relegated to the P2P queue.

There are several diagnostic tools at your disposal. If you need to get an overview of traffic on all queues, navigate to **Status** | **Queues**. This will reveal how much traffic is on each queue, both graphically (in the form of bar graphs) and numerically—it will tell you the **packets per second** (**PPS**) of the queue, bandwidth, queue length, and much more. At the very least, the **Queues** page will indicate what traffic, if any, is in the queues. In some cases, this may be all you need to diagnose the traffic shaping problem.

The **Queues** page offers a snapshot of the current traffic. If you need a cumulative summary of traffic, navigate to **Diagnostics** | **pfTop** and select queue in the **View** drop-down box. This will provide similar information to what you get from the **Queues** page, but expressed in raw totals.

If you are using limiters, navigate to **Diagnostics** | **Limiter Info**. This page will show configuration information and data for limiters and child queues.

One resource that can be useful are the logs, so,e if all else fails, navigate to **Status** | **System Logs**. The **Firewall** tab is the one that is most likely to yield information relevant to solving your problem. You can also click on the + button and use the **Advanced Log Filter** bar to further filter results. Finally, although logging of rules is not generally recommended, you can enable logging on relevant traffic shaping rules, at least temporarily, and see whether the generated logs help you to diagnose the problem.

Summary

In this chapter, we introduced the concept of traffic shaping, discussed some basic traffic shaping algorithms, and introduced the pfSense traffic shaping wizard. We also discussed how to edit queues, how to add limiters, and how to add and edit traffic shaping rules. We showed how Snort can be used for Layer 7 (deep packet inspection) traffic shaping. Finally, we discussed some ways to troubleshoot traffic shaping issues.

Traffic shaping is one of a number of powerful tools that helps us to extend the functionality and security of our networks. In the next chapter, we will cover another such tool, one that enables us to send and receive data over public networks as if they are part of our private network: **virtual public networks** (**VPNs**).

Questions

1. (a) Identify one example of an application that requires low latency. (b) Identify one example of an application where latency is less important than bandwidth.
2. Identify the three types of queuing supported by the pfSense traffic shaper.
3. What option in the traffic shaping wizard allows us to limit the bandwidth of a certain IP address?
4. What queue was developed to address perceived shortcomings in Random Early Detection, and Random Early Detection In and Out?
5. Why are large buffers problematic when detecting congestion on TCP connections?
6. What settings do traffic shaping rules have in the Action drop-down box?
7. We are creating a rule to prioritize VoIP traffic. What protocol is this rule likely to use?
8. What option should we choose if blocking P2P traffic on our network is important?

Further reading

- The purpose of traffic shaping: A document explaining why traffic shaping is used: http://help.fortinet.com/fos50hlp/54/Content/FortiOS/fortigate-traffic-shaping-54/TS_About.htm
- Comparing Traffic Policing and Traffic Shaping for Bandwidth Limiting: The difference between policing and shaping: https://www.cisco.com/c/en/us/support/docs/quality-of-service-qos/qos-policing/19645-policevsshape.html

Virtual Private Networks

8

As computer networking becomes more commonplace and we begin to take network connectivity for granted, users increasingly find the need to connect to private networks from remote locations. At one point, the only way to provide such connectivity was through private WAN circuits. In some cases, private WAN circuits may still be the best option, as they provide low latency and reliability; but they also have high monthly costs, and can be prohibitively expensive for many users.

Fortunately, they aren't the only option available to us. **Virtual private networks (VPNs)** provide us with a means of accessing a private network over a shared public network. The public network is, more often than not, the internet. Access to the private network is provided through an encrypted tunnel and, as a result, it is as if we have a point-to-point connection between the remote system and our private network. Moreover, all of this can be done with some rather generic computer hardware, such as the type of hardware that can run pfSense. Therefore, VPNs provide us with a secure means of accessing a private network from a remote location in a manner that is cost effective.

pfSense provides you with a means of easily implementing VPN connectivity. While we have to concede that a computer that barely meets the minimum specifications for pfSense is a poor candidate for VPN use—establishing and maintaining a VPN tunnel is rather CPU-intensive—pfSense can still enable you to set up a VPN much more cheaply than you would with most commercial equipment. Moreover, with third-party hardware add-ons, much of the encryption work can be offloaded from the CPU.

In this chapter, we will cover the following topics:

- VPN fundamentals
- Configuring a VPN tunnel
- Troubleshooting VPNs

Technical requirements

This chapter will provide examples of both peer-to-peer and client-server VPN connections. As a result, to follow along with the examples in this chapter, you will need two fully functional pfSense firewalls, with at least one node behind each firewall; each of the firewalls will be serving as a peer. This can be done in either a real-world or a virtual environment. The examples provided in this chapter are not particularly resource intensive, but you may need something more than a system that meets the bare minimum requirements for pfSense.

VPN fundamentals

By definition, a VPN is a connection that enables a remote user to securely connect to a private network or server over a public network. From the end user's perspective, it is as if the data is being sent and received over a dedicated private connection—hence, the term virtual private network. One common scenario in which a VPN is used is called client-server: the end user connects to a private network over the internet. Another common scenario is peer-to-peer, or network-to-network communication. A prime example of this would be a case where a branch office of a corporation needs to connect its local network with the private network at corporate headquarters. In such a case, the company is using the internet as if it is a WAN. In either case, client-server or peer-to-peer, the end users of the VPN take advantage of the fact that a VPN connection is an encrypted tunnel, enabling them to use the public internet as a private tunnel for a point-to-point circuit.

The introduction to this chapter briefly discussed private WAN circuits as an alternative to VPNs. In fact, they were the only way to securely connect to a private network before VPNs. They may still be the only way to meet certain bandwidth and latency requirements. A private WAN circuit will usually provide a latency of 3 ms or less. Anyone who has run the ping or traceroute utilities to measure the latency of a connection will know how good that is. With a VPN (or indeed, any other connection that uses the public internet), you will get that much latency with the first hop through your ISP. Running ping tests on your connection will give you a better idea of the latency of VPN connections in specific cases, but in general, you can expect such connections to have latencies of anywhere from 30 to 60 ms. This latency can vary, based on two important factors:

- The type of connection that is being used
- The distance between the remote node and the private network

One of our objectives is to minimize latency, and you can do that by using the same ISP on both ends of the connection. However, that is not always possible. In some cases, using a VPN may actually decrease latency. A good example of this is one in which your ISP uses traffic shaping. In such cases, encrypting traffic may thwart the ISP's attempts to classify the traffic. As a result, the ISP will not throttle the traffic and, therefore, latency will decrease.

In many cases, you will need to use due diligence before implementing a VPN connection. Determine what applications you are likely to use over a VPN, and find out how well such applications perform over connections with latency. Obviously, online games and VoIP applications can suffer from higher latency. Microsoft file sharing (SMB) and Microsoft's Remote Desktop Protocol are protocols that fall into the category of latency-sensitive. Depending on which side of the cost-benefit analysis you fall on, you may find that the improved performance justifies the cost of a private WAN circuit, or you may find that the improved savings justify the performance degradation of a VPN connection. Should you opt for a VPN, you needn't accept poor performance, however. Later in the chapter, we will discuss ways of tweaking network settings to improve performance.

There are several different types of VPN deployment:

- **Client-server**: We have already discussed this briefly. A VPN tunnel is used to connect one or more mobile clients to a company's (or individual's) local network. The encryption provided by the VPN guarantees that data privacy is maintained. This is probably the most likely use case, if you are setting up a VPN for use with pfSense. It should be noted that the client-server relationship can be inverted: pfSense can act as the client and connect to a remote server. This is one of the ways that we can connect to a VPN provider.
- **Peer-to-peer**: A VPN tunnel is created between two private networks. An example of this would be connecting a main corporate office with a satellite office location. In this case, setting up a VPN between the two locations is cheaper than a leased line. The beauty of this setup is that if the tunnel fails for any reason, we can re-establish the connection from either end.
- **Hidden network**: There may be cases where data is too sensitive or confidential to place on the main corporate network. This data might be located on a subnet that is physically disconnected from the rest of the network. In such cases, a VPN can provide us with a means of connecting to this subnet, establishing a private network within a private network.

VPNs can also be utilized to provide additional security for wireless connections. We can require wireless clients to log in through a VPN. By doing so, we can force them to provide additional authentication. The VPN will also provide a layer of encryption in addition to the encryption that the wireless protocol gives us, making the connection that much more secure.

No discussion of VPN fundamentals would be complete without an overview of the VPN protocols that can be used, as well as the advantages and disadvantages of each one. Our overview will cover the three protocols currently supported by pfSense: IPsec, L2TP, and OpenVPN.

Prior to pfSense 2.3, **Point-to-Point Tunneling Protocol (PPTP)** was also supported by pfSense. It was easy to set up and very popular, and implementations of it can be found for Windows, Linux, and macOS. It has, however, been shown to be insecure. This is primarily because most implementations of PPTP rely on MS-CHAPv1 or MS-CHAPv2 for authentication, and both methods are insecure. For example, it has been demonstrated that the complexity of a brute-force attack on a single MS-CHAPv2 key is equivalent to a brute-force attack on a single DES key. An MS-CHAPv2 key can be decrypted in 23 hours. The alternative to MS-CHAPv2 is EAP-TLS, which requires a public key infrastructure that many remote access installations may not have. PPTP has thus been increasingly seen as insecure, and therefore, pfSense dropped support for it in version 2.3.

IPsec

IPsec, as you may have guessed, operates on the network layer of the seven-layer OSI model. It also resides on the internet layer of the four-layer network model. It is the only protocol (of the ones discussed in this section) that resides on this layer. The advantage of using this protocol is precisely the fact that it operates on the internet/network layer. Because of this, it is capable of authenticating the entire IP packet. As a result, not only is the privacy of our data ensured, but our packet's final destination is kept private, as well. It differs significantly from the two other VPN protocols supported by pfSense. OpenVPN offers encryption, but does so on the application layer of the OSI model. The **Layer 2 Tunneling Protocol (L2TP)** does not encrypt data at all.

The four-layer network model, sometimes referred to as the TCP/IP model, is comparable to the seven-layer OSI model, but simpler. In the TCP/IP model, the application, presentation, and session layers are combined into a single application layer. The transport layer is identical to the OSI model's transport layer (this is where the TCP portion of TCP/IP resides), and the internet layer is identical to the OSI model's network layer (where the IP portion of TCP/IP resides). Finally, the OSI's data link and physical layers have been combined into a single network access layer.

IPsec is actually a protocol suite; therefore, it is a group of protocols that combine to provide the functionality we need in an encryption protocol. We can divide this suite into the following groups:

- **Authentication Header (AH)**: This is a 32-bit header; it provides both authentication and connection-less data integrity.
- **Encapsulating Security Payload (ESP)**: A protocol within the IPsec protocol, ESP provides authentication, integrity, and confidentiality. ESP exists in both authentication-only and encryption-only mode. It is responsible for encrypting the payload (in transport mode, which is the more common use of ESP), and, in some cases, the entire payload (in what is known as tunnel mode).
- **Security Association (SA)**: This is the set of security attributes used in a connection. This can include things such as the encryption algorithm, encryption key, and other attributes.

Security associations are established through the **Internet Security and Key Management Protocol (ISAKMP)**, a protocol that is defined in RFC 2408 and provides a framework for authentication and key exchange. Key exchange is usually done via **Internet Key Exchange (IKE)** versions 1 or 2. This protocol was developed by the IETF in November 1998, and is defined in RFCs 2407, 2408, and 2409. Other protocols are available for key exchange. For example, **Kerberized Internet Negotiation of Keys (KINK)** uses the Kerberos protocol for key negotiation. However, the only methods currently supported by pfSense are IKE and IKEv2.

We have already briefly mentioned the modes for establishing an IPsec connection. They are:

- **Transport mode**: The payload of the packet is encrypted, but the header is not encrypted. This mode does not support NAT traversal. As a result, it is a poor choice for IPsec connections that must traverse more than one router.
- **Tunnel mode**: The entire packet is encrypted. As you may have guessed, this mode does support NAT traversal.

If your main criteria for selecting a VPN protocol is the number of encryption algorithms supported, then IPsec is a good choice, since it supports several such algorithms. Advanced Encryption Standard (with a key size of 256 bits) is the most commonly used option, and 256-bit keys are generally considered secure. Other options are available, however. 3DES is offered as an option; this is useful, as many systems only support DES. For those who need a bigger key than AES offers, there's SHA-2, with a 512-bit key. More information about the cryptographic options available with IPsec can be found in RFC 7321 (`http://tools.ietf.org/html/rfc7321`).

L2TP

Layer 2 Tunneling Protocol (L2TP), as the name implies, operates on the data link layer of the seven-layer OSI model. It does not provide any encryption or confidentiality. For those, it must rely on whatever encryption protocol is passing through its tunnel. For that reason, it is often used in combination with IPsec, which does provide both encryption and confidentiality. The proposed standard for L2TP can be found in RFC 2661.

Each L2TP connection has a client end and a server end. The client end is called the **L2TP Access Concentrator (LAC)**, and the server end is called the **L2TP Network Server (LNS)**. We configure the LNS end, and this then waits for new connections. The LNS end can also initiate connections. The packets within an L2TP are either control packets or data packets. The exchange of control packets is what initiates an L2TP connection; L2TP provides reliability for the control packets. No reliability is provided for data packets; such reliability can be provided by protocols running inside the L2TP tunnel. Once an L2TP tunnel is established, the network traffic between the two ends is bidirectional. It is also possible to have multiple virtual networks within a single L2TP tunnel, as L2TP will isolate each connection within the tunnel.

The combination of IPsec running within an L2TP tunnel is known as L2TP/IPsec. Establishing such a connection involves several steps. First, an IPsec Security Association is negotiated, typically (but not always) with IKE or IKEv2. Second, ESP communication is established in transport mode. Finally, an L2TP tunnel is established. L2TP uses UDP as its transport layer protocol, and its default port is `1701`.

When L2TP is used without any other protocols, it is often called native L2TP. You are unlikely to ever use L2TP in native mode, because of the aforementioned lack of encryption or confidentiality. L2TP is often used in conjunction with IPsec, and it can be combined with other protocols, in order to provide the confidentiality and encryption needed (for example, L2TP/PPP).

OpenVPN

A relative newcomer to the family of VPN protocols, OpenVPN is an open source protocol. It is published under the GNU General Public License, or GPL. It is based on **Transport Layer Security/Secure Sockets Layer (TLS/SSL)**, the same cryptographic protocols that websites use to secure communications between their servers and web browsers. Since it is based on TLS, and TLS operates at just above the transport layer, it exists between the session and transport layers in the seven-layer OSI model. It exists between the application and transport layers in the four-layer network model. Currently, OpenVPN software is available for Windows, Linux, and macOS.

Since OpenVPN uses the OpenSSL library for encryption, all of the cryptographic algorithms available in OpenSSL are also available in OpenVPN. It can also use HMAC packet authentication. Support for the mbed TLS, an implementation of TLS/SSL that is dual-licensed with the Apache License and the GPL, has also been added.

There are different ways of performing authentication in OpenVPN. It can be done via certificates or via a user/password combination. It can be implemented with either TCP or UDP. Whichever protocol is used, the default port for OpenVPN is 1194 (this is the IANA assigned port number). Version 2.0 supports several simultaneous connections per process, and, starting with version 2.3, OpenVPN fully supports IPv6 as a protocol inside the tunnel, and OpenVPN connections can also be established with IPv6. It can work through most proxy servers, and it is also good at working through NAT and getting through firewalls. Many network configuration options can be pushed to the client, such as IP addresses and routing commands.

OpenVPN uses two types of interfaces for networking; both use the universal TUN/TAP driver. It can create either a Layer 3 TUN tunnel or a Layer 2 TAP connection. (Layer 2 is the data link layer, and Layer 3 is the network layer.)

OpenVPN seems to be most heavily supported in Linux, with UNIX variants (such as FreeBSD) not far behind. There are clients available for Windows, however (XP and later), and also for macOS X. If support for mobile devices is important to you, take into account the fact that OpenVPN also has clients for iOS and Android.

Choosing a VPN protocol

What factors should you consider when choosing a VPN protocol? This will depend on your circumstances, but some of the likely factors will include:

- Interoperability with other firewalls and routers
- The type of authentication used
- Ease of configuration
- The number of WAN-type interfaces
- The operating systems supported
- The complexity of your networks
- Security needs

Although you might set up VPN tunnels between two pfSense systems when working through the examples in this book, in real-world scenarios, it is very likely that you will be connecting to other firewalls or routers, and therefore, interoperability will become a factor. If this is the case, then IPsec is probably the best choice, since it is included with just about every VPN-capable device. (We used to be able to say the same thing about PPTP, but support for it is being phased out, for reasons discussed earlier in this section). Using IPsec is also a good way of avoiding being locked into a single product or vendor. OpenVPN is gaining acceptance, and the fact that it is an open source protocol helps, but the usage of OpenVPN isn't nearly as widespread as that of IPsec.

You might consider the authentication that the protocol uses when choosing a protocol. IPsec allows you to used pre-shared keys or certificates, as well as username/password combinations. L2TP does not provide for any authentication, so if you require authentication, you won't be using L2TP, or you will be using it in combination with another protocol. OpenVPN supports both pre-shared keys and certificates.

Another factor that you might take into account is the ease of configuration. Fortunately, all of the VPN protocols available for the current version of pfSense are fairly easy to configure. Of these, I have found that OpenVPN is the easiest to configure. It requires the use of certificates for remote access in many environments, but otherwise, it seems relatively easy to configure. IPsec can be challenging to set up for the first time because of all of the options that are available and the fact that the settings on both sides of the connection must match. L2TP is not too difficult to configure on the server side; finding a client that is easy to configure can be difficult.

If you have more than one WAN interface, this may prove to be a factor in your decision. Both IPsec and OpenVPN work well with multi-WAN setups.

There is also the issue of which operating systems you will be supporting, and, of course, which clients are available for those operating systems. If your network consists of mostly (or exclusively) Windows nodes, IPsec may be the ideal protocol to use, since support for IPsec is built directly into Windows, and has been since Windows Vista (2007). Thus, connecting to a VPN under Windows is relatively easy:

1. Navigate to **Settings** | **Control Panel**
2. Click on **Network and Sharing Center**
3. In the **Network and Sharing Center**, click on **Set up a new connection or network**
4. Use the wizard to set up an IPsec/L2TP connection

If you prefer, you can use third-party VPN clients, such as the Shrew Soft VPN client, which works with all versions of Windows (from Windows 2000).

Unfortunately, most Linux distributions do not have built-in VPN support. Ubuntu and Ubuntu-derivative distributions seem to be a little better, with Ubuntu having built-in support for PPTP (which is no longer supported by pfSense). Fortunately, clients are available from third parties, and at least some of these clients are available from Linux repositories. These clients vary in their degrees of robustness, user friendliness, and overall utility. Some are very bare-bones command-line utilities. If your network has to support Linux nodes, you should be able to use IPsec, although OpenVPN is probably a better choice.

For many years, macOS has had support for the IPsec protocol. Now, it even has a user-friendly interface for IPsec. macOS 10.6 (Snow Leopard) and later versions of macOS have a built-in Cisco IPsec VPN client that provides a graphical interface and enables you to connect to an IPsec network. Earlier versions of macOS do not have this client. Nonetheless, you can install the Cisco Remote Access IPsec client on these earlier versions. You can also use the Cisco AnyConnect Secure Mobility Client on these earlier versions. You should be aware, however, that support for macOS 10.5 (Leopard) was dropped with AnyConnect version 3.1; so, if you want to use this client on 10.5 or previous versions of macOS, you'll be stuck with earlier versions.

If your network is likely to support a variety of platforms, your best choices are IPsec or L2TP. The latter is usually implemented in conjunction with IPsec, but there are also several clients on a variety of platforms that support L2TP without IPsec, such as Windows (Windows Vista and later). There is a Microsoft Management Console snap-in called **Windows Firewall with Advanced Security (WFAS)**; this can be used for L2TP configuration. It can be found in **Control Panel** | **Administrative Tools**.

If command-line utilities are your forte, you can use the following command:

```
netsh.exe advfirewall
```

Support for L2TP is not built into Linux. However, there are third-party clients available for popular distributions, such as Arch Linux and Ubuntu. The configuration of most of these clients is fairly easy.

The Cisco IPsec client for macOS supports L2TP. Unfortunately, it seems to only support L2TP over IPsec. As of the time of writing, I do not know of a third-party client for macOS that supports native L2TP (that is, L2TP without another protocol, such as IPsec). Thus, it seems that you should not rely exclusively on L2TP if you have to support computers running macOS on your network.

Linux offers good support for OpenVPN, with OpenVPN support being built into many popular Linux distributions. For example, you can configure an OpenVPN connection through the Network Connections applet in Ubuntu and Ubuntu variants rather easily. The Network Connections applet supports authentication with both certificates and a pre-shared key. This makes OpenVPN a good choice for a VPN protocol, if you are supporting mainly Linux clients.

If you are running Linux and the ability to create an Open VPN connection does not appear as one of the VPN options, no worries: you can always install OpenVPN. In most cases, you should be able to download OpenVPN from your distribution's repositories, although the version that you find in the repositories may not be the latest version. In any case, you can download OpenVPN from your distribution's repositories with one of the following commands: `sudo apt-get install openvpn` (for Debian-based distros) or `sudo yum install openvpn` (for Red Hat-based distros). This should result in the successful installation of OpenVPN and its dependencies. If it does not, check the official OpenVPN site at `http://openvpn.net/`. You may also want to consult your distro's documentation.

Unfortunately, macOS does not have built-in support for OpenVPN; further compounding the difficulty is the fact that the OpenVPN project does not provide a macOS version of their client. As of the time of writing, I do not know of anyone who has successfully compiled the source code of the client under macOS, although it is at least theoretically possible, since the code is open source. There is, however, an open source project, called **Tunnelblick**. This provides the necessary drivers for implementing OpenVPN under macOS. Tunnelblick has a graphical interface; the software provides a way to control both client and server connections, and it can be used on its own or with commercial software (for example, Viscosity). You can find more information about Tunnelblick on its website at `http://tunnelblick.net`.

Another factor is the complexity of your network. In particular, if your VPN tunnel must traverse multiple firewalls, you need to take that into account. IPsec uses UDP port 500 for IKE traffic and the ESP protocol. Unfortunately, not all firewalls handle ESP traffic well when NAT is being used. This is because the ESP protocol does not use port numbers that are easily traceable by NAT devices. In such cases, IPsec clients behind firewalls may need to use NAT-T to function. NAT-T encapsulates ESP traffic over port 4500, using the UDP protocol. PfSense has supported NAT-T since version 2.0, so you should be able to use NAT traversal with IPsec.

If your VPN tunnel is going to traverse multiple firewalls, take into account that OpenVPN is more firewall-friendly than IPsec. OpenVPN uses TCP and UDP (it does not use ESP), and thus, it is not affected by NAT activity, such as changing source ports. One possible issue with OpenVPN is that the port and the protocol can be blocked; OpenVPN uses port `1194` by default. If that port is blocked, you may want to use a port commonly used for something other than OpenVPN—this will help to avoid egress filtering. Ports `80` and `43` are assigned for HTTP and HTTPs, respectively. Since TCP traffic will normally pass freely through these ports, you can use them for OpenVPN traffic, using the TCP protocol.

L2TP uses UDP, and should not pose any particular problems with multiple firewalls. It is, however, commonly used in conjunction with IPsec. Therefore, all of the problems with traversing multiple firewalls with IPsec come into play when using L2TP/IPsec.

Cryptographic security can also be an important issue. L2TP has no encryption capabilities, so if you want encryption, you will have to use it in combination with another protocol. If you are using pfSense, that means a choice between IPsec and OpenVPN.

OpenVPN uses the SSL encryption library. This library provides several different ciphers. You can find out which ciphers are available with the version of OpenVPN installed with pfSense by typing the following command (either at the pfSense console's Command Prompt, or from **Diagnostics** | **Command Prompt**):

```
openvpn –show–ciphers
```

OpenVPN's default encryption algorithm is BF-CBC. This is Blowfish, a block cipher with a 128-bit key size. This is not a terrible cipher, but you may want to choose a stronger cipher, such as AES-256 CBC or CAMELLIA-256 OFB.

Another advantage of OpenVPN is that it supports a number of different digests for message authentication. Among the digests supported are many of the digests supported by IPsec. To list the digests supported by OpenVPN, type the following command:

```
openvpn –show–digests
```

The main disadvantage of OpenVPN, regarding cryptographic security, is that it seems to favor backward compatibility with previous versions of OpenVPN over security. Furthermore, it operates at the application layer of the OSI model. Since IPsec operates at the network layer of the OSI model, it provides encryption on the IP level. For that reason, I would give IPsec a slight advantage over OpenVPN in the area of cryptographic security.

To summarize this subsection's findings, here is a table with some of the features of each VPN protocol supported by the current version of pfSense:

Protocol	Client included in OS	Client available for OS	Supports multi-WAN	Firewall friendly?	Cryptographically secure?
IPsec	Windows, macOS	Windows, Linux, macOS	Yes	Only with NAT-T	Yes
L2TP	None of the major desktop OSes have clients that support native L2TP; Windows and macOS support L2TP/IPsec	Windows, Linux	Yes	Yes	No (no encryption at all)
OpenVPN	Linux	Windows, Linux, macOS	Yes	Yes	Yes

VPN hardware

If you plan on using VPNs on your network, then ensuring that you have hardware capable of creating and maintaining VPN tunnels is important. A system that only meets the specifications of pfSense will likely be inadequate. A typical desktop system will be more than capable. Since VPNs use encryption, and encryption (not to mention compression) is a CPU-intensive affair, if you are going to use VPNs, then your budgeting should allow for a more powerful CPU than what you would use otherwise. Researching benchmarks on CPUs is not a bad idea. This will tend to ensure that you not only get a powerful enough CPU, but that you also get the best return on your investment.

One of the factors to consider when choosing a CPU is the fact that pfSense 2.5 will require a processor that supports AES-NI hardware acceleration. Most Intel and AMD processors made since 2013 support AES-NI. For Intel, Westmere and later processors support it, and for AMD, Jaguar and later processors support it. Use due diligence in selecting an AES-NI-compatible processor, before purchasing your hardware.

If you are going to maintain several VPN tunnels simultaneously, you might consider purchasing specialized hardware. Accelerator cards will offload from the computing-intensive tasks of encryption and compression from the CPU. One company that makes such cards that are compatible with pfSense is Soekris, which had the VPN 14x1 product line. Unfortunately, Soekris USA suspended operations in 2017; however, VPN cards are still available (at least for now) from Soekris Europe.

Configuring a VPN tunnel

Now that we have covered the basics of VPNs, we can discuss how to set up a VPN tunnel. Both peer-to-peer and client-server VPN tunnels will be covered, and, for client-server tunnels, we will discuss how to configure the tunnel from both the server side and the client side. IPsec is the most difficult to configure, and you might not get it to work the first time, whereas OpenVPN and L2TP are somewhat easier.

IPsec configuration

Depending on your deployment scenario, you may want to configure IPsec as a peer that can connect to or accept a connection from another peer, or you may want to set up IPsec as a server that accepts connections from remote clients. We will cover both cases in this subsection.

If you want to set up IPsec to act as a server with multiple mobile clients, you might want to skip to the subsection called *IPsec mobile client configuration*. Such configuration begins at the **Mobile Clients** tab. The process automatically generates a Phase 1 IPsec entry, which you can then use in conjunction with a Phase 2 entry.

IPsec peer/server congfiguration

IPsec configuration starts with navigating to **VPN | IPsec.** The **Tunnels** page displays a table of existing IPsec tunnels. Each IPsec tunnel requires a Phase 1 configuration, as well as at least one Phase 2 configuration (you can have more than one Phase 2 configuration corresponding to a single Phase 1 configuration). Click on the **Add P1** button to start Phase 1 configuration.

The **Phase 1** configuration page has four sections. The first section is **General Information**, and the first option under this section is the **Disabled** checkbox; if you check this box, the Phase 1 entry will be disabled, but will remain in the table. The next option, the **Key Exchange** version drop-down box, allows you to choose between **IKEv1 (V1)**, **IKEv2 (V2)**, or **Auto**. When **Auto** is chosen, **IKEv2** will be used when initiating a connection. If IPsec is accepting a connection, however, either **IKEv1** or **IKEv2** will be accepted.

The **Internet Protocol** drop-down box allows you to choose between **IPv4** and **IPv6**, while the **Interface** drop-down box lets you select the interface that is the local endpoint of the tunnel. As you may have guessed, you will usually want to leave this set to **WAN**, unless you have a multi-WAN setup. The **Remote Gateway** edit box is where you enter the public IP address/hostname of the remote gateway. In most cases, unless you are configuring IPsec on a router that is behind one or more routers, this should match the IP address of the WAN interface (or the domain name that matches the IP address).

The next section is **Phase 1 Proposal (Authentication)**, and the first option in this section is the **Authentication Method** drop-down box. **Mutual PSK** allows for authentication using a **pre-shared key** (PSK). **Mutual RSA** allows for authentication using certificates. These are currently the only methods supported. The **Negotiation Mode** drop-down menu allows you to choose the authentication security, and what differentiates the two options is what happens when the VPN tunnel is down and has to be rebuilt. **Main** will force the peer to re-authenticate, while **Aggressive** will rebuild the tunnel quickly, without forcing re-authentication. The advantage of **Main**, obviously, is that it is more secure, while **Aggressive** will rebuild the tunnel more quickly, sacrificing security. **Aggressive** is generally the favored setting, and seems to work with more clients, although obviously, **Main** is the better option if security is crucial. The **My identifier** drop-down menu identifies the router to the other side of the connection; you can usually leave it as **My IP address**. The **Peer identifier** drop-down box is where you select what will identify the router on the far side. This can usually be left set to **Peer IP address**.

If you selected **Mutual PSK**, the next field will be **Pre-Shared Key**. Here, you enter the PSK string; choose a long key, and it might be a good idea to use special characters. If you chose **Mutual RSA** as the **Authentication Method**, there will be two options. The first is **My Certificate**, where you select a certificate that was previously configured in the pfSense certificate manager. The second is the **Peer Certificate Authority** drop-down box, where you select a **Certificate Authority** (CA), which also will have been configured in the certificate manager.

The next section, **Phase 1 Proposal (Encryption),** contains the encryption options. The **Encryption Algorithm** drop-down box is where you choose the encryption method. If you require strong encryption, you should probably select either **AES** or **Blowfish**, which both support 128-bit, 192-bit, and 256-bit encryption. **3DES** and **CAST128** do not have these options. The **Hash Algorithm** drop-down box allows you to choose the hash function used to ensure the integrity of the data. **MD5** is considered less secure than the other options, but some devices only support **MD5**.

The next option is **DH Group**. This allows you to select the **Diffie-Hellman** (DH) group that is used to generate session keys; the default value is 1,024 bits. This is generally considered safe; you can use a greater number of bits, but it may affect the performance. The last option in this section, the **Lifetime (Seconds)** edit box, allows you to control how long pfSense waits for Phase 1 to complete; the default value is 28,800 seconds, which should be long enough, although you can increase it here.

The **Advanced Options** section has several options. The **Disable Rekey** option, if enabled, prevents IPsec from renegotiating a connection that is about to expire. The **Responder Only** option, if checked, will prevent IPsec from initiating a connection; it will only respond to incoming requests.

The next option is the **NAT Traversal** drop-down box. This allows you to enable the encapsulation of ESP in UDP packets on port `4500`. This only needs to be set if both sides of the connection are behind restrictive firewalls, in which case, you can set this parameter to **force**.

The **DPD (Dead Peer Detection)** option, if enabled, will try to detect whether the other side of the connection is having a problem. If it is, IPsec will try to rebuild the tunnel. If you check this option, you should also set values for **Delay** and **Max failures**. **Delay** is the delay between requesting per acknowledgement, and **Max failures** is the number of consecutive failures allowed before a disconnect. The default values are adequate for most cases. When you are done making changes, click on the **Save** button, and then, when the page reloads, click on **Apply Changes** on the main **IPsec** page.

Phase 1 configuration is now complete, but you must create at least one Phase 2 entry to complete the process of setting up an IPsec connection. The table on the main **IPsec** page should have an entry for the newly-created Phase 1 connection. To begin Phase 2 configuration, click on the **Show Phase 2 Entries** button, and then click on the **Add P2** button.

There are three sections on the Phase 2 configuration page. The first section is called **General Information**. The first option in this section is the **Disabled** checkbox. As with Phase 1 configuration, this option allows you to disable the entry without removing it from the table. The next option is the **Mode** drop-down box, which has the choices **Tunnel IPv4, Tunnel IPv6**, and **Transport**. If you choose tunnel mode, which encrypts the entire IP packet and adds a new IP header, your choice should be identical to the IP protocol set in **Internet Protocol** during Phase 1 configuration. Transport mode encrypts the payload, but not the IP header.

The **Local Network** option gives you the ability to choose which subnet or host can be accessed from the other side of the VPN tunnel. For example, if you select **LAN subnet**, all of the LAN will be accessible from the other end; if you select **DMZ subnet**, all of the DMZ will be accessible, and so on. The other end of the tunnel's VPN settings should have the same setting; however, the setting will be **Remote Network** or **Remote Subnet**.

The **NAT/BINAT translation** drop-down box is the next option. This is where you specify settings that will be presented to the other side of the connection, when the local network is hidden. One of the options is **Address or Network**, in which you can specify the IP address or subnet. The **Remote Network** option is where you can specify the network or address on the other side of the tunnel, which will be accessible from this side of the tunnel; it must match the setting in the **Local Network** setting for the peer. Finally, you can enter a brief, non-parsed description in the **Description** edit box.

The second section on the page is **Phase 2 Proposal (SA/Key Exchange)**. The **Protocol** drop-down box allows you to select the protocol for key exchange. The de facto standard is **ESP**, but you can select **AH** instead. Be aware that ESP uses port 50, and AH uses port 51. pfSense will automatically generate a rule to allow ESP or AH to the endpoint of the IPsec tunnel, and the rule will appear under the **Floating** tab of the **Rules** page.

The next option is **Encryption Algorithm**, and you can choose more than one algorithm. The default is **AES**. It is recommended that you only check the one that you will use, at least at first. The remote peer must select the same algorithm (or at least one of the algorithms chosen).

The next option is **Hash Algorithms**; as with **Encryption Algorithm**, you may choose more than one. Some devices only support **MD5**; you can check that, if that is the case. The default setting is **SHA1**.

The **PFS Key Group** is the next setting. PFS stands for **Perfect Forward Security**; if this option is set, the remote peer must perform a PFS key exchange, or the negotiation will fail. As with the **Phase 1 DH Group**, there is a trade-off between security and performance. Turning off the **PFS Key Group** makes the process of establishing a tunnel faster, but at the cost of security. The **Lifetime** field is where you set the lifetime of the negotiated keys.

The **Advanced Configuration** section has only one setting. The **Automatically ping host** field is where you can enter an IP address for a remote Phase 2 network to ping, to keep the tunnel alive. When you are done, click on **Save**, and then click on **Apply Changes** on the main IPsec page.

Once you have completed Phase 1 and Phase 2 configuration, you will probably want to navigate to **Firewall** | **Rules** and click on the **Floating** tab, to make sure that the rules necessary for your configuration exist. Port 500 (UDP) is used for IKE, and must be open with all configurations. Port 4500 (also UDP) must be open if you use NAT traversal, and either 50 (for ESP) or 51 (for AH) must be open for Phase 2 key exchange.

IPsec mobile client configuration

The previous section involved the configuration of an IPsec tunnel in which authentication is done through either a PSK or certificates. This is acceptable for peer-to-peer connections, and will even work with a client-server connection. However, what if there are multiple mobile clients? Wouldn't it make more sense to configure different settings for each individual user? In such cases, we can use the **Mobile Clients** tab.

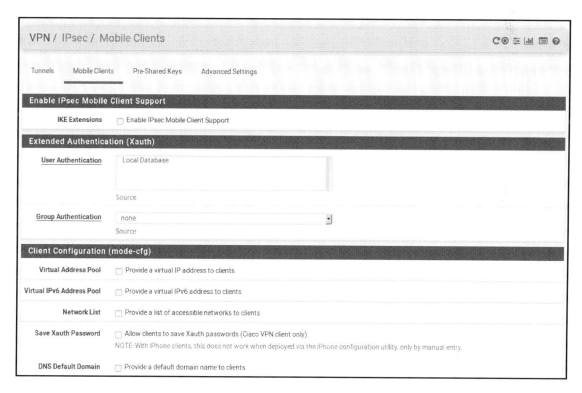

There are three sections on the **Mobile Clients** configuration page: **Enable IPsec Mobile Client Support, Extended Authentication (Xauth),** and **Client Configuration (mode-cfg)**. The first (and only) option in the first section is the **IKE extensions** checkbox; enabling this option enables support for mobile clients. The next section contains two options. The **User authentication** box is where you choose what database is used for user authentication. There only seems to be one option here: **Local Database**. This option allows for user authentication via pfSense's user manager. The second option is **Group Authentication**. Here, you should select **system** for user manager authentication.

The final section of the page has several options. If **Virtual Address Pool** is enabled, pfSense will provide virtual IP addresses to clients; using this option requires that you enter a network mask and the corresponding CIDR. The **Virtual IPv6 Address Pool** option, if enabled, also allows you to provide virtual IP addresses. In this case, however, they will be IPv6 addresses instead of IPv4 addresses.

If the **Network List** option is enabled, a list of accessible networks will be presented to the mobile clients. If **Save Xauth password** is enabled, clients will be allowed to save Xauth passwords. This option will only work if the mobile client is using a Cisco VPN client. If **DNS Default domain** is enabled, pfSense will provide a default domain to clients; you must specify the default domain for this option to work. If **Split DNS** is enabled, you can provide a list of split DNS domain names to the clients. Thus, you can provide different sets of DNS information, based on the source address of the DNS query. If you enable this option, you must enter the domain names in the edit box below the checkbox. The domain names should be separated by commas.

If **DNS servers** is enabled, you can provide a list of DNS servers to clients. You must then enter the DNS servers into an edit box below this checkbox. The **WINS Servers** option is similar, but in this case, you are providing a list of WINS servers to WINS clients. Checking **Phase 2 PFS Group** allows you to set a **Perfect Forward Security** group for clients; this setting will override whatever is set during Phase 2 configuration. If **Login Banner** is enabled, you can provide a login banner to clients (enter it in the corresponding edit box). When you are done, click on the **Save** button, and then the **Apply Changes** button.

Pre-shared keys

The next tab, after **Mobile Clients,** is **Pre-Shared Keys**. On this tab, you can add new keys and edit existing keys. The landing page for this tab displays a table with all previously entered keys. You can add a new key by clicking on the **Add** button, which will load the **Pre-Shared Keys** edit page.

The first option on this page is the **Identifier** edit box; the identifier can be an IP address, a fully qualified domain name, or an email address. In the **Secret** type drop-down box, you can select either **PSK** or **EAP** as the type. Finally, in the **Pre-Shared Key** edit box, you can enter the PSK. It can then be used by anyone who uses the identifier in the **Identifier** field. The PSK can be used by anyone, if one was entered in the **Identifier** field. When you are finished making changes, click on the **Save** button, and when the page reloads, click on **Apply Changes**.

Advanced settings

Finally, there is the **Advanced Settings** tab. There are two sections on this page. The first section is **IPsec Logging Controls**. This section allows you to control different levels of logging for different components of IPsec. Each component has its own drop-down box; you can set the level of logging in the drop-down box. Levels range from **Silent** (no logging at all) to **Highest** (display all logs), with several options in between.

The second section of the page is labeled **Advanced IPsec Settings. Configure Unique IDs** controls whether a participant's IKE ID should be kept unique. If the **IP Compression** checkbox is enabled, IPComp compression of content will take place. The **Strict interface binding** option allows you to enable strongSwan's `interface_use` option, to bind only to specific interfaces. The **Unencrypted payloads in IKEv1** option, if enabled, allows IPsec to send unencrypted ID and HASH playloads in IKEv1 main mode.

If **Enable Maximum MSS** is checked, MSS clamping is enabled, which is useful if you are having trouble sending large packets over the tunnel. If you check **Enable Cisco Extensions**, the Cisco Unity plugin will be enabled, providing support for Cisco extensions.

The **Strict CRL Checking** option will require the availability of a fresh **Certificate Revocation List (CRL)** for peer authentication, if enabled. If **Make before Break** is enabled, pfSense will create new SaS before deleting the old ones during the re-authentication process.

The **Auto-exclude LAN address** option, if enabled, causes traffic from the LAN subnet to the LAN IP address to be excluded from IPsec, addressing cases where the remote subnet overlaps with the local subnet. When you are done making changes, click on the **Save** button, and then click on **Apply Changes.**

Example 1 – Site-to-site IPsec configuration

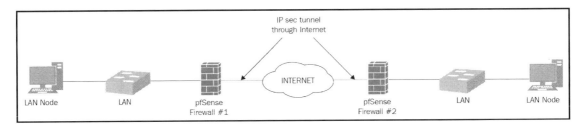

As mentioned earlier, a VPN tunnel can be peer-to-peer or client-server, and in this example, we will simulate a VPN tunnel that might be set up if we had to connect two facilities—likely run by the same company—that both have their own private networks, but are separated by a considerable distance. There are two pfSense firewalls at the boundary of each private network and the internet; therefore, the endpoint for each tunnel will be the firewall's WAN interface, and the configurations at either end will be identical. Setting up our site-to-site IPsec tunnel involves creating Phase 1 and Phase 2 entries, adding firewall rules to allow IPsec traffic, and repeating the process on the second firewall. We will begin by outlining the steps needed to create the Phase 1 and Phase 2 entries:

1. Navigate to **VPN | IPsec**. On the default tab, click the **Add P1** button.
2. In the **General Information** section of the **Edit Phase 1** page, change **Key Exchange** to IKEv2.
3. Set **Remote gateway** to the IP address of the second pfSense firewall.
4. Enter a brief description in the **Description** edit box.
5. Enter a key in the **Pre-Shared Key** edit box.
6. Set the **Hash Algorithm** to **SHA256**.
7. All other values can be kept as their defaults. Click on the **Save** button.
8. When the page reloads, click on the **Show Phase 2 Entries** button. In the Phase 2 section, there should be an **Add P2** button. Click on this button.
9. In the **General Information** section of the page, keep **Local Network** set to **LAN.**
10. Set **Remote Network** to the LAN subnet and CIDR of the remote network's LAN.
11. Enter a brief description in the **Description** edit box.

12. In the **Phase 2 Configuration (SA/Key Exchange)** section, make sure **AES256-GCM** is selected as an **Encryption Algorithm**.
13. Select **SHA256** as the **Hash Algorithm**.
14. Click on the **Save** button when done.

This completes the process of configuring the Phase 1 and Phase 2 entries, but we must still add a firewall rule to allow IPsec traffic. Having covered firewall rules in `Chapter 6`, *Firewall and NAT*, this should be easy:

1. Navigate to **Firewall | Rules** and click on the **IPsec** tab.
2. Click on one of the **Add** buttons at the bottom of the page to add a rule.
3. On the **Edit** page for the rule, select **Network** in the **Source** drop-down box. Enter the subnet and CIDR of the remote network. This should be the same as the information entered for **Remote Network** in the Phase 2 configuration.
4. All other values can be kept as their defaults. Click on the **Save** button.

You can make firewall rules as permissive or as restrictive as you wish. The only limitation is that your rules should not be so restrictive that they block traffic that needs to pass. In the preceding rule, we could have left the **Source** set to **Any**. It is good practice, however, to restrict traffic to the remote subnet, even if it is unlikely that our overly permissive access will be exploited.

Now, all that is left to do is to repeat the process on the second firewall:

1. Navigate to **VPN | IPsec** on the second firewall and set up the Phase 1 configuration. The settings should be identical to the other firewall, with the exception that the **Remote gateway** should be set to the first pfSense firewall.
2. Create the Phase 2 entry on the second firewall. Again, the settings should be identical to the settings on the first firewall, but make sure the **Remote Network** is set to the subnet and CIDR of the network behind the first firewall.
3. Create an IPsec firewall rule on the second firewall. This should be identical to the rule created on the first firewall.

Some guides for setting up a peer-to-peer IPsec connection on pfSense firewalls have included the step of adding a gateway for IPsec traffic. I have found this to be an unnecessary step; peer-to-peer IPsec tunnels seem to work equally well without such gateways.

Now that we have configured IPsec, and have completed configuration on each side, we should be able to establish a connection between the firewalls. To do this, from either firewall, navigate to **Status** | **IPsec**. On the landing page, there will be a table with all available IPsec configurations; click on the **Connect VPN** button that corresponds to the newly-created configuration. Within seconds, the IPsec tunnel should be up. The **Status** column should change from **Disconnected** to **ESTABLISHED,** to reflect the current state of the tunnel. Navigate to **Status** | **IPsec** on the other firewall. The table on that page should also read **ESTABLISHED** in the **Status** column.

This IPsec peer-to-peer connection can be initiated from either firewall. Once the connection is established, however, it can only be terminated from the side on which the connection was initiated.

Now that the tunnel is established, we should be able to access resources on the LAN side of the remote connection as if they were local resources. The only limitations will be our bandwidth, latency, and the processing overhead of maintaining the tunnel.

Example 2 – IPsec tunnel for mobile remote access

Our second example involves a scenario in which we need to set up an IPsec tunnel to provide a means for remote mobile users to connect to our network using an IPsec client on their computer. The users might be workers on site at a client's workplace, or perhaps on a business trip, or working at home. Fortunately, we can set up such a connection with relative ease, and, although not all IPsec clients are easy to configure, there are IPsec clients for all of the major desktop operating systems, so we should be able to get our remote users up and running.

To set up a client-server tunnel for mobile access, we must first complete Phase 1 and Phase 2 IPsec configuration, and then add users to the user manager. To complete IPsec configuration, follow these steps:

1. Navigate to **VPN** | **IPsec** and click on the **Mobile Clients** tab.
2. Check the **Enable IPsec Mobile Client support** checkbox.
3. Even though there is only one choice in the **User Authentication** box, we have to select it. **Select Local Database** in this box.
4. In the **Group Authentication** drop-down box, select **system.**
5. Check the **Provide a virtual IP address to clients** checkbox, and enter a subnet and CIDR for the virtual address pool.
6. Check the **Save Xauth Password** checkbox.

7. Check the **DNS Default Domain** checkbox, and enter **localdomain** as the default domain name.

8. Check the **Provide a DNS server list** checkbox. For **Server #1**, enter 1.1.1.1, and for **Server #2**, enter 1.0.0.1.

9. Check the **Login banner** checkbox and enter a login banner.

10. Click the **Save** button at the bottom of the page.

11. pfSense will prompt you to create a Phase 1 entry for the mobile client configuration. Click on the **Create Phase 1** button to begin IPsec tunnel configuration. This will take you to the **Edit Phase 1** page.

12. On the **Edit Phase 1** page, you will probably want to keep the **Key Exchange** version set to **IKEv1**, because it works with a greater range of clients.

13. Set the **Authentication Mode** to **Mutual PSK + Xauth.**

14. Change **Peer identifier** to **User distinguished name,** and enter an appropriate string, such as your email address.

15. In the **Pre-Shared Key** box, enter a pre-shared key.

16. Scroll down to **Advanced Options**, and change the **NAT Traversal** setting to **Force**. This will force the use of NAT-T on port 4500.

17. When you are finished, click the **Save** button, and then click on **Apply Changes.**

18. On the main IPsec page, click on the **Show phase 2 Entries** button, and then click on **Add P2.**

19. Most of the default settings for the Phase 2 entry can be kept. It is recommended, however, to change the value in **Encryption Algorithms** to 256. (You can keep the algorithm set to **AES**; you may want to set a longer **Lifetime,** as well.)

20. Click on the **Save** button when done, and then click on **Apply Changes**.

That completes Phase 1 and Phase 2 configuration, but we still must create a user group and users for the VPN tunnel:

1. Navigate to **System | User Manager** and click on the **Groups** tab.

2. Click on the **Add** button to add a new group.

3. Enter a group name of **vpnusers**, and, in the **Scope** drop-down box, select **Remote.**

4. Click on the **Save** button.

5. When the page reloads, the newly-created group should be listed in the table. Click on the **Edit** icon for **vpnusers** in this table.

6. There will now be a section on the configuration page for the group called **Assigned Privileges**. Click on the **Add** button in this section.

7. In the **Assigned Privileges** box, select **User – VPN: IPsecxauthDialin** and click on **Save.**

8. From the main configuration page, click on **Save.**

9. The group is now created, but it needs some users. Click on the **Users** tab, and then click on the **Add** button to create a new user.

10. Set an appropriate **Username** and **Password** for the new user.

11. Under **Group Memberships,** select the **vpnusers** group.

12. For the **IPsec Pre-Shared Key**, enter the key you entered during Phase 1 configuration.

13. Click on the **Save** button.

14. Repeat steps 9 through 13 for as many users as you wish to add.

This completes both the mobile client IPsec configuration and the **User Manager** configuration. Now, all that remains is to configure the mobile client. There are many different IPsec mobile clients available, and it is beyond the scope of this chapter to show you how to configure them, but the following guidelines should help:

- The settings made during Phase 1 and Phase 2 configuration must be matched in the settings on the client end. For example, **Key Exchange** must be set to **IKEv1** and **Exchange Type** must be set to **aggressive**. Also, the encryption algorithms must match.

- Since we are using NAT traversal, this must be enabled on the client's end.

- There should be fields for the username and password. Enter the username/password combination for one of the users created during **User Manager** configuration.

L2TP

It is unlikely that you will set up L2TP as a standalone protocol, as it has no authentication and encryption on its own. The more likely scenario is setting up an L2TP/IPsec tunnel. L2TP configuration is not difficult, as we shall see.

L2TP configuration starts by navigating to **VPN | L2TP**. On the **Configuration** tab, there are several options. The **Enable** checkbox enables the L2TP server, if checked. In the next section (**Configuration**), the **Interface** drop-down menu lets you select the interface on which the L2TP server is listening for connections. As with IPsec, this is almost always the WAN interface.

The **Server address** field is the IP address of the L2TP server. This IP address should be an unused one. It is typically on the same subnet as the client IP address subnet. The next field, the **Remote address range** edit box, is for entering the starting IP address of the client subnet. The **Number of L2TP users** drop-down box is where you select the number of clients allowed to connect. To calculate the ending IP address, take the starting IP address plus the number of L2TP users allowed, minus one.

In the **Secret** edit boxes, enter the shared secret (you must enter it twice). In the **Authentication type** drop-down box, you can choose the authentication protocol. There are currently three choices:

- **Challenge Handshake Authentication Protocol (CHAP)**: A peer trying to establish a connection to the server is sent a challenge message, which along with the secret, becomes an input into a one-way hash function. The authenticator performs checks based on its calculation of what the hash value should be. If they match the peer's reply, the peer is authenticated. This is the default choice.
- **MS-CHAPv2**: This is Microsoft's version of CHAP, considered weak because it uses 56-bit DES encryption.
- **Password Authentication Protocol (PAP)**: This involves sending un-encrypted passwords over the network, and is easily the least secure of all available protocols.

The last two options in this section are for the **Primary L2TP DNS Server** and the **Secondary L2TP DNS Server**.

The next section is labeled **RADIUS**. There is a checkbox in this section that allows you to enable RADIUS authentication. If you check this box, you must enter a series of RADIUS options. When you are done making changes on this page, click on the **Save** button.

There is also a **Users** tab. From this tab, you can add L2TP clients. To do so, click on the **Add** button on the page. The configuration page for users is simple: enter an appropriate **Username** and **Password** in the corresponding fields. The password must be entered twice. The **IP Address** field is optional; it allows you to assign the user to a specific IP address. Click on the **Save** button when you are finished.

OpenVPN

The third VPN protocol supported by the current release of pfSense is OpenVPN, and it is an excellent choice if your users primarily use Linux, thanks to the excellent support for OpenVPN that most Linux distros have. It is also a good choice if you have to support mobile devices; there are clients for both iOS and Android.

OpenVPN configuration begins by navigating to **VPN** I **OpenVPN**. While in IPsec, both ends of the tunnels can be configured as peers. OpenVPN tunnels tend to have one end defined as a client and the other end as a server, even when making site-to-site connections. Thus, there are separate tabs for **Servers** and **Clients**. There are also tabs labeled **Client-Specific Overrides** and **Wizards**.

OpenVPN server configuration

To begin server configuration, click on the **Server** tab, and click on the **Add** button. The first option on the server configuration page is the **Disable** checkbox. This, if checked, allows you to disable a server entry without removing it. The **Server Mode** drop-down box allows you to choose between several modes. The two **Peer to Peer** options allow either side of the connection to **Keyinitiate** the connection. If **Remote Access** is selected, only the remote client can initiate the connection. **SSL/TLS, Shared,** and **User Auth** are the authentication options. **SSL/TLS** uses a certificate for authentication; **Shared Key** uses a shared key, and **User Auth** uses a username/password combination.

In the **Protocol** drop-down box, you can set the protocol. Both UDP and TCP are supported, as well as UDP6 and TCP6, for IPv6 connections. The **Device mode** option allows you to chose between **Tun** (a virtual point-to-point link) and **Tap** (a virtual Ethernet adapter).

The **Local port** field lets you choose the port for the connection (the default is **1194**). You may also enter a description in the **Description** field.

If you need to configure options for certificates, you can do this under **Cryptographic Settings**. You can enable **Use a TLS key** and enter your own TLS key, or enable this option as well as **Automatically generate a TLS key,** and let pfSense generate a key. **Peer Certificate Authority** is where you can choose from defined certificate authorities. You can choose a revocation list under **Peer Certificate Revocation** list, if one has been created. You can set the size of the Diffie Hellman key at **DH Parameter Length** (or use **ECDH**). You can also select the **Encryption Algorithm** and **Auth** digest algorithm. It is recommended, however, that you keep this value set to the default for **OpenVPN**, which is **SHA1**. The **Hardware Crypto** checkbox allows you to enable hardware crypto.

pfSense 2.4 has seen the addition of several new OpenVPN options, especially under server configuration. One of these is **ECDH Curve**; to enable the use of this curve, select **ECDH only** in the **DH Parameter Length** drop-down box. ECDH, or **Elliptic-curve Diffie-Hellman**, uses a different algorithm than standard Diffie-Hellman when calculating the secret key.

Standard Diffie-Hellman performs a modulus operation on a group of multiplicative integers. ECDH uses a group of multiplicative points on a curve to calculate the key. The **Default** option for ECDH uses the curve from either the server certificate or secp384r1. You can, however, choose from a variety of different curves in the drop-down box.

Enable NCP is also a new option. NCP, or **Negotiable Cryptographic Parameters**, allows you to override the algorithm selected in **Encryption Algorithm**. Instead, the algorithm will be chosen from the list of **Allowed NCP Algorithms**. This, in turn, is a subset of **Available NCP Algorithms**. These two textboxes are next to each other, and below the **Enable NCP** checkbox. If one peer supports NCP and the other peer does not, pfSense will attempt to establish a connection using the algorithm requested by the non-NCP peer. The algorithm must be on the **Available NCP Algorithms** list, however.

You can use the **Certificate Depth** drop-down box to select the certificate depth. pfSense will not accept any certificate-based logins from clients that are below the depth set here. Certificate depth is the maximum number of intermediate certificate issuers that are allowed to be followed during certificate verification. A depth of **0** means that only self-signed certificates are permitted. A depth of **1** means that the certificate may be self-signed, or signed by a CA known to pfSense.

The next section is **Tunnel Settings**. The **IPv4 Tunnel Network** and **IPv6 Tunnel Network** edit boxes allow you to set the IPv4/IPv6 virtual networks that provide address pools for the clients. The **Redirect Gateway** option allows you to force all client-generated traffic through the VPN tunnel. The **IPv4 Remote network(s)** and **IPv6 Remote network(s)** fields are where you can enter the remote networks that will be accessible from the remote end of the VPN.

Concurrent connections is where you can specify the maximum number of clients allowed to connect to the server concurrently. The **Compression** option gives you the ability to set the compression option for the channel. The options are **No Preference, Disabled (no compression), Enabled with Adaptive Compression,** or **Enabled without Adaptive Compression**. The **Disable IPv6** option allows you to prevent IPv6 traffic from being forwarded.

The next section is **Advanced Configuration**. This section has two options. The **Custom options** box is where you can enter additional options to add to the OpenVPN server. The **Verbosity level** drop-down box allows you to set the logging level (**2** through **11**, with higher numbers offering greater levels of verbosity). When you are done making changes, click on the **Save** button, and then click on **Apply Changes**.

OpenVPN client configuration

If you need to configure pfSense to act as a client to connect to a remote VPN server, click on the **Client** tab. This is ideal if you want to connect to a VPN provider, ensuring that all outgoing and incoming traffic is filtered through a VPN. To begin, click on the **Add** button.

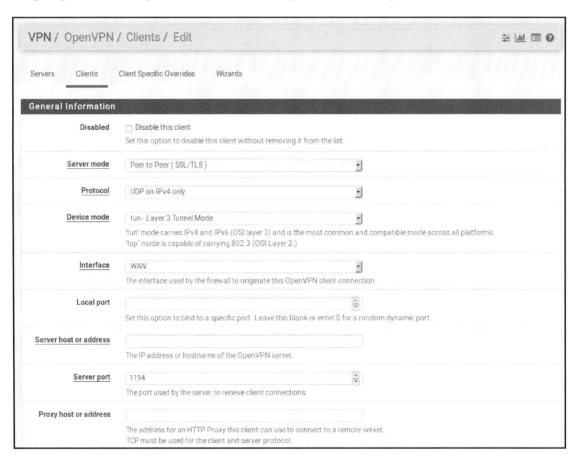

Most of the options on the client configuration page are similar to options found on the server configuration page. There are, however, some notable exceptions. In the **User Authentication Settings** section, you can set the username and password for the remote VPN server. The **Tunnel Configuration** section also has some interesting options. The **Don't pull routes** option, if enabled, will prevent the server from adding routes to pfSense's routing table. If **Don't add/remove routes** is enabled, then routes will be passed using environmental variables. When you want to save the new client configuration, click on the **Save** button, and then click on **Apply Changes**.

Server configuration with the wizard

One way that you can set up an OpenVPN server is with pfSense's server configuration wizard, which you can find by clicking on the **Wizards** tab. The only option on the first page is the **Type of Server** drop-down box. It allows you to choose between **Local User Access** (authentication through certificates), **LDAP** (authentication through **Lightweight Directory Access Protocol**), or **RADIUS** (authentication through a **Remote Authentication Dial-In User Service** server).

Whichever setting you choose for **Type of Server** determines what the next page of the wizard contains. If you select **Local User Access**, you will have to enter certificate and certificate authority information; if you select **LDAP**, you will have to provide information about the LDAP server; and if you choose **RADIUS**, you will have to provide information about the RADIUS server. After that, you will be directed to the **Server Setup** screen, where you can enter information about the OpenVPN server. This is similar to the OpenVPN server configuration page that we covered earlier in this section, with some notable exceptions. The **Inter-Client Communication** option, if enabled, allows for communication between different clients connected to the server. If **Duplicate Connections** is enabled, multiple concurrent connections using the same common name will be allowed.

For more examples of options not available on the server configuration page, scroll down to **Client Settings**. **Dynamic IP**, if enabled, will allow connected clients to retain their connections, even if their IP address changes. The **Topology** drop-down menu allows you to select a method used to supply virtual IP addresses to clients when using IPv4 TUN mode. You can choose **Subnet – One IP address per client in a common subnet** (the default) or **net30 – Isolated /30 network per client**, giving each client two IP addresses. This option may be necessary for older clients (before version 2.0.9 of OpenVPN).

The next step of the wizard covers configuration of the necessary firewall rules. You will need, at a minimum, a rule to permit connections on the OpenVPN port, and another rule to allow traffic to pass inside the VPN tunnel. This page allows you to easily create either or both rules, by just checking the appropriate checkboxes. When you are done, click on **Next**. You should see a message acknowledging that configuration is complete. When you do, click on **Finish**.

OpenVPN Client Export Utility

If you want to make the process of setting up OpenVPN clients, you might consider the OpenVPN **Client Export Utility**. This allows you to export a preconfigured OpenVPN Windows client, or a macOS Viscosity configuration bundle, directly from pfSense.

You can install the OpenVPN Client Export Utility by navigating to **Packages | OpenVPN**, clicking on the **Available Packages** tab, and scrolling down to **openvpn-client-export**. Click on the corresponding **Install** button, and then click on the **Confirm** button on the next page.

Once the client is installed, there should be two new tabs on the OpenVPN page at **Protocols | OpenVPN: Client Export** and **Shared Key Export. Shared Key Export** is mainly for site-to-site connections, while **Client Export** is for clients connecting to an OpenVPN server.

It is beyond the scope of this chapter to provide a detailed discussion of this utility. You should, however, be aware that it is available, and that it can streamline the process of configuring different clients to connect to your network, especially if you are supporting users that use Windows and/or MacOS.

Troubleshooting VPNs

Troubleshooting a VPN connection may be some of the most challenging work you will ever do. Establishing a VPN tunnel involves multiple steps. A failure at any of these steps will result in a failure to establish a VPN connection. In such cases, it may help to use the following guidelines for troubleshooting:

1. If the remote client or peer is not able to connect to pfSense, then it is possible that the VPN service is not running at the local end of the connection. Check to make sure that it is running.
2. If the VPN service is running at either end, it is possible that one or more ports are blocked and need to be unblocked. Check to make sure that the rules allowing traffic through the necessary ports are unblocked, and that they are taking effect. Even if the rules exist, the order of the rules may be such that they are not taking effect. Consult the following table when checking to see whether the correct ports are open:

Protocol	Ports
IPsec	UDP on 500 for ISAKMP (necessary for all configurations), 50 for ESP, 51 for AH, UDP on 4500 for NAT-T
L2TP	UDP on 1701 (default port)
OpenVPN	TCP or UDP on 1194 (default port)

3. If the remote client is able to connect to the server, but the connection ultimately fails, then often, the best source for information about what has happened is in the log files. If you navigate to **Status | System Logs**, you will be able to find OpenVPN and IPsec log entries in separate tabs. In many cases, the source of the problem is a mismatch between the client and server settings (or peer settings).

While a lot of VPN problems stem from client-server settings mismatches, in other cases, you may be experiencing problems because of the nuances of certain clients. For example, the ShrewSoft VPN Client seems to require IKEv1 for key exchange, and a negotiation mode of Aggressive. The Windows built-in VPN client, however, seems to require IKev2. Consulting the client software documentation will help, as will looking for additional information online.

One aspect of IPsec configuration that may cause problems (if configuring IPsec in pfSense is new to you) is what happens when you switch from IKEv1 to IKEv2, and then back to IKEv1. The negotiation mode will change to Main, even if you originally set it to Aggressive. Therefore, if you change the Key Exchange Method, make sure that you have the right setting for Negotiation mode before saving your settings.

Summary

In this chapter, we began by discussing the basics of VPNs and how they provide a cost-effective way of connecting clients to private networks across the internet (client-server) and private networks to other private networks across the internet (peer-to-peer). We then introduced the three protocols currently supported by pfSense (IPsec, L2TP, and OpenVPN), and the advantages and disadvantages of each. We then covered how to configure each of these protocols. Finally, we discussed how to troubleshoot a VPN connection. We built heavily on some of the concepts covered in previous chapters, especially the firewall rules covered in `Chapter 6`, *Firewall and NAT*.

In the next chapter, we will cover something that many pfSense users will likely want to implement in their ongoing quest to make their networks more robust: multiple WANs.

Questions

1. What are the two main types of VPN connections?
2. (a) If we need to select a VPN protocol and we need to ensure that it works with a variety of firewalls, what is the best option? (b) If we are supporting only Linux clients and security is not our main concern, what is the best option? (c) If we can only use TCP for our VPN tunnel, what is the best option?
3. What port must be open on all firewalls that are endpoints of IPsec connections?
4. If we are setting up an IPsec server and need to support multiple clients with separate logins, where should we start configuration?
5. (a) What encryption options does L2TP have? (b) What authentication protocols are available as options in pfSense's L2TP configuration?
6. If we are setting up an OpenVPN server and don't want to use the standard Diffie-Hellman algorithm for key generation, what options do we have?
7. What option is available to make OpenVPN server configuration easier?
8. What port must be open for NAT traversal to work?

Further reading

- Virtual Private Networking: *An Overview* – A Microsoft TechNet article: `https://docs.microsoft.com/en-us/previous-versions/windows/it-pro/windows-2000-server/bb742566(v=technet.10)`
- Encryption and Security Protocols in a VPN: A good HowStuffWorks article: `https://computer.howstuffworks.com/vpn7.htm`

9
Multiple WANs

We have not addressed the issue of redundancy and high availability in this volume so far, and topics such as redundancy and load balancing are, for the most part, beyond the scope of this book. Nonetheless, ensuring that our networks have a reliable connection to the internet is something which we should be concerned about. If you operate a business, you will want to ensure that access to the internet is always available, and you will want to eliminate single points of failure and make sure that you are getting the most out of the available bandwidth. We can do this by implementing a multi-WAN setup. Fortunately, pfSense makes the task of setting up multiple WAN interfaces easy.

In this chapter, we will cover the following topics:

- Multi-WAN fundamentals
- Configuring multiple WANs
- Troubleshooting WANs

Technical requirements

Working through the examples in this chapter will require at least one working pfSense firewall with multiple WAN interfaces, either in a real world or virtual environment. It will also help to have two separate internet connections. This can be simulated in a virtual environment. You can also use your home and mobile internet connections, if you have both of these.

Multi-WAN fundamentals

When we want improved uptime and improved throughput with our internet connection, multiple WAN interfaces providing multiple internet connections provide an effective way of accomplishing this. When you first configure pfSense, you must set up a working LAN and WAN interface. You can have more than one WAN interface, and these interfaces are referred to as OPT WAN interfaces.

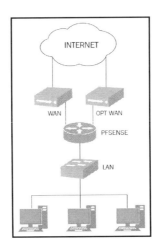

To take full advantage of a system that utilizes multiple WANs, you should have separate internet connections. The ideal scenario is one in which you have separate internet connections from separate internet providers. This is because there is a higher likelihood of a connectivity issue between your network and an internet service provider, thus affecting all connections that go to that provider compared to a connectivity issue affecting multiple providers at the same point in time. In addition, if you have two connections to the same ISP and there is a failure of the entire ISP, then both of your connections will go down. Needless to say, this is nowhere close to the redundancy we seek to achieve. Still, if there is only one ISP in your area, two connections will at least provide more bandwidth than one.

In such a case, if you opt for two connections from the same provider, you should try to obtain a second connection that has a different type and path of cabling than the first connection has. Even if you have connections from different providers, this is good practice. Often, connections carried on the same cabling are subject to the same cable cut (and therefore the same outage).

If you have multiple connections, your connections should not only use different cabling, but they should also have different paths to the internet. This might lessen the risk of using the same ISP. This is because in many cases, different types of connections from the same provider use completely different networks and, therefore, take different paths.

Service-level agreement

After you have done your initial research and have narrowed down your choices but before you have made a final decision on which provider or providers to use, you will probably want to see each provider's **service-level agreement** (**SLA**). The SLA, as we mentioned in Chapter 7, *Traffic Shaping*, is the official commitment between the ISP and the client. This document defines particular aspects of the service that should be provided to the client. An ISP is not required to have an SLA. Nevertheless, many providers have an SLA, and many that do make their SLA available on their website.

Although the SLA might be part of the contract between an ISP and their clients, it might not be part of it. There are several aspects of service that can be defined by the SLA. These can include throughput, mean time between failures, mean times between recovery, mean times between repair, percentage of up-time, and much more. It can also specify which party is responsible for recording faults and paying fees. It may also delineate the procedure for supervising/monitoring performance levels, who to contact when there are issues, and finally, the time frame in which problems will be resolved. Typically, an SLA will also specify the consequences for an ISP not fulfilling its SLA obligations, and in some cases, if the service provider does not abide by its obligations, the client may have the right to terminate the contract, or at least receive a refund for the time during which connectivity is not available.

Redundancy and high availability for internet connections is often more important in a business environment, and this is the most typical scenario in which you will be configuring a multi-WAN setup. In such cases, you may consider acquiring a T1 service, since such connections have been held in high regard for a number of years. In general, the SLA for a T1 connection is more favorable than SLAs for other types of connections. Moreover, a T1 service is seen as more reliable. With pfSense, however, you needn't necessarily lease a T1; you can achieve high levels of reliability at a lesser cost via a multi-WAN setup. Two low-cost broadband connections can provide greater bandwidth and the same or greater level of reliability than a single T1 connection.

Policy-based routing

Another reason for implementing a multi-WAN setup is that such setups make **policy-based routing** possible. This is a form of routing in which routing decisions are made based on administrative policies rather than other criteria such as speed. In this context, it means that pfSense can divert traffic that matches a certain firewall rule to a specific gateway. A simple example of this would be a rule that directs outbound traffic from a certain subnet (for example, the DMZ) to a certain gateway. We can also direct traffic from a specific host instead of a network, or maybe just traffic that uses a certain protocol. Another use for policy-based routing is segregating services based on their priority. You may have a high-quality connection with little bandwidth, such as a T1 connection (1.544 Mbps), and a low-quality connection with a much higher level of bandwidth, such as a typical broadband connection. You could use policy-based routing to send high-priority traffic to the T1, while leaving other permitted (but lower priority) traffic relegated to the broadband connection.

Failover and load balancing

There are two forms of redundancy/high availability associated with multi-WAN setups. The first is **failover** and the second is **load balancing**. Failover involves some gateways having priority over other gateways. Only when all higher priority gateways fail do the lower priority gateways come online. With load balancing, multiple gateways are online at the same time, and each of the online gateways are handling some share of the total WAN traffic. Thus, we have the option of either using additional connections, but only when our primary connection goes down (failover), or using multiple connections to increase total bandwidth (load balancing).

There is, however, one significant limitation regarding bandwidth aggregation. While we are able to use multiple connections in a load balancing gateway group in order to increase overall bandwidth, a single connection will still be routed through a single WAN interface. Assume that we have two connections, each with x Mbps of bandwidth. Combining the two into a load balancing gateway group gives us $2x$ Mbps of aggregate bandwidth. But if one node on our network is downloading a file from an FTP server, this connection will only be able to use x Mbps of bandwidth. Applications that use multiple connections (for example, a BitTorrent client that usually establishes multiple peer-to-peer connections when downloading a file) should be able to utilize the full aggregate bandwidth, and of course, the more users you have on your network, the greater the likelihood is that you will utilize the total available bandwidth.

There are many different algorithms that could potentially be used to determine a gateway group's behavior. pfSense load balancing uses a round-robin algorithm; therefore, requests are distributed sequentially. By default, each gateway handles an equal share of traffic, but different weights can be assigned to each gateway if necessary.

When is a gateway down?

Having multiple WAN interfaces necessitates a means of determining when a gateway is down. In pfSense, this is done by assigning each WAN interface its own monitor IP. pfSense pings the monitor IP continuously. If the monitor IP stops responding, then the gateway is assumed to be down. If the monitor IP is for an OPT WAN interface (in other words, not the primary WAN interface), then pfSense will automatically add a static route, which will divert traffic to the correct gateway within the gateway group. A gateway IP should be an IP on a reliable site; moreover, each WAN interface within a gateway group should have a unique monitor IP so that the monitor IP's failure to respond will not result in multiple gateways going down. WAN interfaces in different gateway groups, however, can have the same monitor IP.

You might be wondering what constitutes a ping failure in the case of gateway monitoring. pfSense uses the following defaults:

- If packet loss in one of the criteria used for determining when a gateway is down and packet loss reaches a rate of 20%, the gateway will go down
- We know that a packet is lost if we send one and do not receive a reply after 2 seconds
- An ICMP probe is sent every half a second
- If latency averages 0.5 seconds and high latency is one of the criteria used for determining when a gateway is down, then the gateway will go down
- The criteria used to determine when a gateway is down can be set by editing the settings for a gateway group (this will be shown later in this chapter)

A gateway will reach alert status when packet loss reaches 10% or latency reaches 0.2 seconds. Alert status means the gateway will remain up, but the background of its listing in **Status | Gateways** will change to yellow. If these default settings are unacceptable, you can adjust them. You can do so by navigating to **System | Routing**, clicking on the **Gateways** tab, and editing the gateway whose values you wish to change. On the **Edit** page for the gateway, click on the **Advanced** button to reveal these settings.

Configuring multiple WANs

Gateway load balancing requires that you set up at least one gateway group, which consists of two or more WAN interfaces. This involves several steps:

1. Adding WAN interfaces and configuring them
2. Configuring DNS servers for each of the newly-created WAN interfaces
3. Forming gateway groups and adding the new interfaces to them
4. Adding firewall rules for each new gateway group

Adding and configuring additional WAN interfaces is not difficult. When you first set up pfSense, the WAN interface is automatically created and configured in the setup wizard. Configuring additional WAN interfaces is not that much different. It involves the following steps:

1. Navigate to **Interfaces | (assign)**, and on the **Interface Assignment** tabs, there will be a tab showing all the existing interface assignments—at a minimum, the WAN and LAN interfaces will be listed here.
2. Select an unused network interface from the **Available network ports** drop-down box and click on the **Add** button corresponding to that drop-down box (on the right side of the row). This will add a new interface; the interface will have a generic name at first, such as OPT1. Hover over the leftmost column in the table and click on the new interface's name.
3. You can also select the new interface from the **Interfaces** menu.
4. On the interface configuration page, check the **Enable** checkbox. Enter an appropriate description for the interface in the **Description** field; this will become the interface's new name.
5. The **IPv4 Configuration Type** and **IPv6 Configuraton Type** drop-down boxes are where you select the appropriate configuration types for the interface IP. If the interface will be receiving an IP address from your ISP—and this likely represents the majority of cases—then the correct selection is either **DHCP**, **DHCP6**, or **SLAAC** for IPv6. If you choose either of these options or both, then there isn't much more you have to do as far as interface configuration goes. pfSense will automatically set up this interface as a gateway.

6. On the other hand, if you chose **Static IPv4** and/or **Static IPv6**, you will have to manually configure the new interface as a gateway. To do so, scroll down to the **Static IPv4/IPv6 Configuration** section of the page and click on the **Add new gateway** button.

7. Clicking on this button will launch a dialog box; this will allow you to configure the most basic options for the gateway. Since the first WAN interface is already the default gateway, you should leave the **Default gateway option** disabled.

8. In the **Gateway name** edit box, you should give the gateway an appropriate name and enter a gateway IP address in the **Gateway IPv4** or **Gateway IPv6** edit box. The IP address of the gateway should be different compared to the interface's IP address, but on the same subnet as the interface.

9. Enter a brief description in the **Description** field.

10. Click on the **Add** button when you're done. There isn't much more that needs to be done for the secondary WAN configuration, unless you have some other options you need to enter that are specific to your connection. For example, you may need to configure advanced DHCP options; if you have a PPP or PPPoE connection, you may have to enter a username and password.

11. You should probably check the **Block private networks and loopback addresses** checkbox and the **Block bogon networks** checkbox (to block non-IANA-assigned networks), as blocking such networks on WAN interfaces is a good practice. When you are done, click on the **Save** button at the bottom of the page, and when the page reloads, click on the **Apply Changes** button.

12. Repeats steps 1 through 11 for as many WAN-type interfaces as you have. If you are configuring interfaces for use with different ISPs, the options you choose in each case may be different.

Next, you must configure the DNS settings for each of the newly-created gateways. To do so, perform these steps:

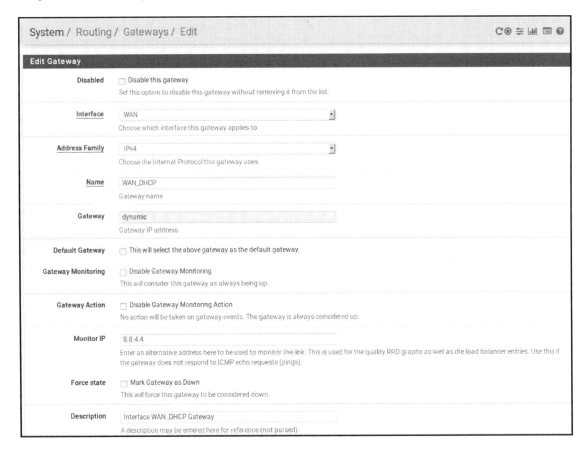

1. Navigate to **System | General Setup**.
2. On the **General Setup** page, in the **DNS Server Settings** section, you should enter a DNS server for each of the new gateways (you can choose the gateway in the drop-down box adjacent to the edit box where you enter the IP address of the DNS server). There should be at least one unique DNS server per gateway in a multi-WAN setup. This is because we are looking to eliminate single points of failure in our configuration.
3. When you have finished configuring the DNS settings, click on the **Save** button at the bottom of the page.
4. Navigate to **System | Routing** and begin gateway configuration.

5. The **Gateways** tab should be the default tab, and on this tab, the newly created gateways should be listed in the table. The gateways will have the names you assigned to them when you created the gateways in the previous series of steps, but only if you configured the gateways manually. Otherwise, they will have names such as WAN2_DHCP or WAN2_DHCP6 (for gateways with interfaces that get their IPs from the ISP), and so on:

   - Two other options on the **Gateways** tab, new to pfSense 2.4, are the **Default gateway IPv4** and **Default gateway IPv6** dropdown boxes. This replaces the **Default Gateway** checkbox on the gateway **Edit** page, and provides an easy way of selecting and changing the default gateway.

6. Click on the **Edit** icon for any of the newly created gateways, and you will notice that there are many more options than there were in the dialog box when you click on the **Add new gateway** button on the interface configuration page:

   - The **Disable this gateway** option allows you to save the gateway configuration while forcing the gateway offline. This can be useful for troubleshooting.
   - The **Interface** drop-down box allows you to change the interface being configured.
   - **Address Family** lets you choose between **IPv4** and **IPv6** addresses.
   - **Gateway** allows you to enter the gateway IP address. If the interface is configured to use DHCP or DHCPv6, this field will be read-only.
   - There is a **Default Gateway** option which allows you to set this gateway as the default.
   - There is a **Disable Gateway Monitoring** option, which, if enabled, causes pfSense to consider the gateway to always be up.
   - There is a **Monitor IP** field, in which you may enter an alternative IP address to monitor the gateway. To determine whether a gateway is up or down, pfSense first pings a gateway; however, having the gateway ping a remote address is often a better indicator of whether a gateway is up. Therefore, if a gateway fails to respond to a ping and a monitor IP is specified, pfSense will have the gateway ping the monitor IP. It is useful to have this as a fallback when a gateway doesn't respond to this ping; therefore, you should probably configure this option. To do so, enter a non-local IP address to ping. If you cannot think of a reliable site to ping, just enter the DNS server's IP address.
   - If the **Mark Gateway as down** option is enabled, pfSense will consider the gateway to be down.

- There is a **Description** field where you can enter a brief, non-parsed description.
- The **Advanced** section, which displays when you click the **Display Advanced** button, also has some interesting options. The **Weight** drop-down box allows you to select the weight for the gateway within a gateway group; higher numbers indicate that the gateway has more weight. As an example, consider a gateway group in which one gateway has a weight of 1 and the other gateway has a weight of 2. The gateway with a weight of 2 will have twice as many connections going through it than the gateway with a weight of 1.
- The **Data Payload** field lets you set the -s parameter of the ping command. This allows you to set the number of data bytes to send (the default is 1).
- The **Latency** thresholds edit boxes are the fields you can set to determine the low and high thresholds for latency in milliseconds. If the low threshold value is met, pfSense sends an alarm, while if the high threshold value is reached when pinging, the gateway's status will be set to down. The defaults of 200/500 should be fine in most cases. There may be other cases where setting the right latency is critical, however, for example, you may have a high latency connection such as a satellite internet connection, and in such a case, you don't want the gateway's status changing to down when the connection is still good.
- The **Packet Loss** threshold fields are where you can specify the low and high thresholds for packet loss. As with **Latency**, if the low threshold value is met, an alarm is sent, while if the high threshold value is met, the gateway is set to down.
- The **Probe Interval** field lets you specify how often an ICMP ping probe is sent; the default value for this parameter is 500 ms.
- The **Loss Interval** is the allowed latency of ping replies—this is the time interval allowed to lapse before packets are considered lost. The default is 2,000 ms.

- The **Time Period** is the period over which results are averaged for packet loss. The default is 60,000 ms.
- The **Alert** interval field lets you enter the time period between checking for an alert condition. The default is 1 second.
- The final option on the page is **Use non-local gateway**. If this option is enabled, a gateway outside of the interface's subnet can be used.
- Click on the **Save** button when you have finished making changes, and then click on the **Apply Changes** button on the main **Routing** page.

As you may have gathered, the settings at the top part of the page for **Gateway** settings contains most of the options you are likely to have to change, and the options under **Advanced Settings** are mostly options that can be kept at their default values. Nonetheless, it's good to know that you can change these values if needed. Once upon a time, pfSense gateway pings were hardcoded in such a way that a reply was received 5 seconds after a ping request was considered successful. Moreover, a ping request was considered successful if at least 1 reply was received from every 5 requests. This meant that pfSense tolerated up to 80% packet loss (and a high level of latency) before a gateway was considered to be down. These extremely tolerant settings were designed to eliminate false positives and flapping (a case where an interface is alternatively advertised as up and down in rapid succession, due to the criteria for an interface being down not being met consistently). However, these settings also meant that a gateway could still be up when in reality the packet loss was so high that the connection was unusable. The default packet loss setting of 20% is probably good for most cases. The value you are most likely to have to adjust is **Latency** thresholds, and even then only for certain types of connections.

Once the gateways are configured, we can set up the actual gateway group. This can be done by following this procedure:

1. From the main **Routing** page, click on the **Gateway Groups** tab. This tab will display a table that shows all the configured gateways (it should be empty at first).
2. Click on the **Add** button at the bottom of the table to add a new gateway.

3. On the **Edit** page for the gateway group, you have a few options:
   - In the **Group Name** field, enter the name of the group.
   - Under **Gateway Priority**, you have two configurable options, each with its own set of drop-down boxes. The **Tier** drop-down box allows you to select the tier on which a gateway exists. You might recall that with tiers, lower numbers have priority over higher numbers. Therefore, gateways on the same tier are load balanced with each other, while gateways on a higher tier are inactive as long as a gateway on a lower tier is still up (a failover setup). If we set WAN_DHCP to **Tier 1** and WAN2_DHCP to **Tier 2**, then WAN_DHCP will get all the traffic for the gateway group while WAN2_DHCP will not be used unless WAN_DHCP goes down. But if both WAN_DHCP and WAN2_DHCP are set to **Tier 1**, both gateways will be active at the same time and handle a share of the total traffic. Set the tiers to the same or different values depending on whether you want a load balancing or failover gateway group.
   - The **Virtual IP** drop-down box is where you can select the virtual IP for each gateway; however, this only applies to instances in which the gateway group is used as an endpoint for a local Dynamic DNS (DDNS), IPsec, or OpenVPN connection. In most cases, you can leave it set to **Interface Address**.
   - There is only one **Trigger Level** drop-down box for each gateway group. Here, you can specify when to trigger the exclusion of a gateway member. You have the following choices:
       - **Member down**: This one is obvious. A member is excluded when it fails to respond to a ping attempt/fails to ping the monitor IP.
       - **Packet Loss**: Exclusion is triggered when packet loss is unacceptably high (the actual threshold is set during gateway configuration; see the previous points for more details).
       - **High Latency**: Exclusion is triggered when latency is unacceptably high (again, the actual threshold is set during gateway configuration).
       - **Packet Loss or High Latency**: In this case, a group member is excluded when either packet loss or high latency is too high.

- You can enter a brief description in the **Description** field. When you are done making changes, click on the **Save** button, and then click the **Apply Changes** button on the main **Routing** page.

One procedure you can follow for the sake of completeness is to configure failover groups for each of the gateways (assuming you didn't configure the first group as a failover). This is a relatively simple process:

1. On the **Gateway Groups** tab of the **Routing** page, click on the **Add** button.
2. In the **Group Name** edit box, type an appropriate name for the group (for example, FAILOVER1). In the **Gateway Priority Tier** drop-down box, select the appropriate tier for each connection. The first WAN connection should be set to **Tier 1**, and the second should be set to **Tier 2**.
3. In the **Trigger Level** drop-down box, set the desired trigger level.
4. Type an appropriate description in the **Description** field. Then, click on the **Save** button and click on the **Apply Changes** button.
5. Now, you want to create another failover group, only this time reverse the settings for the tiers so that they are the opposite of what they were for the first group. Click on the **Add** button again, or, if you want to make life even easier, click on the **Copy** icon in the entry for the first failover group. This will make a new gateway group, with all values defaulting to the values of the first failover group. Configure another gateway group, but set the second WAN connection to **Tier 1** and the first WAN connection to **Tier 2**. When you are done, click on the **Save** button, and then on the main **Routing** page, click on **Apply Changes**.

The gateway group is now configured, but without firewall rules for the group, no network traffic will be directed through the group. You could create a rule for each interface that will be using the group, but in cases where the group will be used on more than a single network, this would seem to be a good opportunity to use a floating rule. To create a floating rule for the gateway group, follow these steps:

1. Navigate to **Firewall | Rules**, and from there, click on the **Floating** tab. To add a new rule, click on one of the **Add** buttons.
2. Keep the **Action** set to **Pass**; we are, after all, trying to pass traffic.
3. In the **Interface** listbox, select every interface that will be using the gateway group (this is potentially every non-WAN interface, but isn't necessarily so).
4. Rules involving gateways can only be one-way rules, so in the **Direction** drop-down box, select **out** (it applies to traffic leaving the interface).
5. In the **Protocol** drop-down box, select **any**.

2. The **Source** field should be set to an alias that refers to all the interfaces selected in the **Interface** listbox. If you want to keep things simple, then leave **Source** set to **any**. The **Destination** field can be left set to **any**.

3. Scroll down to the **Advanced Options** found in the **Extra Options** section. Click on the **Show Advanced** button to show additional options.

4. The third-to-last option will be the **Gateway** drop-down box. In this drop-down box, select the first gateway group you created previously.

5. Click the **Save** button on the main **Firewall** page and click **Apply Changes**.

Although it is easier to set up a floating rule, if you want to set up per-interface policy-based routing, you can do that as well:

1. Navigate to **Firewall** | **Rules** and click on the tab for the interface for which you want to set the policy. On that page, click on one of the **Add** buttons at the bottom of the page.

2. If all you want to do is create a general rule directing all interface traffic to a specific gateway, there are very few default values that need to be changed. Change the default **Protocol** from **TCP** to **any**, and change the **Gateway** to the interface that you want to direct traffic to (again, this can be found by clicking on the **Display Advanced** button and scrolling down).

3. If your policies are more granular, you should make the necessary changes to the rule so that the rule only matches traffic you want to be directed to the gateway.

4. You can enter a brief **Description** in the description field.

5. Click on the **Save** button when finished.

6. Although you are making specific rules for each interface, you may still want to have a floating rule as a fallback. This way, all traffic that doesn't match the policy-based routing rules will go to the gateway group. If you create such a floating rule, make sure that the **Quick** option on the floating rule is disabled. Otherwise, the floating rule will take precedence over all other policy rules. As always with rules, make sure the order is correct.

7. To be completely thorough, you will need to create rules for the two failover gateway groups (if you created such groups previously). To do so, click the **Copy** icon in the table entry for the new rule, and create a new rule for each of the failover groups. The only changes you need to make are in the **Gateway** drop-down box and you also probably want to change the **Description** field). Click on **Save** when you have finished created all the necessary rules.

8. On the main **Rules** page, click on the **Apply Changes** button when you are done creating and editing rules.

In most cases, you will not have to configure static routes. This is because when a route needs to change as a result of a gateway going offline, pfSense will automatically create a temporary static route to re-route traffic to a gateway that is up. In some cases, however, we will need static routes. As an example, consider traffic that originates from pfSense. This includes such traffic as traffic from services, ping requests, and similar things. Policy-based routing only works with traffic that enters the router from the outside. It does not apply to traffic that originates from pfSense. Such traffic cannot be tagged for alternate routing. The solution in such cases is to create a static route. Fortunately, adding a static route is easy:

1. Navigate to **System | Routing**; from there, click on the **Static Routes** tab.
2. At the bottom of the page, click on the **Add** button. This will take you to the **Edit** page for the static route.
3. On this page, enter the destination network for the route in the **Destination** network field. This involves entering an IP address and a CIDR.
4. Select the correct gateway for the route in the **Gateway** drop-down box. There is also a link that allows you to create a new gateway.
5. Note that there is a **Disable this static route** option if we ever have to disable this route. You can enter a description in the **Description** field.
6. When finished, click on the **Save** button and then the **Apply Changes** button.

There are also two settings of interest available by navigating to **System | Advanced**, clicking on the **Miscellaneous** tab, and scrolling to the **Gateway Monitoring** section:

- The **State Killing on Gateway Failure** option, if enabled, causes all states to be flushed when a gateway goes down. If this option is not enabled, active states from a gateway that goes down will be transferred to other gateways in the gateway group. This may be undesirable if you don't want persistent connections to be transferred; hence, this option is available.
- The **Skip rules when gateway is down** option, if enabled, will change the default behavior regarding what happens to a rule specifying a gateway in cases where the gateway is down. The default behavior is to make an implicit rule without the gateway that is down. However, you may want to just skip the rule, so this option is provided.

If you completed the preceding steps, then your gateway group should be fully functional. Nevertheless, you will probably want to check to ensure that the gateway group is functional. To do so, follow these steps:

1. First navigate to **Status | Gateways**; there are two tabs on this page: **Gateways** and **Gateway Groups**. Stay on the **Gateways** tab first.

2. On the **Gateways** tab, there is a table showing all configured gateways. The meaning of the **Name**, **Gateway**, **Monitor**, and **Description** fields should be pretty obvious by now. The following not-as-obvious fields also contain critical information:
   - **RTT (Round Trip Time)**: This measures the ping round trip time in milliseconds. RTT is averaged over the calculation interval specified for the gateway.
   - **RTTsd (Round Trip Time standard deviation)**: Introduced in pfSense 2.3, this is the standard deviation of the round trip time. Once again, RTTsd is averaged over the calculation interval specified for the gateway.
   - **Loss**: Packet loss (over the calculation interval)
   - **Status**: Only two values—either online or offline

3. You can also test the gateway group monitoring by unplugging each of the WAN interfaces one by one. Then, see how long it takes for the **Gateway** status page to report the gateway as offline.

4. If the amount of time it takes to report a gateway as down, you may have to revisit the **Gateway Groups** page and adjust the **Trigger Level** setting for the group. You may also have to adjust the **Latency or Packet Loss** threshold for the gateway.

DNS considerations

Since policy-based routing does not apply to traffic generated by pfSense, the router's internal routing table determines the route to DNS servers. Because of this, if static routes are not configured, pfSense will only use the primary WAN interface to access DNS servers. Although this may be what you want, you must configure static routes if you want pfSense to use the correct WAN interface for DNS queries.

If you do not configure status routes for these WAN interfaces, then you will face the following issues:

- It can be a problem if you are using your ISP's DNS servers. This is because ISPs will often block recursive DNS queries from outside of their network. You can eliminate this problem by using alternative DNS servers, such as the ones run by OpenDNS, or the privacy-friendly DNS servers operated by CloudFlare.
- If no static routes are configured and the primary WAN interface goes down, then you will have lost the only interface with a route to DNS servers, and therefore would be left with no means of DNS resolution.

One of the ways to solve this problem is to use the DNS server for a secondary WAN gateway as the monitor IP address for the gateway. In this case, pfSense will automatically add a static route for the gateway's DNS server, and we needn't add a static route manually.

You can always add a new rule, though. To add a static route to 1.1.1.1, for example, navigate to **System | Routing**, click on the **Static Routes** tab, and from there, click on the **Add** button. The **Destination network** field should have 1.1.1.1/32 (1.1.1.1 with a CIDR of 32). Select the secondary gateway in the **Gateway** drop-down box. Then, enter a brief description in the **Description** field and click the **Save** button and **Apply Changes**.

NAT considerations

If you use **Network Address Translation (NAT)** in your setup, then you should make sure that there is a set of outbound rules for each additional WAN interface. If **Outbound NAT** is set to **Automatic outbound NAT rule generation**, then you do not have anything to worry about, as the necessary outbound NAT rules will be generated automatically. If **Outbound NAT** is set to **Manual outbound NAT rule generation**, then you will find it necessary to edit the rules in order to direct traffic. This would be the case, for example, if you have a **CARP (Common Address Redundancy Protocol)** setup, and **Outbound NAT** is set up to direct outbound traffic to a WAN virtual IP. Basically, you will have to create a new set of outbound NAT rules for each additional WAN interface. You can use the existing outbound NAT rules as a template for the new rules. Use the **Copy** option and just change the **Interface** setting to the secondary WAN interface and the **Address** to the secondary WAN's virtual IP address.

If you have any 1:1 NAT mappings, take into consideration that each of these mappings specifies a unique WAN interface. Furthermore, such mappings override any other outbound NAT settings for the interface on which they are configured. If you want these mappings to work on additional WAN interfaces, you will have to add new entries for them.

Finally, if you have any Port Forwarding entries, note that these entries also specify a unique WAN interface. If you want to open a port on multiple WAN interfaces, you can do this. The easiest way is to use the **Copy** option to create a new rule based on the old rule. Change the interface to the new secondary WAN interface; the **Destination** will automatically update the secondary WAN interface's address when you do so. Update the description in the **Description** field if you like. Then, click on the **Save** button; on the main NAT page, click on **Apply Changes**.

Third-party packages

Unfortunately, there aren't many packages available that enhance pfSense's multi-WAN capabilities. The only package I know of that currently exists is **gwled**, which allows you to use LEDs on certain embedded devices to monitor gateways. After you install gwled, a new option will appear on the **Interfaces** menu called **Gateway Status LEDs**. If you navigate to this option, you can control the options for this package. Checking the **Enable gwled** checkbox enables this package—it is not enabled by default. The package allows you to monitor the gateways using LEDs #2 and #3 on supported devices. You need to enable each LED individually, and you must also specify to which gateway each LED corresponds using the drop-down box for each LED.

Troubleshooting

Multi-WAN gateway groups are not difficult to add and configure, but you may nevertheless have to troubleshoot such a setup. If you do, there are several problems you are likely to encounter:

- You may encounter a connectivity issue with your primary or secondary connection
- You may encounter a misconfiguration in your setup
- You may encounter a situation where pfSense thinks a gateway is up when it is actually down, or vice-versa

The first point seems fairly obvious—that connectivity issues may cause problems with multi-WAN setups—but you will want to make sure that both (or all, if you have more than two connections) connections are working, independent of the gateway group. If the secondary connection represents a low percentage of our overall bandwidth, or if it is part of a failure group and therefore is inactive as long as the primary connection is up, then we might not notice that it is not working until the primary connection fails. Thus, ensuring that both connections work when we first set up multiple WAN connections will potentially save us some grief. If we are troubleshooting, ensuring that both connections work first can easily save us a significant amount of troubleshooting time.

Testing your multi-WAN setup before declaring it to be functional is a good idea. First, simulate a WAN interface going down. In the first case, you should disconnect the cable between pfSense and your primary connection and confirm that you are still connected to the internet. Confirm that the DNS resolution is still working. Then, reconnect the primary connection, disconnect the secondary connection, and repeat this process.

You may have a cable, DSL, or some other connection with a modem. Try unplugging the modem and also unplugging the connection between the modem and the demarcation point and see what happens. For a T1 connection, try unplugging the internet connection from the router—then, either unplug or power off the router. If you have more than two WAN interfaces in your setup, you may want to perform this test with different combinations of interfaces being up and down—as long as one interface in a gateway group is up, you should still have some level of internet connectivity and also be able to perform DNS resolution.

 The **point of demarcation** is the physical point at which the public network of a telecommunications network ends and where the private network of a customer begins. It is usually at this point where the cable physically enters the building.

This testing is often invaluable; you will often uncover a configuration error that you would not have uncovered under normal circumstances. For example, what if the secondary WAN interface uses the public IP address of the primary WAN connection as a monitor IP? If this is the case, when you power off the modem connected to the primary WAN connection, the secondary WAN connection will go down, even though the secondary connection is solid and should still be up.

Misconfiguration can be a problem. Although creating a gateway group is easy enough, there are many steps needed to make sure that everything works. There must be NAT rules for each new WAN interface and there must be firewall rules to direct traffic to the appropriate gateway group. Check to make sure that any policy-based rules work as well. By default, the rules will direct traffic to the default gateway—so when the primary WAN interface is still up, everything might seem to be working. But when the primary WAN interface goes down, internet connectivity will be lost, even though there are still functional interfaces within the gateway group. You should check the firewall and NAT rules to make sure that they are doing what they are intended to do.

If the flow of traffic seems to work as it should, but DNS resolution does not work, then the issue may be that pfSense does not apply its internal routing tables to internal traffic. For that reason, you may have to configure a static route for the secondary WAN's DNS server.

There may be a failure with gateway load balancing in which one of the WAN connections in a gateway group no longer has internet connectivity, but remains up. The reason for this may be that the monitor IP is still responding—this would be the case if you set the monitor IP to an IP on your internal network. As a result, pfSense thinks the connection is still good. If this is the case, make sure that the monitor IP is correct and specifies an external IP address.

But alas, even if the monitor IP is an external IP, our problems may not be over. The network administrator at the external site we are pinging may see pfSense's pings to the site. The admin might suspect that these pings are the beginning of a denial-of-service attack, and might then block your pings. When the monitor pings fail, your gateway will go down, even though the network interface is still functioning and has internet connectivity. This could happen whenever you set a monitor IP you don't control. The best solution is to use a site for the monitor IP that is external to your network, but is a site that you control. If you cannot do this, the next best solution is to use a DNS server as your monitor IP, since a DNS server normally will not block your pings.

In many cases, when you connect to certain websites, they will store session information such as your public IP address. This includes such sites as e-commerce sites. If you subsequently connect to the same site through a different public IP address, then the site might not function as it should, because it will see a different IP address and assume that a new session should be started. The **Use Sticky Connections** option is designed to eliminate this problem. This option directs traffic from such websites to the same WAN address, as long as there are states that refer to the connection in the state table.

If you have implemented load balancing with your gateway group, you should verify that it works. One way to do this is to visit a website that tells you what your public IP address is. If you don't know the URL of any of these sites, just do a web search for `what is my IP address`. If you refresh the page several times, you should see your public IP address change. You may have to reload this page several times before you see a change. There may be other traffic on your network, and you may have set the weights on your gateway group to favor one gateway heavily.

If your IP address never changes, you should make sure that you are really reloading the page and not accessing the page from a cache. This might be the case if you have a browser cache or are using a web proxy. In addition, make sure that you do not have sticky connections enabled or some other option that enables persistent connections. If your IP address does not change, try deleting your web cache, visiting different what is my IP-type sites, and trying different web browsers. If you still can't get your IP address to change, you might have to troubleshoot further.

Another way to test load balancing is with command-line utilities such as **traceroute**. The **traceroute** utility is a command that displays the route a packet trackets to a site. It also displays the transit delay at each step, and is available on Windows, Linux/BSD, and macOS. We will cover **traceroute** in greater detail in `Chapter 11`, *Diagnostics and Troubleshooting*.

Finally, there is the possibility that your packet loss and latency settings are generating false positives. The opposite could also be true, and one or more of your connections could be down without pfSnese detecting it. If one of your gateways is generating false positives, then navigate to **System | Routing** and on the **Gateways** tab, edit the **Advanced Settings** for the gateway that is generating the false positives. Sometimes, increasing the time period over which results are averaged can eliminate this problem.

Summary

In this chapter, we discussed how multi-WAN configurations can be used to improve your bandwidth and increase the reliability of your internet connection. We covered some of the basics of choosing ISPs to improve the likelihood that multiple connections leads to increased uptime. Then, we explained in detail the various steps required to configure a multi-WAN connection in pfSense. Finally, we enumerated some of the things than can go wrong with a gateway group, and how to troubleshoot such issues.

Setting up multiple WAN interfaces requires configuring some static routes. In the next chapter, `Chapter 10`, *Routing and Bridging*, we will cover routing in greater detail.

Questions

1. What is the official agreement between an ISP and a customer referred to as?
2. Suppose we have a multi-WAN setup. If our primary connection goes down and we find we cannot access a site through its name, but can access it through its IP address, what is the likely cause?
3. Again, suppose we have a multi-WAN setup. If our primary connection goes down and our secondary connection is up, but we cannot access the internet, what are the possible causes? Identify at least one cause.
4. Suppose we have a multi-WAN setup with a satellite internet connection as our secondary connection. If the secondary connection is set to down by pfSense even though internet connectivity is possible through this connection, what is the likely cause?
5. (a) Why do we normally have to create static routes for DNS servers in a multi-WAN setup? (b) How can we avoid having to create static routes for DNS servers in a way that ensures DNS resolution will work with all WAN connections?
6. How can we prevent states from being transferred to a secondary gateway when the primary gateway goes down?
7. Assume we have a multi-WAN setup with two WAN connections. (a) What tier do we set the gateways to if we want to set up the gateway group for load balancing? (b) What tier do we set the gateways to if we want to set up the gateway group for failover?
8. (a) What problem might result from setting the monitor IP to an IP address that is within the internal network? (b) What problem might result from setting the monitor IP to an IP address that is external to our network, but is not within our control?

Further reading

- Configuring multi-WAN load balancing (an excerpt from the pfSense 2 Cookbook): `https://www.packtpub.com/mapt/book/networking_and_servers/9781849514866/6/ch06lvl1sec49/configuring-multi-wan-load-balancing`
- Using Multiple IPv4 WAN Connections (part of Netgate's pfSense documentation): `https://www.netgate.com/docs/pfsense/routing/multi-wan.html`

10
Routing and Bridging

No primer on pfSense would be complete without some discussion of routing and bridging. These two networking concepts are often employed for similar reasons, but there are some significant differences between them. **Routing** is the process of moving packets between two or more networks. It is most commonly used to move traffic between the public internet and private networks. **Bridging** is the process of connecting two network segments together. The most significant difference is that routing involves inter-network traffic, while bridging involves intra-network traffic.

When pfSense is initially installed and configured, WAN and LAN interfaces are created, and pfSense can route traffic between these two networks with ease. In fact, it can easily route traffic between any interfaces directly connected to it. It will not, however, know how to route traffic to networks not directly connected to it unless you define a static route for it. Bridging, however, is not something that is done in typical network conditions. It allows us to extend a network beyond a single segment. Broadcast traffic will still flood both sides of the bridge, but each side of the bridge will form its own collision domain. In the days before switches (in which each port forms its own collision domain), this was an effective way of expanding a single network while ensuring a smooth flow of traffic. One significant limitation of bridging in pfSense is that two bridged interfaces can only pass traffic if the firewall rules allow it, at least by default.

This chapter will cover the following topics:

- Routing and bridging fundamentals
- Routing
- Bridging
- Troubleshooting

Technical requirements

To work through the examples in this chapter, you will need at least one working pfSense router (in either a real or virtual environment), and one other router. The second router need not be a pfSense router (any consumer-grade router will do).

Routing and bridging fundamentals

This chapter deals with both bridging (joining network segments together) and routing (sending data from one network to another). Bridging is the simpler of the two concepts, so we will cover it first.

Bridging fundamentals

Network bridging occurs at the Data link layer (Layer 2) of the OSI model and the Link layer of the Network model. A simple bridge is simple to a repeater, which extends a network segment beyond the length that would normally be allowed by amplifying the signal. One of the differences is that the two network segments connected by a bridge may use different forms of media (with repeaters, the media must be the same, so you won't see a 100-Base-T segment and a 1000 Base-T segment connected by a repeater). Another difference is that bridges use a store-and-forward mechanism to forward packets. This creates two collision domains, making it possible to add more nodes to the network without the number of collisions becoming unacceptably high.

A simple bridge forwards packets to the other side of the bridge, and doesn't care whether the destination host is on the other side of the bridge. Another type of bridge is a transparent bridge. Such bridges have the capability of learning which side of the bridge hosts are on, and then use this information to decide whether or not to forward packets. Transparent bridges contain a database. This database is empty at first, and packets are sent to both sides of the bridge regardless of the location of the destination host. A transparent bridge will gradually learn which side of the bridge a host is on, by observing which side of the bridge from which the host sends. This information gets entered into the database, and eventually, the bridge will only forward packets to the other side of the bridge if the target host is on the other side of the bridge.

An example of a transparent bridge at work involves an imaginary network with three nodes, which we will call A, B, and C. Assume A and B are on one side of the bridge, and C is on the other side. Imagine A begins a session with B. Packets reach the bridge, and the bridge, not knowing initially that B is on the same side of the bridge as A, floods both sides of the bridge with B's packets. When B replies, the bridge learns that B is on the same side of the bridge as A. As a result, the bridge will no longer forward traffic between B and A to the other side. If B begins a session with C, then the bridge will initially flood both sides with B's packets once again, not knowing C's location. Once the bridge learns where C is, traffic between B and C across the bridge.

Bridges can, in the form of hubs and switches, be used to partition networks. You might recall from the previous chapters that we normally create different subnets by giving each subnet their own interface. Nodes on the same subnet connect to the same switch, which in turn connects to the interface for that subnet. Another way of partitioning the network into different subnets is to use VLANs, which enables us to have multiple subnets on the same interface. A third possibility, however, is to use stackable hubs or switches, with each backbone hub/switch acting as a bridge between network segments on the same subnet. This entails the following steps:

1. Our private network is partitioned into different subnets that represent parts of the network we want to keep separate, for example, a DEVELOPERS subnet and ENGINEERING subnet. Each subnet gets its own interface (for example, fxp0 for DEVELOPERS and fxp1 for ENGINEERING).
2. A backbone hub is connected into each interface.
3. Two or more switches are connected to each backbone hub, thus partitioning the subnets into different segments.

This configuration may not be quite as advantageous as using VLANs to partition networks into subnets, but it does provide several advantages:

- VLANs require managed switches. A configuration using backbone hubs can be implemented with unmanaged switches, which are less expensive.
- The backbone hub allows nodes on the same network to communicate with each other, regardless of what segment they are on. At the same time, traffic between two nodes on the same segment does not reach the backbone hub, and it does not affect users on other segments, making this setup superior to one in which the entire network shares a single switch.

- Providing each network with its own backbone hub acts to extend the total maximum allowed distance between a node and the router. On a 1000BASE-T network, for example, the maximum distance between devices is 100 meters (a device can be a node, a switch, a hub, a repeater or a bridge). If a network has a single switch, and the switch connects to the router, then a node can be at most 200 meters from the router or from another node on the subnet. Adding a backbone hub extends the total possible distance between a node and the router by another 100 meters, and between two nodes on the same subnet by 200 meters.
- If a nonbackbone switch fails, the backbone hub will detect the problem. It will then disable the port on the backbone to which it is connected. As a result, the malfunctioning switch will not affect the rest of the network, and nodes on the other network segment will still be able to communicate with each other.
- We can add network segments to each of the networks by plugging another switch into the backbone hub for that network. Thus this configuration is relatively scalable.
- Our subnets are separate; the DEVELOPERS subnet cannot communicate with the ENGINEERING subnet and vice versa unless we create firewall rules to allow it; thus the configuration provides security.

This type of configuration still isn't quite as flexible as partitioning networks into VLANs. With this configuration, if we want to add network segments, we must plug them into the backbone for that subnet, limiting the new segment's total distance from the router. With VLANs, we can add to a subnet by plugging a managed switch into one of the trunk ports of any switch on the network. In addition, we are without the advantages of VLANs, which is that we could make VLAN assignments based on MAC addresses. As a result, with VLANs we can move nodes around, and pfSense will assign the node to the correct VLAN. With a configuration involving stackable hubs, such automatic assignment is not possible, and a node must be connected to a switch that is physically connected to the correct interface.

Another weakness of using stackable hubs is that the backbone hub for each network represents a single point of failure. If the stackable hub for a subnet goes down, connectivity between different segments is lost, and so is connectivity to the router (and, therefore to the internet). We can solve this problem by introducing redundant backbones to our network.

Adding redundant backbone hubs, however, creates a new problem. If a node on DEVELOPERS1 wants to start a session with a node on DEVELOPERS2, then the switch for DEVELOPERS1 will generate two copies of the frame whose target is the node on DEVELOPERS2. One copy goes to the first backbone hub for the subnet, and the other copy goes to the second backbone hub for the subnet. Then each of these hubs sends the frame to DEVELOPERS2. If there are only two network segments, but what if there is another network segment? If two nodes on the same segment establish a session, then traffic doesn't reach the backbone hubs, so there is no problem. But if a node on DEVELOPERS1 wants to establish a session with a node on the same network but a different segment, the backbone hub will not know whether the destination node is on DEVELOPERS2 or DEVELOPERS3, so each hub will send a copy to both, for a total of four frames. Thus, we can see how the number of frames generated can easily get out of hand and crash the network. Even if the backbone hubs are capable of learning where the nodes reside, initially, they don't know where any node is, so the same problem exists.

The solution to this problem is to avoid loops within the subnet, and the way to do this is with a spanning tree protocol. With such a protocol, bridges communicate with each other to determine a spanning tree; this is a subset of the original network topology that does not contain any loops. When the spanning tree algorithm is run, certain interfaces will be disconnected, creating the spanning tree. If one of the network devices fail, then the algorithm can be run again. Running it again will determine what interfaces need to be activated to make the new spanning tree.

It might be useful to discuss how **Spanning Tree Protocol** (**STP**) works, since you may make use of it if you implement bridges. The following diagram illustrates the process:

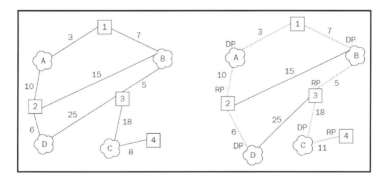

The figure on the left is the network before the spanning tree has been generated. In this diagram, there is a network with several bridges and several network segments. The bridges are represented with boxes and segments are represented with clouds.

The numbers in the boxes represent the bridge IDs. For the sake of completeness, assume that each network segment has a cost metric of 1. The spanning tree is generated using the following procedure:

1. The algorithm starts by choosing a root bridge; the root bridge is simply the bridge with the lowest bridge ID. This is Bridge 1.
2. Each bridge determines the least cost path to the root bridge. The cost of traversing a certain path is simply the sum of the cost metrics of each segment along the path. The port that provides a path to the least cost path to the root bridge becomes designated as the **root port** (**RP**) for that bridge.
3. The next step is the bridges determining the least cost path running from each segment to the root bridge. The port connecting each segment to the root bridge becomes designated as the **designated port** (**DP**) for each network segment.
4. Each port that is not a root port or a designated port then becomes a blocked port. Blocked ports are not part of the spanning tree.

The figure on the right represents the spanning tree after root ports and designated ports have been assigned. The spanning tree is outlined in red and all ports not connected to a red segment are blocked ports.

Routing fundamentals

Routing takes place on the Network layer (Layer 3) of the OSI model, and on the Network layer of the Network model. While switches are store-and-forward devices that use MAC addresses to identify nodes, routers are also store-and-forward devices, but they use IP addresses to identify nodes. Routers (and Layer 3 switches, for that matter) allow us to move data between networks. A router is also responsible for maintaining information about other routers on the network, which it stores in tables. There are also several different protocols that enable a router to learn the topology of a network.

A router can do everything a switch or hub can, and has more functionality. The obvious difference is that it is capable of handling internetwork traffic, but many routers also have firewall capabilities and the ability to use the shortest path to a node. As our networks become more complex, these features become tremendously useful.

There are two broad categories of routing, and both of them will be discussed in this chapter:

- **Static routing**: A static route is a routing entry that we enter manually into the router's routing table. Sometimes adding a static route is unavoidable. In the previous chapter, we needed to add a static route for DNS traffic for additional WAN interfaces. We may also have networks that are not directly connected to pfSense. In this case, pfSense will not know where to send traffic to this network; creating a static route would solve this problem. It is not an ideal solution, though: a router that relies on static routes is not very fault tolerant; it cannot detect changes on the network. This brings us to dynamic routing.

- **Dynamic routing**: This is implemented by dynamically configuring routing tables through an algorithm. The means by which this is done is through dynamic routing protocols. This includes **Routing Information Protocol** (RIP) and **Open Shortest Path First** (OSPF). Both of these protocols work on Layer 3 of the OSI model and the Network layer of the Network model. We can divide routing protocols into the following two broad categories:

    - **Distance-vector routing protocols**: This group of protocols determine the best path to a node based on distance. These protocols count the number of routers through which a packet must pass in order to reach the destination, with each router having a hop count of one. It has the advantage of only having to communicate with neighboring routers that are configured to use the same distance-vector protocol. A router sends all or part of its routing table to such routers, who then amend their routing tables and inform their neighbors of the changes. Algorithms used in distance-vector protocols include the Bellman-Ford algorithm, the Ford-Fulkerson algorithm, and DUAL FSM. One of the problems with this method is the possibility of infinite loops. For example, consider the case of routers A, B, and C. A is connected to B, while B is connected to both A and C. B advertises its route to C back to A, which in turn updates its routing tables and advertises its route to C back to B, even though the route runs through B. If the link between B and C goes down, B will consult its routing table, sees that A has a route to C, and sends traffic destined for C to A. A will in turn send this traffic back to B, resulting in an infinite loop. Two ways of avoiding this outcome are split-horizon and split-horizon with poison reverse. Split horizon simply means that a router will not advertise a route back to the router from which it learned the route. This would solve the case in our example; A would not advertise its route to C back to B, since it learned the route from B.

Split-horizon with poison-reverse allows a router to advertise a route back to the router from which it learned the route, but the route metric is set to infinity, which also solves the problem. Once the link between B and C goes down, B will not send packets destined for C to A, since A's path to C has a route metric of infinity. Some examples of distance-vector protocols include RIPv1, RIPv2, and **Interior Gateway Routing Protocol** (**IGRP**).

- **Link-state routing protocols**: This is the other main class of routing protocols and involves each router constructing a map of its connectivity to the entire network. This map takes the form of a graph. Thus, each router independently calculates the best logical path to each destination and adds the information to its routing table. These protocols have advantages over distance-vector protocols: each router has a complete map of the network, making it less likely that there will be a loop. It is easier to troubleshoot networks using link-state protocols, and changes in the network will tend to be detected more quickly. There are also some disadvantages. The database of paths requires more memory and processor power than a distance-vector routing table would. The database size, however, can be minimized if it is carefully designed. The initial discovery process generates a great deal of traffic as well. This can degrade network performance during this initial period. One example of such a protocol is OSPF.

There are several dynamic routing protocols available; not all of them are available with pfSense. They are explained as follows:

- **RIP**: This is an old—in fact, it's the oldest—and popular distance-vector protocol. RIPv1 used classful routing. Since the routing updates did not have subnet information, all subnets had to be of the same size within the same network class. The distance between routers was known as a hop. The maximum distance between hops was 15; 16 hops represented infinity, or an unreachable route. RIPv1 also did not have support for router authentication. Updates were done via broadcast packets. RIP uses UDP over port 520. RIPv2 improved upon RIPv1 in many ways. It introduced support for classless routing, and also support for using multicasts to send the routing table, as well as MD5 authentication. The maximum hop count remained at 15, primarily to maintain compatibility with RIPv1. The latest version of RIP, RIP next generation (RIPng), is an extension of RIPv2, which supports IPv6, does not support RIPv1 update authentication, and sends updates on port 521 instead of the reserved RIP port 520.

- **OSPF**: This link-state protocol constructs a topology map of the network using link-state information, in other words, which routers have turned on, off, or restarted.
- **IGRP**: This is a proprietary distance-vector protocol. It was developed by Cisco and increases the maximum hop count to 255. It also allows multiple metrics for each route, and is a classful routing protocol (so all addresses within an address class must have the same subnet mask). The increase of the maximum hop count addressed one of the main shortcomings of RIP.
- **Enhanced Interior Gateway Routing Protocol (EIGRP)**: This is an update to IGRP, and as with RIPv2, it supports classless routing. Furthermore, it does not send the entire routing table to neighboring routers. Rather, it only sends incremental updates. Although EIGRP began life as a proprietary protocol, parts of the protocol were converted to an open standard in 2013.
- **Border Gateway Protocol (BGP)**: This is a distance-vector protocol that uses TCP and is used for routing within an autonomous system.

Routing

pfSense does most of its routing transparently. For example, if we have two local networks, LAN and DMZ, the firewall rules allow traffic between the networks. If a node on LAN tries to establish a session with a node on DMZ, pfSense will send packets to the right network, assuming that the network is directly connected to pfSense. If a node on LAN is trying to establish a session with a remote node, then packets that have the remote node as their destination will be sent to a gateway. There are some special cases, however, where this form of transparent routing isn't enough, and we will discuss them in this section.

Static routes

We may have local networks that are reachable through a router other than pfSense's default gateway. In such cases, we need to configure a static route. To illustrate this, we will present a simple example of a router connected to the LAN network.

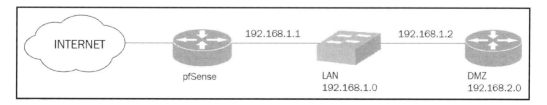

In this case, the LAN interface has an IP address of `192.168.1.1`; this is a static IP address. We also have the DMZ router connected to the switch for the LAN network. DMZ's WAN-side interface has an IP address of `192.168.1.2` (assume this is also a static IP address). DMZ is not directly connected to pfSense, and the DMZ network is not reachable through pfSense's default gateway. In fact, the gateway will block the DMZ's packet, since as a WAN interface, it has been configured to block private networks. In order for routing to the DMZ network to work, we must define a static route.

To set up a static route, we must first add `192.168.1.2` as a gateway and then add a static route to that gateway. The process is relatively easy:

1. Navigate to **System** | **Routing**. The default tab should be the **Gateway** tab.
2. On the **Gateway** tab, click on **Add**.
3. On the gateway **Edit** page, select the correct interface using the **Interface** drop-down box, matching the interface on which the gateway resides (in our case, LAN).
4. Enter an IP for monitoring the gateway in the **Monitor IP** edit box, if desired. This will help pfSense mark the gateway as down, if it stops responding to pings from the IP address entered.
5. Enter a brief, nonparsed description in the **Description** field, if desired.
6. When done, click on the **Save** button and on the main **Routing** page, click on **Apply Changes**.
7. We now have our gateway, but we need to add a static route. To do so, click on the **Static Routes** tab and click on the **Add** button.
8. On the static routes Edit page, enter the network that will be reached, as well as the correct CIDR, in the Destination network edit box (in our case, it would be `192.168.2.0/24`).
9. In the **Gateway** drop-down box, select the gateway you created in steps 1-6.
10. Again, you may enter a brief description in the **Description** field.
11. When done, click on the **Save** button.

pfSense now has a route to the DMZ router, which is good. However, there is a problem with this configuration. As an example, imagine that there is a node attached to the LAN switch and that this node has an IP address of `192.168.1.3`. This node is trying to establish a session with a node on the DMZ router that has an IP address of 192.168.2.3.

The LAN node's default gateway should be the LAN interface IP, that is, `192.168.1.1`. It therefore sends packets whose destination is `192.168.2.3` to pfSense, which in turn uses the static route we just created to send packets to the DMZ via the `192.168.1.2` gateway. When the DMZ node sends return traffic, however, it won't find `192.168.1.3` on the local network, and then will try the default gateway (`192.168.1.2`). The LAN switch, seeing that the target node is on the LAN, will forward the packets to `192.168.1.2` without the intervention of pfSense, as pfSense only filters traffic between networks directly connected to it. As far as pfSense is concerned, the connection was never completed. Thus, the entry gets dropped from the state table and the connection between the LAN node and the DMZ node gets dropped. This diagram illustrates the asymmetrical routing that takes place.

Yet another possibility is a situation you may have with ICMP redirects. This is a type of redirect that is sent by a gateway when it knows a more direct route to a destination. If the sending node allows such redirects, then their routing table will temporarily add the new route. Again, consider the example in which our LAN node at `192.168.1.3` tries to communicate with our DMZ node at `192.168.2.3`. The request goes through the LAN's default gateway and reaches pfSense. Since pfSense realizes there is a more direct route to `192.168.2.3` via `192.168.1.2`, it sends an ICMP redirect back to 192.168.1.3, informing it of this more direct route. At the same time, it sends the initial TCP SYN packet to `192.168.2.3` via the static route; pfSense also creates a state table for this entry. All subsequent communication between `192.168.1.3` and `192.168.2.3`, however, will take place through the DMZ gateway (`192.168.1.2`). pfSense will not see this traffic, since as far as it is concerned, it is intra-network traffic. The state table entry created for this connection will eventually expire and be deleted. If the ICMP redirect-learned route between `192.168.1.3` and `192.168.2.3` expires as well, then `192.168.1.3` will send the next packet after its expiration to pfSense. Since this is not a packet establishing a new connection, pfSense will reject it. The connection between `192.168.1.3` and `192.168.2.3` will then be dropped.

There are two ways we can deal with these situations. One is to navigate to **System | Advanced**, click on the **Firewall & NAT** tab, scroll down to **Firewall Advanced**, and enable the **Static route filtering** option. If this option is enabled when one or more static routes have been defined, traffic that enters and leaves through the same interface will not be checked by pfSense. This would apply to traffic sent to `192.168.2.3` from `192.168.1.3`, since it enters through the LAN interface (`192.168.1.3`) and exits via a static route that again sends it to the LAN interface (`192.168.1.2`).

Enabling this option will solve the immediate problem, but it will also apply to all cases in which traffic enters and leaves through the same interface, not just this instance. It would be better if we had a rule that only applied to interfaces that have static routes associated with them. We can get this done by creating two rules: a rule on the interface through which the static route passes, and a floating rule that will cover the return traffic. This can be done by following this procedure:

1. Navigate to **Firewall | Rules** and click on the tab of whichever interface the static route passes through (in our example, it would be LAN).
2. Click on one of the **Add** buttons at the bottom of the page to add a rule.
3. Make sure the **Action** drop-down box is set to **Pass** (the default) and the **Protocol** drop-down box is set to **TCP** (also the default).
4. The **Source** should be set to match the setting in the **Interface** drop-down box (in our example, it would be **LAN net**).
5. For **Destination**, choose **Single host or alias** in the drop-down box. In the adjacent edit box, enter the IP address of the static route's gateway (in our example, it would be **192.168.1.2**).
6. Scroll down to the **Extra Options** section and click on the **Show Advanced** button.
7. In the **Advanced** section, set the **TCP Flags** option to **Any Flags**. This will cause the rule to match traffic on the interface regardless of what TCP flags are set or not set.
8. In the **State type** drop-down box, change the setting to **Sloppy**. This will cause pfSense to perform a less strict state match on return traffic.
9. When you are done making changes, click on the **Save** button. You should place this rule at the top of the firewall rules table for the interface to ensure that it always gets applied.
10. The next step is creating a floating rule for the return traffic. To do this, click on the **Floating** tab, and from that tab, click on the **Add** button.
11. Again, make sure the **Action** column is set to Pass, and that **Protocol** is set to **TCP**.
12. In the **Interface** listbox, the same interface selected in the first rule should be selected (in our example, LAN).
13. The direction set in the **Direction** drop-down should be set to out.
14. As with the first rule, scroll down to **Extra Options** and click on the **Show Advanced** button.
15. Set the **TCP Flags** option to **Any Flags**.

16. Set the **State** type to **Sloppy**.
17. When you are done, click on the **Save** button, then on the main **Rules** page, and finally on **Apply Changes**. You now have rules covering traffic in both directions.

One other potential issue that may arise is nodes on our DMZ network trying to connect to the internet. Our static routes and firewall rules have taken into account the asymmetric nature of sessions between the LAN and DMZ. Yet we didn't consider what happens if the DMZ tries to connect to the internet, and it will likely fail. This is because the default **Allow LAN to any** rule only matches traffic whose source is the LAN net. While this rule may be entirely consistent with your intended policy, you may, after all, want to keep nodes on the DMZ from accessing the internet. If you want to change this outcome, you will have to change the default allow rule. Specifically, you will have to alter the source setting from LAN net to any, so that LAN traffic can pass to the internet regardless of its source.

Public IP addresses behind a firewall

Another situation that is close enough to static routing to justify inclusion in this section is a situation in which you have one or more public IP addresses on an internal interface. You might just have a single public IP address on an internal interface, but more commonly, you will have an entire subnet allocated by the ISP. In either case, you would follow a four step procedure to setting things up:

1. Configuration of the WAN interface
2. Configuration of the internal interface
3. Configuration of outbound NAT rules
4. Configuration of firewall rules

Suppose our ISP has provided several IPs. One is an IP for their router, which is directly connected to the internet. Another is an IP for the WAN interface of pfSense. Finally, there is a block of eight IP addresses used by an interface that is part of our internal network. The following table illustrates these assignments:

IP address	Description
192.0.10.10	This is the IP address for the ISP router
192.0.10.11	This is the pfSense WAN IP
192.0.20.0/29	This is the ISP-assigned public IP for use on internal interface

Although we were assigned eight IP addresses, only six of them are usable; the first address becomes the network ID, and the last address becomes the broadcast address. Also, note that the public addresses in this example are actually private addresses, for the purpose of this example only.

First, we set up the WAN interface:

1. Navigate to **Interfaces** | **WAN**.
2. Since our ISP assigned an IP address for the WAN interface, we choose **Static IPv4** in the **Configuration type** drop-down box, and enter the assigned IP address (192.0.10.11) in the appropriate edit box.
3. In the **IPv4 Upstream** gateway field, we enter the IP address of the ISP's router.
4. We haven't yet added the upstream router as a gateway. Therefore, we click on the **Add new gateway** button and enter the ISP router's IP address and a description, then click on the **Add** button.
5. When we are done, we click on the **Save** button and then on **Apply Changes**.

If we haven't added the internal interface yet, we need to do that as follows:

1. Navigate to **Interfaces** | **(assign)**.
2. Add an interface by selecting an available one from the **Available network ports** drop-down box and clicking on the **Add** button. Then, click on the name of the interface (for example, OPT1) and begin configuration.
3. On the interface's configuration page, click on the **Enable** checkbox.
4. You can change the name of the interface in the **Description** field.
5. The **Configuration type** should be set to **Static IPv4**.
6. For **IPv4 Address**, we enter one of the public IP addresses assigned by our ISP. It might as well be the first usable address, so we enter 192.0.20.1/29. One IP address is assigned to the interface, and five IP addresses are available for internal hosts that require public IP addresses.
7. When we are done, we click on the **Save** button and then **Apply Changes**.

Next, we must complete outbound NAT configuration. By default, outbound traffic on internal interfaces is translated to the WAN IP. Obviously, we will want to disable this behavior on the new interface. Doing so requires us to perform the following steps:

1. Navigate to **Firewall** | **NAT** and click on the **Outbound** tab.
2. Under **General Logging Options**, select the **Manual Outbound NAT** rule generation radio button.

3. Click on the **Save** button. You should now be able to add, edit, and delete outbound NAT mappings.

4. In the **Mappings** section, there should be an autocreated rule for the internal interface to which a public IP address has been assigned (for example, Auto created rule – OPT1 to WAN). We don't want to map outbound traffic on this interface to the WAN IP, so this rule should be deleted.

5. Once you have deleted the autocreated rule for the new interface, click on the **Apply Changes** button on the **NAT** page.

The last step in setting up the public IP addresses is firewall rule configuration. Users on the internet trying to reach the public IPs on the internal interface will be coming through the WAN interface. Therefore, at a minimum, we will have to create a rule on the WAN interface to allow traffic to pass to one or more of the public IPs. We will walk through one such example for setting up a web server, which is as follows:

1. Navigate to **Firewall | Rules**. The **WAN** tab is the default tab.
2. Click on one of the **Add** buttons.
3. On the rule **Edit** page, keep **Action** set to **Pass** and **Protocol** set to **TCP**. The Source should remain set to **any**.
4. Set **Destination** to **Single Host or alias** using the **Destination** drop-down box, and set the destination address to `192.0.20.2`. Set the **Port** to `80`.
5. Click on **Save** when done, and on the main **Rules** page, click on **Apply Changes**.

You may want to create other rules for the internal interface. For example, you'll probably want to block access to local networks, and perhaps create a rule allowing access to the WAN interface so that access to the internet is possible.

Dynamic routing

Although dynamic routing is not supported natively in pfSense, implementing dynamic routing is still possible through the use of third-party packages. As of version 2.4, these packages are available:

Package name	Routing protocol(s) supported
OpenBGPD	BGP
Quagga OSPF	OSPF, BGP, and RIP (RIP supported by the Zebra daemon)
Routed	RIP v1 and v2
FRR	BGP and OSPF

With the release of pfSense version 2.3, many packages were dropped. One of them was the Optimized Link State Routing Protocol. Still, several distance-vector and link-state protocols are available.

RIP (routed)

The routed package is actually a frontend—a frontend to FreeBSD's routed daemon. To install it, navigate to **System** | **Packages**. Then, scroll down to the table listing for routed, click on the **Add** icon, and then when pfSense asks you to confirm installation, click on the **Confirm** button. Installation seldom takes more than 2 minutes.

Once routed is installed, you can begin using it by navigating to **Services** | **RIP**. The RIP configuration page has a number of options. The **Enable RIP** checkbox allows you to start routed, which by default is not running when RIP is first installed. The **Interfaces** list-box is where you choose the interfaces to which RIP will bind. Any interfaces that provide a path to another RIP-enabled router should be selected here. The **RIP Version** drop-down box is where you select either **RIP Version 1** or **RIP Version 2**. The RIP daemon will advertise and listen using whichever version you select. If you use Version 2, you should specify a password in the **RIPv2 password** field. The **no_ag** option, if enabled, will turn off aggregation of subnets in RIP responses. The **no_super_ag** option, if enabled, turns off aggregation of super networks. When you are done making changes, click on the **Save** button.

OpenBGPD

OpenBGPD is a daemon that implements Border Gateway Protocol, or BGP. You can install OpenBGPD by navigating to **System** | **Packages**, clicking on the **Add** icon next to the OpenBGPD entry, and then clicking on the **Confirm** button on the confirmation page.

Navigate to **Services** | **OpenBGPD** to begin OpenBGPD configuration. You will see several configuration tabs, the first of which is **Settings**. On this tab, the **autonomous systems (AS) Number** field lets you enter the local autonomous system number. The **Holdtime** field lets you enter the time a session with a neighboring OpenBGPD router will be kept active without receiving either a KEEPALIVE or UPDATE message from the neighbor. **Holdtime** is measured in seconds. The **fib-update dropdown** box enables you to determine whether OpenBGPD will keep updating the Forwarding Information Base. This is the kernel routing table.

The **Listen on IP** field allows you to specify the local IP address on which the BGP daemon will listen. If this field is left blank, the daemon will bind on all IPs. The **Router IP** edit box allows you to set the router IP. This IP must be local to pfSense. The **CARP Status IP** field is where you can specify the IP address for determining the CARP status. If OpenBGPD checks the CARP status and finds the interface to which the IP address corresponds is in BACKUP status, then the BGP daemon will not start until the status changes to MASTER. Finally, in the **Networks** field, you can identify a network that will be announced as belonging to the AS. This can be **(inet | inet6) connected** to announce all IPv4- or IPv6-attached networks, or **(inet | inet6) static** to announce IPv4 or IPv6 static routes.

The next tab, **Neighbors**, is where you can add neighboring routers. Clicking on the **Add** button below the table enables you to add another router. On the router configuration page, there are several parameters you can enter. You can enter a description in the **Description** field, and the **Neighbor** field is where you enter the neighbor router's IP address. The **TCP-MD5 key** edit box is where you enter the MD5 key for communicating with the other router. This does not work with Cisco routers. However, you can enter a password in the **TCP-MD5 password** field, which should enable OpenBGPD to authenticate with a Cisco router. The **Group** drop-down box is where you can add the neighbor to a BGP group. If you want to do this, however, you must first add a group at the **Group** tab. The **Neighbor** parameters setting dropdown allows you to set certain parameters on the neighboring router. Some of these parameters have numerical values that can be set. If they do, then the **Value** edit box will be enabled when the said parameters are selected. You add parameters by clicking on the **Add** button. When you are done, click the **Save** button.

As mentioned earlier, the **Groups** tab is where you can define groups into which neighboring routers can then be placed. In order to add a group, click on the **Add** button below the table. On the group configuration page, enter a name in the **Name** field. The **Remote AS** field allows you to enter an AS for the group. You can also enter a brief nonparsed description in the **Description** field. There is also a **Save** button for saving changes; if you don't want to save the changes, click on the **Cancel** button.

The **Raw config** tab allows you to manually edit the `bgpd.conf`, which may be necessary in some cases. If you do, any changes you make to `bgpd.conf` will override any changes you made on the other tabs, so take that into account. At the bottom of the page, there are two buttons: **Save** and **Cancel**. There is one other tab, that is, the **Status** tab, which provides information about the OpenBGP daemon as it runs.

Quagga OSPF

Another package that makes a link-state routing protocol available is Quagga OSPF. This implementation of the OSPF protocol is available as a package. It can be installed by going to **System | Packages** in the same manner as other packages described in this section. If you read the package description, however, you will notice that it mentions that QuaggaOSPF is installed in the same location as OpenBPGD. Installing both packages will break things. If you are going to install Quagga OSPF and you already have OpenBGPD installed, it is recommended that you uninstall OpenBGPD first.

Once Quagga OSPF is installed, you can begin configuration by navigating to **Services | Quagga OSPFd**. There are several tabs; the first is **Global Settings**. You must enter the password for the Zebra and OSPFd daemons, which you can do in the **Master Password** field. The **Logging** option, if enabled, will cause OSPF information to be written to the syslog, which can be useful in diagnosing and troubleshooting issues. Similarly, the **Log Adjacency Changes** option allows you to have OSPF daemon write adjacency changes to the syslog. The router ID is entered in the Router ID field. This ID is customarily written in the dotted decimal format in which IP addresses are written (for example, 1.1.1.1); however, the router ID does not represent an actual IP address, and expressing the router ID in this form is optional.

The **Area** field is where you enter the OSPFd area; we differentiate OSPF areas by the fact that each area has its own link-state database. As with router IDs, areas are usually expressed in IPv4 format, but they do not have to be. The **Disable FIB updates** option, if enabled, allows you to turn the router into a stub router. A stub router only receives route advertisements within the **autonomous system** (**AS**).

The **Redistribute connected networks** option, as the name implies, enables redistribution of connected networks. The **Redistribute default route** option enables redistribution of a default route to pfSense. **Redistribute static** enables the redistribution of static routes, but only if you are using Quagga static routes. **Redistribute Kernel** enables redistribution of the kernel routing table. It is required if you are using pfSense static routes.

In the **SPF Hold Time** edit box, you can specify the SPF hold time in milliseconds. This is the minimum time between two consecutive shortest path first calculations. The default value of **SPF Hold Time** is 5 seconds. In the **SPF Delay** field, you can specify the delay between receiving an update to the link-state database and starting the shortest path first calculation (the default is 1 second).

Enabling the **RFC 1583** option causes decisions regarding AS-external routes to be evaluated according to RFC 1583. If this option is not enabled, intra-area routes will always be favored over inter-area routes, regardless of the cost.

In the next section, you can generate rules for certain areas that will take precedence over any redistribute options otherwise specified. Each entry must have a subnet to the route and an area ID. You can also disable redistribution for each entry and disable acceptance. Clicking on the **Add** button adds an entry. The CARP Status IP edit box is essentially identical to this setting in OpenBGPD, and it allows you to specify the IP address used to determine the CARP status. When you are done, click on the **Save** button.

On the **Interface Settings** tab, you can specify which interfaces will send and receive OSPF data. Click on the **Add** button under the table to add a new interface; the configuration page has several options. The **Interface** dropdown is where you can specify the participating interface. The **Network Type** drop-down box is where you enter the participating interface. And the **Network Type** drop-down box is where you specify the OSPF network type. The following are the options:

- **Broadcast**: Router data is sent to a large number of routers. To run in broadcast mode, you must elect a **designated router (DR)** and a backup designated router (BDR). All non-designated routers will form an adjacency with the DR.
- **Non-Broadcast**: The router will be able to receive OSPF data; it will not make it available to other routers, though.
- **Point-to-Multipoint**: Sends OSPF data to a collection of point-to-point networks without the necessity of having a DR or BDR.
- **Point-to-Point**: Sends OSPF data to one router at a time instead of to a group of routers or to all routers.

Take note of the fact that the only two modes officially supported by OSPF are nonbroadcast and point-to-multipoint networks. Broadcast and point-to-point modes were defined by Cisco for use in **non-broadcast multi-access (NBMA)** networks. OSPF was defined in RFC 2328.

The **Metric** field is where you can enter the cost for the OSPF interface, and the **Area** field is where you can specify the area. You can enter a description in the **Description** field. Enabling Interface is Passive prevents the transmission/receiving of OSPF packets on the interface, transforming the interface into a stub network. **Enabling Accept Filter** results in the daemon not adding routes for this interface subnet from OSPF into the routing table. This can be helpful in multi-WAN environments. The **Enable MD5 password** checkbox enables the use of an MD5 password on the interface, if checked. To use this option, you must specify a password in the next field.

The **Router Priority** field is where you can specify the router priority in a DR election; the default is 1. The **Hello Interval** field lets you specify the interval at which Hello discovery packets are sent; the default for this interval is 10 seconds. The **Retransmit Interval** edit box is where you can specify the retransmit interval; the default is 5 seconds. Finally, there is the **Dead Time** field, where you can specify the interval at which OSPF will check to see if a neighbor is still alive (therefore, not dead); the default is 40 seconds.

As is the case with OpenBGPD, Quagga OSPF has a **Raw Config** tab. Here, you can edit the OSPF config files manually. There are also fields where you can enter both the physical and virtual IPs of interfaces for CARP configurations. Each configuration file has two text-boxes. The textbox labeled SAVED is where you can make changes to a config file, while the text-box labeled RUNNING is the version of the config that is currently running. Clicking on the Copy X Running to Saved button (where X is the name of the daemon whose configuration file is being edited) causes the contents of the RUNNING edit box to be copied into the SAVED edit box, enabling you to save any changes made.

The **Status** tab is where information about the different daemons is aggregated. There is a summary of data of the OSPF daemon, the BGP daemon, and the Zebra daemon, as well as any routes associated with them.

FRRouting

The **FRRouting** (FRR) package has been available for pfSense since late 2017. It supports BGP, OSPF, and OSPF6, and is intended as a replacement for both OpenBGPD and Quagga OSPF. It allows pfSense users to run both BGPD and OSPF at the same time. Rather conveniently, FRR can be configured both from the web GUI and from the command line.

If FRR is installed and either OpenBGPD or Quagga OSPF are already installed, then pfSense will automatically uninstall them. Once FRR is installed, there will be four new options on the Services menu. These are **FRR BGP**, **FRR Global/Zebra**, **FRR OSPF**, and **FRR OSPF6**. These options can be accessed either by navigating to them on the services menu, or by clicking on the identically marked tabs on the pages for each option.

If you are familiar with OpenBGPD and Quagga OSPF, you should be able to configure FRRouting fairly readily, since it contains many of the functions of these packages. It supports the same protocols; you can also edit the config files of each of the daemons. It also has some features not previously available with other packages. One example is the BGP configuration page, which has a section called Network Distribution. This, among other things, allows you to redistribute OSPF routes to BGP neighbors. The OSPF options, for the most part, are similar to the options found in Quagga OSPF, with some exceptions. Global Settings supports both access lists and prefix lists, which allow you to either allow or deny certain networks or parts of networks in specific contexts that are used by the routing daemons. You can also view the status of each daemon on a separate page.

Bridging

You can bridge two interfaces in pfSense by combining two or more interfaces and thus forming a single broadcast domain. In such a case, two ports on pfSense act as if they are on the same switch, except that firewall rules still apply in controlling traffic between interfaces. The most important consideration when bridging interfaces is to prevent looping. As mentioned earlier, this can be done using the Spanning Tree Protocol (STP).

Older versions of pfSense had filtering turned off by default, but this is no longer the case, and the default behavior of pfSense is to apply firewall rules to bridges. There is no way to selectively disable filtering in the current version of pfSense, but if you want to disable filtering completely, you can navigate to **System** | **Advanced** and check the **Disable Firewall** checkbox. Of course, you should only do this if you intend to use pfSense solely to bridge interfaces, or otherwise have no need to do packet filtering.

There are some issues you should consider when bridging interfaces:

- One interface will have an IP address, the main interface. The bridged interface will not have an IP address.
- For DHCP to work, it should be running only on the main interface, not on the interface being bridged.
- Since the firewall rules still apply, if you want DHCP to work on the bridged interface, you must create a firewall rule to allow DHCP traffic on the bridged interface.

Bridging interfaces

You can bridge interfaces in pfSense by navigating to **Interfaces** | **(assign)** and clicking on the **Bridges** tab. On this tab, there is a table displaying all the configured bridges. To add a new bridge, click on the **Add** button under the table.

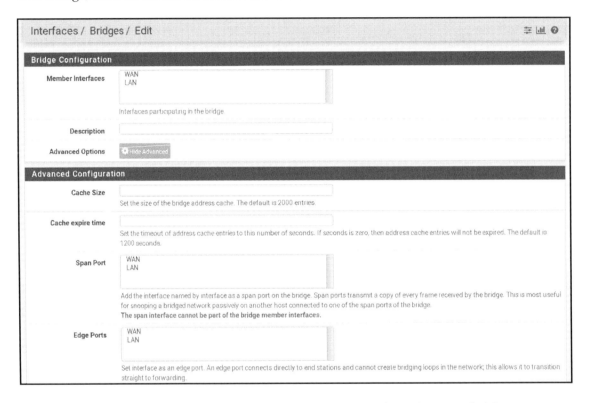

On the Bridge **Edit** page, you need to select at least two interfaces (you can bridge more than two interfaces); you can select them in the **Member Interfaces** listbox. The interfaces selected are the ones that will be bridged. You may also enter a brief description in the **Description** field.

Clicking on the **Display Advanced** button reveals a number of advanced options you can configure. The **Cache size** field is where you can set the size of the bridge address cache; the default size is 2000 entries. The **Cache expire time** field is where you can set the timeout, in seconds, of address cache entries, but the cache entries will not expire if you set this field to zero. The default **Cache expire time** is 1200 seconds.

Next is the **Span Port** listbox; setting an interface as a span port means that it will transmit every frame received by the bridge. This can be useful if you need to monitor bridge traffic. The interface designated as a span port cannot be any of the bridge interfaces.

There is an **Edge Ports** listbox. An edge port is a port that is only connected to one bridge and therefore cannot create bridging loops on the network and can transition directly to the forwarding state. The **Auto Edge Ports** listbox allows you to select interfaces that will automatically detect edge status; this is the default for bridge interfaces.

If you select interfaces in the **PTP Ports** listbox, these interfaces will be designated as point-to-point links. The **Auto PTP Ports** listbox will cause pfSense to automatically detect the point-to-point status. It does this by checking the full duplex link status of the interface.

The **Sticky Ports** listbox allows you to select interfaces that will be marked as sticky. Interfaces that are marked as such will have dynamically learned address entries marked as static once they enter the cache. Such entries will never be aged out of the cache or replaced. This is so even if the learned address is seen on another interface. The **Private Ports** listbox allows you to set selected interfaces as private; these interfaces will not forward traffic to any other interface that is also set as private.

You will need to choose a spanning tree protocol for your bridge, and pfSense gives you two options:

- **STP**: This is the original Spanning Tree Protocol. It creates a spanning tree within a network of bridges, disabling links that are not part of the tree and leaving a single path between any of the two bridges. The protocol was standardized as 802.1D. STP is not particularly fast, and it can take up to a minute for this protocol to respond to a topology change on the network.
- **Rapid Spanning Tree Protocol (RSTP)**: This protocol reduces the convergence time for responding to a topology change to mere seconds, but it is more complex than STP. The original STP protocol had three port designations, namely, root, designated, and disabled. RSTP adds two more port designations – alternate, which represents an alternate path to the bridge, and backup, which is a backup or redundant path to a segment. Switch port states have three designations, namely, discarding, learning, and forwarding. The protocol was standardized by 802.1W.

The STP options can be found by scrolling down to the **RSTP/STP** section. There is an **Enable RSTP/STP** checkbox, which allows you to enable these protocols. You can select either RSTP or STP in the **Protocols** drop-down box. The **STP Interfaces** listbox is where you can choose the interfaces on which either RSTP or STP is enabled. The next two options are the **Valid Time** field and **Forward time** field.

The **Valid time** field specifies how long a spanning tree will be valid, while the **Forward time** field specifies the delay for forwarding packets. The default for **Valid time** is 20 seconds, and the default for **Forward time** is 30 seconds. The **Hello Time** edit box is where you can enter the time between broadcasting STP configuration messages. This only takes effect if STP mode is invoked. In the **Priority** edit box, you can enter the bridge priority, and in the **Hold count** edit box, you can enter the number of packets that will be sent before rate limiting is invoked.

There is one last series of edit boxes, and in these boxes you can set the spanning tree priority for each of the interfaces. The priorities can be set anywhere from 0 to 240, in increments of 16. The default priority is 128. It is also possible to set the path cost for each interface; it can be set from anything to 1 to 200000000. By default, the path cost is calculated from the link speed, and you can change it back to the default behavior by setting it to 0. When you are done, click on **Save**, and then click on the **Apply Changes** button.

There are two additional tasks we must address before bridge configuration is complete. You need to disable DHCP on the bridged interface. To do so, navigate to **Services** | **DHCP Server** (or **DHCPv6 Server/RA**) and click on the tab for the bridged interface. Once there, make sure the **Enable** checkbox is unchecked (thus, disabling DHCP on the interface), and then click on the **Save** button. Taking these steps will ensure that DHCP functions properly on the bridged interface.

Finally, you should create a firewall rule on the bridged interface in order to allow DHCP traffic. You can do this by navigating to **Firewall** | **Rules**, clicking on the tab for the bridged interface, and clicking on one of the **Add** buttons on the page. Normally, we set the **Source** field to a network or IP address; DHCP, however, represents a special case, since DHCP clients do not have IP addresses (at least when the DHCP process begins). Thus, you must set the **Source** to 0.0.0.0, with **Single** host or alias as the type of source (this can be chosen in the **Source** drop-down box). The source port should be set to **68** (one of the IANA-assigned port for DHCP).

In the **Destination** field, set the destination to 255.255.255.255 (the address where DHCPDISCOVER messages are broadcast). Set the destination port to 67 (the other IANA-assigned port for DHCP). Set Protocol to **UDP**, and make sure the **Action** drop-down box is set to **Pass**. Click on the **Save** button when you are done making changes, and then click on **Apply Changes** on the main **Firewall** page. You should place this rule at the top of the list of rules for this interface to ensure that it applies to DHCP traffic. Once this rule has been added and the firewall rules have been reloaded, the clients in the bridged segment should be able to receive DHCP leases, using the DHCP server on the interface to which this interface has been bridged.

The other issues

Since bridged interfaces act somewhat differently than nonbridged interfaces, you may find that there are some things you cannot do with bridges, or you may have to make some modifications to your usual configuration to get a feature to work with a bridge. We already saw an example of this with DHCP when we discussed how to configure a bridge. In this section, we will enumerate some other such cases.

If you are implementing a captive portal, you may be aware that it requires an IP on each interface on which it is active. This IP address is used to serve the portal contents. Bridged interfaces do not have an IP address; therefore, captive portal setups do not work with bridges.

Bridged interfaces can raise issues with mutli-WAN configurations. Nodes on the bridged interfaces often have a different gateway than pfSense. Further, the router that is the default gateway for these nodes is the only device that can route traffic from these notes. Nevertheless, you can configure a multi-WAN setup to work with bridged interfaces if either nodes on the bridged interfaces have pfSense as their default firewall, or if multi-WAN is only used on nonbridged interfaces.

We have not covered **Common Address Redundancy Protocol (CARP)** except in passing, other than to note that it is a method of having a completely redundant firewall or firewalls that can become active when the master firewall goes down, thus eliminating a significant single point of failure on the network and minimizing downtime. That having been said, CARP does not work well with bridging. Take the case of a standard CARP setup with two firewalls, one master and one backup. Both firewalls will be connected to the switch for each internal interface. This is an acceptable setup; each node has one path to each of the switches. The two network segments that are bridged are merged into a larger network and everything works. If interfaces are bridged on a network, then there will be two paths to a node on a bridged interface, namely, the bridge on the master firewall and the bridge on the backup firewall.

If we are using managed switches on the bridged interface, then we can handle this by implementing STP or RSTP on the managed switch.

If we have only unmanaged switches on the bridged interface, we might have issues getting the setup to work, but there is a method:

1. First, configure master and backup firewalls on your CARP setup, and make sure the interface assignments are identical on all firewalls (including bridged interfaces).

2. If you are using managed switches, use STP/RSTP to ensure the port connecting to the switch has priority over the port connecting the switch to the backup firewall. When you have completed the port setup, confirm that the master firewall's port is forwarding traffic and that the same port on the backup firewall is blocking traffic.

3. You may also be able to use a script to ensure the bridge on the firewall is only up if the firewall is designated as the master. You can do this by running the ifconfig command on the carp0 interface. Use the grep command to check the command's output. Once the script is installed, you can run the script automatically using the cron daemon.

4. Another way to ensure sending and receiving data is solid is to use devd. This will tell you when the CARP state transition occurs. You can edit devd.conf to ensure any bridges are brought up and down whenever there is a CARP state transition.

It is not the intention of this book to describe procedures for using bridges with a CARP setup. You can, however, find these issues discussed at the official pfSense documentation site here: `https://www.netgate.com/docs/pfsense/highavailability/carp-cluster-with-bridge-troubleshooting.html`.

Troubleshooting

If you implement static or dynamic routing or bridging on your network, at some point you are likely to encounter a situation that will put your troubleshooting skills to the test. We will first consider how to troubleshoot issues with routing.

The pfSense routing table is often a good place to start troubleshooting routing issues (under **Diagnostics | Routes**). Here, you can learn what routes exist, how they are configured, as well as how many times the route has been used. The table is divided into two sections (one for IPv4 traffic, and the other for IPv6 traffic. There are also several columns in the table. Some of the parameters in these columns are obvious, such as **Destination**, **Use** (which is the number of times a route was used), and **Mtu** (which is short for maximum transmission unit).

There is also a column called **Flags**; some of the more significant flags include the following:

- **U = RTF_UP**: This is when the route is usable
- **G = RTF_GATEWAY**: This is when the destination port requires forwarding by an intermediary
- **H = RTF_HOST**: This entry is a host entry
- **S = RTF_STATIC**: This entry was added manually

Consider the simple static routing example invoked earlier in the chapter, wherein the DMZ network's WAN interface address was `192.168.1.2` (part of the LAN subnet) and the router's LAN interface address was `192.168.2.1`. Suppose a node on the DMZ subnet with an IP address of `192.168.2.3` cannot reach a node on the LAN subnet with an IP of 192.168.1.3. First, we need to consider obvious potential problems, such as an interface in shutdown mode or misconfigured interface. For example, the default gateway for `192.168.2.3` is `192.168.2.1`. If it is not configured as such, then the network interface on 192.168.2.3 will not know where to send inter-network traffic.

If obvious solutions have not worked, you should try testing connectivity. In this case, you could start by pinging the gateway from the DMZ node (`192.168.2.3`). If the ping fails, then there is a good chance you have a local issue, such as a malfunctioning or misconfigured router. If you can ping the router, it's probably time to look elsewhere for the source of your problem.

You can use the traceroute command, which we will also discuss in the next chapter. In our simple networking example, pinging the LAN interface address (`192.168.1.1`) will tell us much, especially if the ping fails. Consider the following possible causes:

- The LAN interface could be down or misconfigured
- The static route to the DMZ is misconfigured, and pfSense does not know where to send the ping replies.

Armed with two hypotheses of the cause of the problem, we can now further narrow it down. If we try pinging 192.168.1.2 from pfSense, and it works, then the LAN interface is up. There is a good possibility the static route to the DMZ network is misconfigured.

Your network may be considerably more complex than this, but the same basic troubleshooting techniques will help you diagnose problems with static routes. Try and employ a divide-and-conquer approach to try to isolate the source of the problem, and remember that ping and traceroute are your friends. If you are using Cisco switches, then you have additional command-line utilities at your disposal; it behooves you to learn which ones are the most helpful and use them.

There are many problems that can arise if you use a dynamic routing protocol, but some of the more common ones include the following:

- Incorrect configuration, such as a switch a port being set to down inadvertently
- The router doesn't have enough memory to hold the routing table
- Looping issues
- Incompatibility between routing protocols on the network (for example, RIPv1 and RIPv2 being used on the same network

Similarly, bridging interfaces can result in a number of common issues:

- The bridge may not be forwarding traffic. Firewall rules may be blocking traffic, or there may be so many topology changes that STP is having trouble keeping up with them.
- There could be a storm of traffic, usually indicative of a loop.

Issues relating to routing and bridging are not always the easiest problems to diagnose and troubleshoot, but by using some common sense and simple command-line tools, you can start to focus in on the source of the problem.

Summary

In this chapter, we considered two fundamental networking concepts—routing and bridging—and the role they play in our networks. Static and dynamic routing may not be something you make much use of in a small network, but if your network starts to grow, odds are that you will employ either static or dynamic routing or both. We discussed some of the dynamic routing protocols available. We covered how to set up a static route in pfSense and how to configure dynamic routing protocols using some of the third-party packages available. Although you may never have an occasion to bridge interfaces, we outlined the process, as well as some of the issues involved with bridges. Finally, we covered how to troubleshoot routing and bridging.

In the next chapter, we will cover diagnostics and troubleshooting in greater depth, including the procedure to follow troubleshooting, as well as the diagnostic tools that are at our disposal when working with pfSense.

Questions

1. (a) What layer of the OSI model does bridging take place at? (b) What layer of the OSI model does routing take place at?
2. Identify the two types of dynamic routing protocols.
3. (a) What options do we have with third-party packages if we want to implement RIP? (b) What options do we have if we want to implement OSPF?
4. (a) What is the maximum hop count in RIPv1? (b) What is the maximum hop count in RIPv2?
5. Is it possible to run Quagga OSPF and FRR at the same time?
6. Identify the spanning tree protocols available in pfSense.
7. What must be done if DHCP traffic is to pass to both sides of a bridged interface?
8. If packets are flooding a bridge, what is the likely cause?

Further reading

- **Difference Between Router and Bridge (Brief article describing the main differences between routers and bridges)**: http://www.differencebetween.net/technology/difference-between-router-and-bridge/
- **"Routing" versus "Bridging" (GRC article describing routing versus bridging in the context of OpenVPN.)**: https://www.grc.com/vpn/routing.htm

11
Diagnostics and Troubleshooting

If you are involved with implementing and maintaining computer networks, then it indicates that one of your networks will not function as it should at some point. This could be the result of human error, such as a configuration mistake or poor network design. It could be the result of a software or hardware failure. It is possible that someone is launching a malicious attack on your network. Finally, there is a possibility that legitimate users on your own network will, perhaps unintentionally, cause the network to malfunction. In each of these cases, you, as the person responsible for maintaining the network, will be called upon to fix the problem, and your troubleshooting skills will be put to the test.

In this chapter, we will first outline a general procedure for troubleshooting networks. We will then discuss some common networking problems and possible causes. We will also cover the most useful troubleshooting tools available in both pfSense and on the command line of most operating systems. In the final section, we will apply what you learned to troubleshoot a real-world networking problem.

In this chapter, you will learn the following topics:

- Troubleshooting fundamentals
- pfSense troubleshooting tools
- A troubleshooting scenario

Technical requirements

In order to work through the examples in this chapter, you will need a functioning pfSense system, in either a real-world or virtual environment, with at least one node attached to the LAN side of pfSense. It will also be helpful to have at least one functioning Windows, Linux, or MacOS computer attached to your network.

Troubleshooting fundamentals

At times, troubleshooting can be a simple process. At some point, perhaps even when working through the examples in this book, you made a change to pfSense's configuration (or perhaps somewhere else on your network), and your network was no longer functioning normally. In such cases, resolving the problem can be as simple as remembering what change you made that caused the malfunction and undoing that change. A good proportion of network problems can be solved in this way.

However, in other cases, troubleshooting is not that easy. The cause may be something outside our control, or even if the cause was something we did, we may not be able to isolate it down to a single cause. The network on which the problem has manifested itself might be a critical resource for a company, and we cannot just troubleshoot it at any time—we might have to wait until after business hours or till the weekend. Finally, even if the problem is relatively simple to solve, documenting the problem and its resolution is useful, as it will potentially save colleagues' time, if the problem ever manifests itself again.

It is therefore generally advantageous to embrace a structured approach to troubleshooting, as it is not only a good practice, but will save us time and potentially help us improve our troubleshooting skills. With this in mind, I will outline a multistep approach to troubleshooting, which should be helpful not just in diagnosing and troubleshooting pfSense issues, but also with networking and information technology in general.

A seven-step approach to troubleshooting

The following seven-step approach should help you zero in on networking problems:

1. **Identifying the problem**: This may seem obvious at first, but in reality, many times we don't know the extent of a problem. In such cases, we would be better off gathering information, identifying symptoms, and, in some cases, questioning users. If there is more than one problem, recognize it as such so you can approach each problem individually. When questioning users, try to elicit information without making them feel defensive (for example, *What did you do to break the network?* is generally not considered a useful line of questioning). You can ask the user how the network functions normally and compare it to how it functions now. Recreate the problem if needed and try to isolate the problem to the best of your ability.

2. **Formulating a theory of probable cause**: A single problem can have several possible causes, and it may not be easy to narrow it down to one cause. However, if you exercised due diligence in gathering information in the previous step, you can often eliminate at least some of the causes you enumerated at first. In many cases, the most obvious cause is the correct one, and starting with the most obvious possible cause is a reasonable approach. At the same time, your initial theory may turn out to be incorrect, and you may have to consider other theories as well. You may even have to revisit step 1 and resume gathering information.

3. **Testing the theory**: Once you have established a theory of probable cause, the next logical step is to attempt to confirm the theory. If you are able to confirm your theory, you can move on to the next step; otherwise, you will have to formulate an alternate theory.

4. **Establishing a plan**: We have formulated a theory of probable cause, and the theory seems to be correct. However, we still need to establish a plan of action to restore the network to full functionality. Establishing a plan is more important in enterprise-level environments, where formal procedures are in place for IT maintenance. The implementation of your solution may involve taking systems offline. If so, you have to determine when they will be taken offline, and for how long, and follow whatever formal or informal procedures the organization has for taking systems offline. At a minimum, it usually involves scheduling a time (often during nonworking hours) when the work will be done.

5. **Implementing the solution**: Now that you have gotten this far, you can make the necessary corrective change to the network, but your work is not done. You cannot assume that the solution will work without testing it, so you need to do that, and you also should take into account that early results might be deceptive. You may need to test your network several times to be sure that the solution you implemented works.

6. **Verifying system functionality**: This is somewhat of a corollary to step 5, but you need to consider that sometimes solutions that fix one problem create another problem. As a result, you need to verify full system functionality. Only when you have done this will you know that the solution was truly a success.

7. **Documenting the problem and its solution**: Now that you have successfully solved the problem, you need to document the problem/solution. This involves keeping a record of all steps taken when solving the problem. Documenting not only your successes but also your failures can save you (and others) time later on. In large organizations, keeping a record of the person who implemented the solution can help; this way, if someone in the organization has a question (and the person in question is still working for the company), it will be easy to find them.

The problem could have been reported by a member of the IT staff, but it may also have been reported by a user. If it was reported by a user, consider providing feedback to this user. If you do, it could encourage them to report problems in the future. It might also provide them with some insight into how to avoid the problem.

We have already introduced the seven-layer OSI model, not to mention the four-layer TCP/IP model for networks, and I see no reason to rehash them in great detail here. Nonetheless, they do provide an effective way of conceptualizing problems. Determining the layer on which the problem resides can help us diagnose and solve the problem:

- **Physical layer/Data link layer (OSI) or Link layer (TCP/IP)**: The physical layer of the OSI model covers problems such as damaged or dirty cabling or terminations, as well as high levels of signal attenuation or poor signal bandwidth. It can also cover problems dealing with wireless networks such as interference or malfunctioning access points. The data link layer of the OSI model covers problems such as MAC address and VLAN misconfigurations, suboptimal VLAN performance, and improper L2TP and/or OSPF configuration. The physical and data link layers of the OSI model are merged into the Link layer of the TCP/IP model.
- **Network Layer**: This covers problems such as damaged or defective networking devices, and also includes misconfigured devices, lack of adequate network bandwidth, and so on.
- **Transport Layer**: This covers problems with the TCP and UDP network protocols.
- **Session/Presentation/Application layers or Application layer (TCP)**: This can cover problems related to applications and their protocols.

Common networking problems

There are some networking issues that are so commonplace that they deserve separate coverage. If our problem falls into one of these categories, we can save considerable time on diagnosis.

Wrong subnet mask or gateway

If the subnet mask specified in a node's network settings does not match the subnet mask for the network, then that node will not be able to communicate with the rest of the network. If there is a problem that only affects a certain node, and the node seems to be physically connected to the network, then this is definitely a possibility.

Finding the subnet mask of a node is usually an easy affair. If the node is running Windows, navigate to **Settings | Network Connections**, right-click on the current network adapter, and select **Properties**. There should be a list box displaying all the available protocols. Select **Internet Protocol Version 6** or **Internet Protocol Version 4**, depending on which version is being used. When you have selected the right protocol, click on the **Properties** button, and a dialog box should appear displaying, among other things, the subnet mask.

You can find the subnet mask in Linux in a similar way. If you are running Ubuntu or Linux Mint, for example, double-click on the networking icon at the right end of the task bar (the icon should look like two connected cables for a wired connection and as a series of arcs for a wireless connection. You should be able to launch the **Network Connections** dialog box. In this box, you should be able to find your connection and double-click on it.

The **Editing** dialog box should appear. This box provides you with the ability to change settings. Click on either the **IPv4 Settings** or **IPv6 Settings** tab. Once you do this, you should be able to see the subnet mask. Make sure that the subnet mask matches whatever it should be for the subnet. For example, if you are on the `192.168.1.0/24` subnet, the mask should be `255.255.255.0`.

The correct configuration of the subnet mask is a necessary precondition of network communications. However, not setting the gateway (or setting it to the wrong value) will prevent the node from communicating with other networks. Confirm that the gateway is set correctly. You can usually find this setting in the same place as the subnet mask.

Wrong DNS configuration

The **Domain Name System** (**DNS**) provides network-connected nodes with a means of translating hostnames into IP addresses. If a DNS server is not specified for a node, then that node will not be able to use DNS services. If the correct DNS server is not specified, then DNS resolution can take longer than the usual, thus creating the impression that there is a great deal of latency in the network.

If you can ping a site by specifying the IP address, but if the ping fails if you specify the hostname (and ping returns an unknown hostname error or a similar error), then there is a good possibility that the DNS configuration is wrong. If this is the case, you should check the DNS configuration on both the host and the firewall. There is the possibility that the DNS server is down, so you may want to to specify alternate DNS serves. Keep in mind that both Google (`8.8.8.8` and `8.8.4.4`) and CloudFlare (`1.1.1.1` and `1.0.0.1`) have their own DNS servers.

Duplicate IP addresses

You are probably aware that all IP addresses on a network must be unique. This requirement holds for networks cards, routers, access points, and so on. If the network device is on the LAN, its IP address must be unique on the LAN. If the device is on the internet, the address must be unique on the internet. In some cases, you will get a warning informing you that there are duplicate IP addresses, but not always.

The use of DHCP, in which assignment of IP addresses is managed by the DHCP server, and IPv6, which greatly increases the address space, both cut down on the possibility of duplicate IP addresses. Duplicate addresses are most likely on IPv4 addresses in which the addresses are statically assigned, so if you are dealing with such a network, consider the possibility.

Network loops

There can only be a single path between two network devices; if there is more than one path, then the resulting loop can generate a broadcast storm that could bring down your network. If you have bridged two interfaces on your network, you should look into the possibility of looping. One way to prevent looping is to manually configure ports, so there is only one path to each device. However, the greater likelihood is that you use a spanning tree protocol such as the original **Spanning Tree Protocol** (**STP**) or **Rapid Spanning Tree Protocol** (**RSTP**).

Another situation where looping might occur is if you are running a spanning tree algorithm, but the information in the routing table is incorrect. This can happen if there is a manual misconfiguration, or if there is a failure in automatic route detection. In either case, the network will get bogged down rather quickly, so it should be easy to detect.

Routing issues

In the previous chapter, we discussed how to set up a static route. Such routes can be a possible source of problems, as a change in network topology can render a static route incorrect. If you make changes to your network and also have static routes, you should consider how such changes make impact static routes and make the necessary changes.

Port configuration

Keep in mind that the default behavior of pfSense is to block all ports on the WAN side of the router. As a result, any remote users who try to connect to a port on a local host will be blocked from doing so. If we want remote users to be able to connect to local hosts, we must add both a port forwarding rule forwarding the traffic to the local host, and a firewall rule, permitting such traffic on the WAN interface. In practice, pfSense has the option to autogenerate a firewall rule from a NAT rule, thus saving us the trouble of having to remember to separately create a firewall rule.

Black holes

Most of the networking errors we have discussed so far involve scenarios where we clearly know when packets are not reaching their destination. However, what if packets are dropped without the source ever being informed that they have not reached their destination? Errors such as these can only be detected by monitoring network traffic, and we refer to such situations in which packets seem to just disappear as black holes.

When do such scenarios occur? One case is where a host tries to connect to another host that is down, or tries to connect to an IP address that has never been assigned to a host. One would think that using TCP would provide the ability to be informed that the packets never reached their destination, but often the packets are simply dropped. It also happens in cases where you are using a connectionless protocol such as UDP; thus, there is no way of communicating back to the original sender that the IP address is dead.

Another possibility is that you have a **Maximum Transmission Unit** (**MTU**) black hole. This happens when MTU exceeds the maximum MTU size allowed on a network (this can happen, for example, if VLAN tags are added to a packet), and the **Don't Fragment** (**DP**) flag is set in the IP header. In this case, any device whose MTU is smaller than the packet's size will drop the packet. The solution, in this case, is to run **Path MTU Discovery** (**PMTUD**) on all network devices. PTMUD solves the issue of packets being too big by sending a *fragmentation needed* ICMP message back to the device sending the large packets. This causes the offending device to reduce its MTU size. The problem with this fix is that some network devices block ICMP messages for security reasons. If this is the case, network devices will complete the TCP three-way handshake, but when data is transferred, the connection will hang because of the MTU size mismatch, and you will still have a black hole connection.

If you have network devices that block ICMP traffic, one possible solution is to use the RFC 4821 version of PTMUD. This version circumvents the problem using TCP or another protocol to probe the device with progressively larger packets. Another solution, which may not be practical in your case, but is still worth mentioning, is to change the **maximum segment size** (**MSS**) of all TCP connections lower than the Ethernet default of 1,500 bytes.

Physical issues

Physical issues can be the origin of many problems. First, there are issues related to cabling. The most common form of network cabling and the form that is used in most homes and offices is **unshielded twisted pair** (**UTP**) cabling. Fiber optic cabling is the more expensive alternative. UTP cabling is prone to various types of interference; one form is crosstalk, when the signal from one cable bleeds into another cable.

Crosstalk is likely to occur when two UTP cables are run too close to each other. **Near end crosstalk** (**NEXT**) refers to when an outgoing data transmission leaks into an incoming one, whereas **far end crosstalk** (**FEXT**) occurs when a transmitting station at the far end of a transmission leaks into the receiving line. The solution, other than separating the cables as much as possible, is to purchase high-quality UTP cable. In these cables, the twisted pairs are twisted more tightly together. The greater the number of twists, the less crosstalk there is.

Electromagnetic interference (**EMI**) can also reduce the signal strength of cabling. Computer monitors, fluorescent lights, and electrical current are just some of the things that create an electromagnetic field and can cause problems with UTP cabling. **Radio frequency interference** (**RFI**) from objects such as cell phones can also be a factor. The best solution, other than buying high-quality UTP cabling, is to run network cabling away from such devices as much as is possible.

Keep in mind that the signal in UTP cabling is susciptible to attenuation, especially if the cable is too long. The maximum length for both Cat 5 and Cat 6 cabling is 100 meters. If you have noted intermittent network problems, you may want to check the length of the cabling. If the cables are too long, this may well be the problem. If you can't shorten the cable run, then try installing a repeater and see if this solves the problem.

Naturally, you can avoid all the problems associated with UTP cabling by installing fiber optic cabling. Fiber-based media uses light transmission instead of electronic signals. As a result, the issues discussed in this section such as crosstalk, EMI, and attenuation become non-issues with fiber optic cabling. It is also a secure medium; this is because accessing the data signals requires tapping into the media, which is usually difficult to accomplish.

Alas, the high cost of fiber optic cabling precludes many organizations from implementing it in their networks. In addition, fiber optic media is incompatible with most electronic equipment. This means that you must purchase fiber-compatible network equipment if you want to utilize it. The net effect of this is that while fiber optic cabling will continue to play a role in networking, particularly in serving as the primary medium for the internet as well as for WANs and MANs, its impact on smaller networks will likely to be limited, at least for the forseeable future.

Above all, be sure to check your cabling on a regular basis. If you suspect that Ethernet cabling is damaged, try swapping it with new cabling and see if it solves the problem. Investing in a network cable tester is also a good idea, there are many cable testers available relatively cheap, which will save you both time and money in the long run. Check to make sure that devices at both ends of the cable are on. Also check to make sure the ports are enabled and functioning. If you suspect that a device on your network is not performing autonegotiation of speeds correctly, you may want to plug in another device and see if it works.

You can spend as little or as much as you want on a cable tester, depending on what functionality you want and how deep your pockets are. Prices range from under $10 for simple cable continuity testers, to several thousand dollars for multifunction testers that can certify your cabling as meeting the TIA/EIA-568 standard and print a report. In recent years, some of the capabilities that previously had only existed in very expensive cable testers can also be found in cheaper units. For example, the cable testers capable of performing TIA/EIA-568 tests and printing reports can be found for as little as $250.

Wireless issues

You may have an issue with a node that relies on a wireless adapter. If so, make sure that the wireless adapter is functioning properly. The wireless adapter should be enabled. If it is an iOS or Android device, make sure that it is not in airplane mode and that the Wi-Fi adapter is on and ready to connect to an access point. Also, check the settings for the wireless **service set identifier (SSID)**; verify that the device is configured to use the SSID that corresponds to the network to which you want it to connect. If the SSID for the network to which you want to connect is not showing up in the list of available wireless networks on the client, then check to make sure that SSID broadcasts are enabled on the access point or router to which the client needs to connect. You can also simply type in the SSID on the client. This should allow you to connect to the network, even if its SSID is hidden. If you do this, then make sure you match the SSID exactly, including the case of the letters.

You may also save some time if you make sure that the device you are trying to connect to your wireless network is capable of connecting to the frequency band supported by the network's wireless access point or router. To make life easier, consult the following table, which lists the bands supported by different 802.11 wireless standards:

802.11 standard	Band	Description
802.11a, 802.11g, 802.11n, 802.11ac	5 GHz	This covers the wireless standards most commonly used
802.11b, 802.11n	2.4 GHz	802.11b extended throughput to 11 Mbps; 802.11n uses multiple antennas to achieve speeds of 600 Mbps and beyond
802.11ad (WiGig)	60 GHz	Multi-gigabit per second wireless delivery
802.11af (White-Fi, Super Wi-Fi)	54-790 GHz	Proposed for longer distance wifi networks
802.11ah	Below 1 GHz	Wi-Fi HaLow; also proposed for longer-distance networks with lower energy consumption, making this standard suitable for **Internet of Things (IoT)** devices
802.11aj	45 GHz	Rebranding of 802.11ad for use in the 45 GHz unlicensed spectrum in some regions of the world (for example, China)
802.11ay (in development)	60 GHz	Extension of 802.11ad with four times the bandwidth (20-40 Gbps) and extended transmission distance of 300-500 meters

As you can see, the most common wireless standards currently in use (802.11b/g/n/ac) use either the 2.4 or 5 GHz band; some of them (such as 802.11n) use both bands. To connect older 802.11a or 802.11b devices to your network, enable Mixed Mode on your wireless access point or router. This will ensure that the slower rates used by these standards are enabled. If the client supports multiple 802.11 modes, but is trying to connect over a long distance, then you may have to enable Mixed Mode, so the client can connect to your network using one of the slower 802.11 modes.

When you are verifying the functionality of your wireless network, you should check to see what IP subnet is assigned to the network corresponding to the SSID, as well as the router that should be reachable via this subnet. Once you have checked this information, verify that the client is receiving an IP address that belongs to this subnet. You should also log in to the router and verify that (a) the client is connecting to the router and (b) an IP address is being assigned to the client. In pfSense, this can easily be confirmed by checking **Status | DHCP Leases** or **Status | DHCPv6 Leases**.

You should also consider whether the security parameters on the client and the access point and router match. As you might have gathered, there are several security algorithms available for wireless networking. It is beyond the scope of this chapter to delve into these standards in any detail, but here is an overview of the most commonly used wireless standards:

- **Wired Equivalent Privacy (WEP)**: This was introduced as part of the original 802.11 standard in 1997. WEP had keys of either 40 or 104 bits. To connect, the client must send an authentication request to the access point. The access point will then reply with a clear-text challenge. The client must then encrypt the challenge and send it back to the access point, which then decrypts the challenge. If it matches the challenge sent, the client is authenticated. This algorithm had a major weakness: the challenge was sent in the clear. As a result, it is possible to intercept the challenge and use this to then derive the keystream used for authentication. WEP also used an encryption key that is manually entered on devices that support it. This key does not change. Because of these weakness, WEP is now generally considered insecure and thus has been deprecated in favor of WPA/WPA2.

- **Wi-Fi Protected Access (WPA)**: This standard was introduced in 2003. The algorithm was designed to address the main weaknesses of WPA; it employs the Temporal Key Integrity Protocol (TKIP). This protocol dynamically generates a new 128-bit encryption key for each packet. There are two versions of WPA: (a) WPA-Personal, which supports both 128-bit encryption keys and 256-bit shared keys, and (b) WPA-Enterprise, which supports the same size keys as WPA-Personal, but requires authentication via a RADIUS server.

- **WPA2**: This standard was introduced in 2004. It added supported for **Counter Mode Cipher Block Chaining Message Code Protocol** (**CCMP**), which is an AES-based encryption protocol. There are WPA2-Personal and WPA2-Enterprise versions of this standard.

- **WPA3**: This algorithm was announced in January 2018. It supports 192-bit encryption keys and per-user encryption.

If your access point and/or router uses WPA-Personal or WPA2-Personal, make sure that the encryption method is set to WPA-PSK or WPA2-PSK. Then, enter the same passphrase on both devices. If you are required to support both WPA and WPA2, then make sure the access point and/or router supports both TKIP and AES encryption. Also, make sure that both are enabled on these devices. If you are using WPA-Enterprise or WPA2-Enterprise, then matters are somewhat more complicated because you must set up the client to use RADIUS authentication. As a concession to those using these algorithms, the next section covers RADIUS issues.

RADIUS issues

If you use WPA-Enterprise or WPA2-Enterprise, your clients must be authenticated via a RADIUS server. Even if you don't use either of these standards and therefore don't have to use a RADIUS server, you might consider using one because RADIUS provides an effective way of providing centralized authentication. Troubleshooting RADIUS is essentially a two-fold process. You need to ensure that the access point and/or router can connect to the RADIUS server, and you must also ensure that the client can log in to the RADIUS server.

You should first verify that the RADIUS server has a secret configured and that it is ready to accept connections from the access point and/or router. You should also verify connectivity between the RADIUS server and the access point and/or router. There are different ways of accomplishing this although using the ping utility is an easy and effective way.

What should you do if you find that the RADIUS server is online, but the client's login attempts are being rejected? In such a case, you should make sure that the client is using the Extensible Authentication Protocol to log in and also that it matches the type that the RADIUS server requires. The following are some of the more common options you may encounter:

- **EAP Transport Layer Security (EAP-TLS)**: The original wireless LAN EAP authentication protocol, this was defined in RFC 5216.
- **Protected Extensible Authentication Protocol (PEAP)**: This type encapsulates an EAP session within an encrypted TLS tunnel for added security.
- **EAP Tunneled Transport Layer Security (EAP-TTLS)**: Authentication takes place within an encrypted tunnel. Supported by Windows, starting with Windows 8.
- **EAP Flexible Authentication via Secure Tunneling (EAP-FAST)**: This is another variant of EAP which creates an encrypted tunnel. This version uses a **Protected Access Credential (PAC)** to establish a tunnel. Within the tunnel, client credentials are checked.

If your RADIUS server uses either EAP-TTLS or EAP-FAST, then you will need to install an 802.11X supplicant program on the client. You should also check to make sure that the other EAP-specific settings match on both the RADIUS server and the client. If you still have issues, then you likely want to refer to your RADIUS server's documentation for help. In such cases, a LAN analyzer or packet sniffer (for example, Wireshark) can be useful, as they can be used to debug protocol issues.

pfSense troubleshooting tools

The first step in our approach to troubleshooting involves gathering information, and we are fortunate in that pfSense provides a good deal of information that relates to the functioning of your network. This information can be extremely helpful when troubleshooting problems. Since the pfSense dashboard provides a good overview of the system, we will begin with it.

Dashboard

You can gather a lot of information from the pfSense dashboard. When you first log in to the web GUI, the default landing page is the dashboard; you can also navigate to it from anywhere else in the web GUI via **Status | Dashboard** on the main menu. This dashboard contains a generous amount of information about pfSense as it runs, including the uptime, CPU usage, memory usage, the version being run, and whether an upgrade is available for the version being run. The dashboard was given a major redesign for version 2.3. Version 2.4 and higher support multiple languages. If you navigate to **System | General Setup**, you can choose the number of columns in the display. However, if you resize the width of your browser, the dashboard will automatically resize to a single column. This ensures that you do not have to scroll left and right. You can add widgets to the page by clicking on the plus side of the title bar; there are many widgets that make it easier to monitor your system. For example, there are widgets for gateways, CARP status, traffic graphs, load balancer status, and so on. Many packages also have their own widgets. The dashboard updates every few seconds, thus eliminating the need of reloading the page.

System logs

To begin accessing the system logs, first navigate to **Status | System Logs**. There are several tabs in this section. The default tab is **System**, but you will likely want to narrow your focus. Fortunately, different subcategories (for example,, **Firewall** and **DHCP**) have their own tabs where you can view only log entries related to such activity. This simultaneously makes it easier to find log activity for a specific subcategory while also reducing clutter on the **System** tab. The **System** tab is itself divided into several subcategories (currently, **General**, **Gateways**, **Routing DNS Resolver**, and **Wireless**).

The way pfSense logs are stored is designed to not overflow available disk space. As a result, the logs have a binary circular log file format. Log files are a fixed size and store a maximum of 50 entries. If this limit of 50 entries is reached, then older log entries will be overwritten by newer ones. If you want or need to save these logs, you can do so by copying them to another server with syslog.

The default log order is chronological; however, you can show log entries in reverse order by clicking on the **Settings** tab and checking the **Forward/Reverse Display** checkbox. There is an **Advanced Log Filter** section at the top of the page—this section can be expanded by clicking on the filter icon to the right of the section heading. **Advanced Log Filter** can save you considerable time, because it allows you to filter log entries by several criteria. These criteria include time, process, **process ID (PID)**, the quantity of entries displayed, and the message contained in the log entry. Each of these fields with the exception of **Quantity** (which can only take an integer, for obvious reasons) can contain a regular expression. To filter these logs, simply click on the **Apply Filter** button in this section.

Many of the log settings can be controlled via the **Settings** tab. The **GUI Log** entries field is where you can enter the number of log entries that will be displayed in the GUI—but not the number of entries in the actual log files. To change the number of entries in the log files, we must use the next option, **Log file size (Bytes)**. This field allows you to change the size of each log file. By default, each log file is about 500 KB; there are 20 log files, so the total disk space used by the log files is 10 MB. If you want to retain more than 50 entries per log file, you can increase this number, at the cost of disk space. If you do so, make sure that you have enough disk space available.

The next subsection is **Log firewall default blocks**. Enabling the **Log packets matched from the default block rules in the ruleset** option will cause pfSense to log packets that are blocked by the implicit default block rule. All internetwork traffic is blocked by the implicit block rule, but traffic blocked is not normally logged – but it will be logged if this option is set. If the log packets matched from the default pass rules put in the ruleset option is checked, then pfSense will log packets that are allowed by the implicit pass rule. The **Log packets blocked by 'Block Bogon Networks' rules** and **Log packets blocked by 'Block Private Networks' rules** options allow you to log packets blocked by those rules, which can be useful if you suspect your network is being attacked and the attacker is using some form of IP spoofing.

If the **Web Server Log** option is checked, then errors from the web server process for the pfSense GUI or the captive portal will appear in the main system log. The **Raw Logs** option, if enabled, will show the logs without them being interpreted by the log parser. Normally, we want the log files to be parsed, so they are easier to read; however, the raw log files, though difficult to read, can often be more helpful in troubleshooting—they provide detailed information that is often left out of the parsed log output. The **IGMP Proxy** option, if enabled, will allow for verbose logging.

The next option, the Where to show rule descriptions dropdown box, allows you to show a description of the rule being applied in the firewall log. You have these options:

- **Don't load descriptions**: The default option
- **Display as column**: The description appears as an additional column
- **Display as second row**: The description will appear below the corresponding log entry

The **Local Logging** option, if enabled, will disable writing log files to the local disk. Clicking on the **Reset Log Files** button will clear all local log files and reinitialize them as empty logs. It will also restart the DHCP daemon. If you have made any changes to the settings on this page, you should click on the **Save** button to make sure that you don't lose these changes before clicking on the **Reset Log Files** button to clear the logs.

The next section is the **Remote Logging Options** section, which is useful if you have a syslog server. Checking the **Enable Remote Logging** checkbox will allow you to send log messages to a remote syslog server, and if you enable this option, several other options will appear on the page. The **Source Address** drop-down box is where you choose to which IP address the syslog daemon will bind. The choices include each interface on your system, localhost, and the default, which is any interface. You can select the protocol to use in the **Protocol** drop-down box. The options are **IPv4** and **IPv6**, but this option will only be used if a nondefault option is used for **Source Address**, and even then, it only expresses a preference. If pfSense cannot connect to the syslog server using the chosen IP protocol, it will try with the other.

The **Remote** log servers fields allow you to specify the IP addresses and ports of the syslog servers. You can specify up to three syslog servers here. The **Remote Syslog Contents** checkboxes are where you can choose which events are sent to the syslog server(s). If you choose to use a remote syslog server, remember to configure the syslog daemon on the remote end to accept syslog messages from pfSense. When you are finished making changes on this page, click on the **Save** button.

Interfaces

You can view information about the status of interfaces by navigating to **Status | Interfaces** on the main menu. You can view the following information:

- The inteface's device name
- Interface status (up or down)
- The interface's MAC addresses
- The IP address, subnet mask, and, if applicable, gateway
- The number of packets that have passed and that have been blocked
- The total number of both errors and collisions

If an interface has been configured to receive its IP address via DHCP (this applies to many WAN-type interfaces), you can renew the DHCP lease from this page.

Services

You can find out the status of most system and package services by navigating to **Status | Services**. You will find a table on this page that lists the name of the service, a brief description, as well as whether the service is running or stopped (**Status**). There is also an **Actions** column from which you can either start a stopped service or restart/stop a running service. You shouldn't have to control services in such a crude fashion under normal circumstances, but it may help during troubleshooting.

There are three additional icons that sometimes appear in the Services table:

- **Related settings**: This links to the settings page for the service (the icon looks like three sliders)
- **Related status**: If the service has its own page on the **Status** menu, it is linked to here (the icon looks like a bar graph)
- **Related log entries**: If the service has its own tab in **Status | Logs**, it will be linked to here (the icon looks like a logbook page)

Monitoring

You can view another useful set of information relating to the real-time operation of pfSense by navigating to **System** | **Monitoring**. There are two sections on this page. The first is a graph, and the second is a summary of the information in the graph. There are several pieces of information available relating to the percentage of CPU usage attributable to different system processes. They are as follows:

- User-related processes
- Nice (low-priority) processes
- Non-nice system processes
- System interrupts

There is also a column representing the grand total of processes for each; each entry also includes the minimum, maximum, and average percentage of CPU usage of each of these categories.

Traffic graphs

By navigating to **Status** | **Traffic Graph**, you will be able to view traffic graphs for each interface. You can select the interface in the **Interface** drop-down box; the interface selected will then be graphed. Information in the table adjacent to the graph will be sorted in descending order based on either bandwidth in or bandwidth out. Whether it is sorted by bandwidth in or bandwidth out depends on what you select in the **Sort by** drop-down box. The **Filter** drop-down box allows you to display either local traffic or remote traffic; otherwise, both will be displayed. The **Display** drop-down lets you control what is displayed in the Host Name or IP column (containing the IP address, hostname, description, or fully qualified domain name).

Firewall states

Needless to say, sometimes, it is helpful to view information about firewall states. Fortunately, there are several different ways of viewing this information from within the pfSense web GUI.

States

If we need to view the states table, the easiest way to do so is to navigate to **Diagnostics** | **States**. This table provides information about each state table entry. Information displayed includes the interface, protocol, the direction of traffic, socket status, and the number of packets/bytes exchanged. You can also filter the state table, either by an interface or by a regular expression, by using options in the **State Filter** section. If you need to clear the state table, you can also do that from this page, using the **Reset States** tab.

State summary

You might need just an overview of state information rather than information about individual states. If so, navigate to **Diagnostics** | **State Summary**. You can find state information organized by source IP, destination IP, total per IP, and IP pair. If you need to see if an IP address has an unusual number of states, you can do it from this page.

pfTop

pfTop is the first utility covered in this section that is available in both the web GUI (via **Diagnostics** | **pfTop**) and from the console/SSH (pfTop is 9 on the console menu). **pfTop** is extremely useful because it provides a live view of the state table as well as the total amount of bandwidth used by each state. If you are using **pfTop** from the console, type q to quit and thus return to the console menu.

pfTop contains several column headings, and you could probably guess what most of them stand for; for the sake of clarity, however, we will enumerate each of the default headings here. **PR** stands for protocol; **D** stands for direction (this can be in or out); **SRC** stands for source; and **DEST** stands for destination. **AGE** is how long since the entry was generated. **EXP** is when the entry expires; **PKTS** is the number of packets that have been handled by the rule; and **BYTES** is the number of bytes handled by the rule.

STATE deserves a bit of an explanation. This column indicates the state of both sides of the connection, using the format client:server. The states will not fit into an 80-column computer display, so pfTop uses integers (for example, 1:0). This is what the numbers signify:

Number	State
0	TCP_CLOSED
1	TCP_LISTEN
2	TCP_SYN_STATE

3	TCP_SYN_RECEIVED
4	TCP_ESTABLISHED
5	TCP_CLOSE_WAIT
6	TCP_FIN_WAIT1
7	TCP_CLOSING
8	TCP_LAST_ACK
9	TCP_FIN_WAIT2
10	TCP_TIME_WAIT

As an example, an entry of 4:4 would indicate that the state on either side of the connection is TCP_ESTABLISHED. An entry of 1:3 would indicate that the state on the client side is TCP_LISTEN and the state on the server side is TCP_SYN_RECEIVED.

Although **pfTop** is quite usable as a command-line utility, if you use **pfTop** within the web GUI, you can very easily change the output to suit your needs. The **View** drop-down menu lets you control how **pfTop** displays its output and provides the following options:

- **label**: This column represents the rule being invoked
- **long**: Display protocol, source, destination, gateway, state, and age
- **queue**: If the traffic shaper is configured, pfTop will display results organized by queue
- **rules**: Display each rule being invoked in the rightmost column

There is also a **Sort by** drop-down box. This allows you to sort output in descending order by several categories. There is a **Maximum # of States** drop-down box. This allows you to set the number of states that appear on each page.

Keep in mind that when you run pfTop from the console, it runs in interactive mode. Thus, **pfTop** reads commands from the terminal and acts upon them accordingly.

For a full listing of commands available for **pfTop** in interactive mode, refer to the **pfTop** man page. This page also includes **pfTop** command-line options.

tcpdump

When you are troubleshooting network problems, you may find it necessary to use packet capturing, which is also known as packet sniffing. One way you can perform packet capturing is to use **tcpdump**, which is a command-line tool. Rather conveniently, **tcpdump** is a command -line tool. It can be used to capture and analyze packets, and details can either be displayed on screen or saved to a file. **tcpdump** uses the libpcap library to implement its packet capturing functionality.

You should give consideration as to which interface's traffic you want to capture, as the results can be very different depending on which interface you monitor. In many cases, you probably want to focus on a single interface, whereas in others, you may want to capture traffic from several interfaces simultaneously. To use **tcpdump**, you will have to know the underlying device names of the interfaces being monitored; if you do not remember what they are, navigate to **Interfaces | (assign)** and view them. You can also find out this information from the console menu, which lists each interface along with its device name. You can also issue the following command at the console shell to find the interface names:

```
tcpdump -D
```

To run tcpdump on a single interface, type this:

```
tcpdump -iinterface_name
```

In this case, interface_name is the device name (for example, fxp0). You can also run **tcpdump** without any command-line options; this will cause **tcpdump** to capture packets from all interfaces.

You might note that if you run **tcpdump**, it normally displays the hostname of both the source and the destination. This is because the default behavior of pfSense is to run a reverse DNS lookup on IP addresses. This means that **tcpdump** may be generating a considerable volume of DNS traffic that you don't want. There are ways to limit this. You can, for example, limit the number of packets captured with the -c option. To limit the number of packets captured to 10, type the following:

```
tcpdump -c 10
```

The default maximum capture size for each packet is 64 K. However, you may only be interested in what is in the header. You can use the $-s$ parameter to limit how many bytes of each packet is captured. To limit the bytes to 96, type the following code:

```
tcpdump -s 96
```

If you want to save packet capure files in pcap format for later analysis, you can so this as well. This can be helpful, especially if you have a graphical network protocol analyzer available on your PC. To save the output to a file, type the following code:

```
tcpdump -w filename
```

Be aware that `tcpdump` puts your network interface in promiscuous mode by default. Thus, it shows every frame on the wire, not just ones being sent to its MAC address. This is less of a problem with modern networks that use switches, and interfaces will generally only get traffic they should receive. If you find you are capturing a lot of traffic not of interest to you, however, you might want to use the p option, which allows you to run `tcpdump` in nonpromiscuous mode.

If you need to control the verbosity of `tcpdump` command's output, you can do so with the $-v$ flag. This flag only controls the output of `tcpdump` on the screen and not the contents of **tcpdump** output that is being saved. You can also choose $-vv$ or $-vvv$, which provides additional verbosity for screen output. If you invoke both one of the verbosity options and $-w$ (to write to a file), `tcpdump` will report the number of packets captured every 10 seconds.

If you invoke the **-e** option, `tcpdump` will display the MAC addresses of the source and destination of the packet. It will also display 802.1Q VLAN tag information.

`tcpdump` displays packet sequence numbers. The first packet in a series of packets always has large sequence numbers; however, by default, all subsequent packets have smaller numbers. The reason for this is that `tcpdump` switches to relative sequence numbers when displaying multiple packets from the same source/destination to save display space. If you only want to see actual sequence numbers, use the $-S$ flag.

If you want a simple frontend for `tcpdump`, you can get that from the web GUI by navigating to **Diagnostics | Packet Capture**. For the most part, it seems like the most common sense options are selected by default, regardless of the default of the command-line `tcpdump` utility. On that page, you can use the **Interface** drop-down box to choose the interface whose packets will be captured. Unfortunately, there does not seem to be an option to capture all interfaces. Enabling **Promiscuous** causes `tcpdump` to enter promiscuous mode. The **Address Family** dropdown allows you to select IPv4 or IPv6 packets (or both). The **Protocol** dropdown has several options in terms of which protocol's packets you choose to capture.

The **Host Address** field allows you to specify a source or destination IP address or subnet; tcpdump will then look for the address specified in either field. You can also perform many Boolean operations on addresses: for example, you can negate the IP address and capture all packets except ones that have the IP address as their source or destination; you can perform a Boolean AND (by separating addresses by a comma), perform a Boolean OR (by separating addresses with a pipe).

If you specify a port in the **Port** edit box, tcpdump will filter by port, looking for the port you specify in either field. The **Packet Length** edit box lets you specify the number of bytes of each packet that will be captured (similar to the -s command-line option). The default value is 0, meaning that the entire packet will be capture. The **Count** field lets you set the number of packets tcpdump will capture. The default value is **100**, whereas a value of **0** will cause tcpdump to continuously capture packets.

The **Level of detail** drop-down box is where you can select the amount of detail that will be displayed after you hit **Stop** when packets have been captured. This option does not, however, affect the level of detail in the packet capture file.

The **Reverse DNS Lookup** option, if enabled, will cause tcpdump to perform a reverse DNS lookup on all addresses. As noted before, this is generally not recommended because reverse DNS lookups can generate considerable DNS traffic. When you finish selecting options, click on the **Start** button.

When **tcpdump** is running, you should see a **Packet capture is running** message across the bottom of the page, and the **Start** button should become a **Stop** button. Once **tcpdump** is finished running, either because it has captured all the packets it was set to capture or because the Stop button was pressed, a **Packets Captured** listbox should appear with information about the packets captured. You can change the level of detain on the page by changing the **Level of Detail** value and clicking on the **View Capture** button. You can also save the packet capture by clicking on **Download Capture**.

tcpflow

Like tcpdump, tcpflow gives you the ability to view the text contents of network packets in real time. However, tcpdump is more suited to capturing packets and protocol information. tcpflow is more suited toward viewing the actual data flow between two hosts. tcpdump displays output to the console by default, whereas tcpflow writes output to a file by default, and you must use the **-c** option if you want to see the tcpflow output on the console.

Other than this, much of the syntax of tcpflow is similar to that of tcpdump. An example of using tcpflow is as follows:

```
tcpflow – i fxp0 –c host 192.168.1.3 and port 80
```

Such a command would capture packets on the fxp0 interface with a source or destination of 192.168.1.3 port 80. Unlike tcpdump, tcpflow is not part of the pfSense's default installation.

ping, traceroute, and netstat

ping, traceroute, and netstat are old command-line utilities, and like many utilities that have stood the test of time, they do their job so well that nobody saw fit to improve upon them in any significant way. These utilities can be used to test the reachability of hosts and provide information about routing and network connections. They are often the first tools used by network technicians and admins when testing networks, and they can be invaluable when troubleshooting network issues. ping and traceroute are both accessible from pfSense's web GUI, but they are more commonly used from the console.

ping

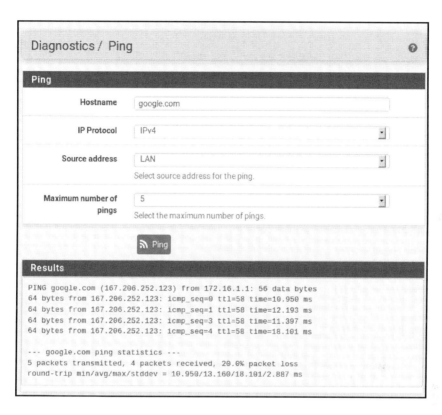

The `ping` utility's main function is to measure the **round-time-trip** (**RTT**) for packets sent from a source to a destination that are echoed back to the source. To do this, it uses **Internet Control Message Protocol** (**ICMP**) and sends ICMP Echo Request packets to the destination host. It then waits for an ICMP Echo Reply.

When `ping` runs, it will report several pieces of information. The first is the size of the packet received. The default size is 56 bytes. However, an ICMP `ECHO_REQUEST` packet contains an additional 8 bytes for an ICMP header; therefore, the size reported is 64 bytes. The next piece of information is the destination IP address (ping does not resolve hostnames by default).

The `icmp_seq` field reveals the ordering of ICMP packets; these packets are not necessarily received in the same order as they are sent although when networks are functioning correctly, they usually are. **TTL** stands for **time to live**, and this field is reduced by one by every router en route to its destination. If TTL reaches zero before the packet arrives at its destination, an ICMP error is sent back (**ICMP Time Exceeded**). The last field is the RTT of each packet, which is generally a good benchmark of the latency of a connection.

At the end of the `ping` session, `ping` reports aggregate statistics. The number of packets transmitted and received is reported, along with the percentage of packet loss. We also see the **minimum RTT**, the **average RTT,** the **maximum RTT**, and the **standard deviation**.

It should be noted that it is increasingly common for firewalls to block ICMP traffic, thus rendering ping useless with these hosts. In fact, pfSense blocks such traffic by default. If you want to ping your hosts from the other side of a pfSense firewall, you will have to explicitly allow such traffic. Adding some well-crafted firewall rules will thus allow us to ping our own networks, but it will be of no help when we are pinging networks we don't control. If you find a need to ping a network that blocks ICMP traffic, you might be better off using a utility that relies on TCP or UDP for sending packets, as these protocols are much less likely to be blocked. One such utility is `tcpping`. It has a similar syntax to ping. If you are pinging to local hosts, you can use `arping`. This utility uses the **Address Resolution Protocol** (**ARP**) request method to resolve IP addresses.

To install **tcpping**, first install the **tcptraceroute** script. It can be found in most Linux repositories. If you are using Debian/Ubuntu/Mint Linux, use this command:

```
sudo apt-get install tcptraceroute
```

For CentOS/Red Hat Enterprise Level, we are using yum for package installation as follows:

```
sudo yum install tcptraceroute
```

To install tcpping, do the following:

```
cd /usr/bin

sudo wget http://www.vdberg.org/~richard/tcpping

sudo chmod 755 tcpping
```

The `chmod` command is to set the proper permissions for `tcpping`.

In spite of these difficulties, the ping utility can be useful in a number of different scenarios:

- It can help us determine if there is network connectivity between two hosts
- It can help us determine if there is an unacceptable level of packet loss
- It is a good tool for measuring latency between any two hosts

traceroute

`traceroute` is a network diagnostic tool for IP networks. Like many simple network utilities, it is available on multiple platforms and under Windows as `tracert`. Its purpose is to display the path of packets and the transit delays in each step. A step is referred to as a hop. The RTT of each hop is recorded; the sum of the mean times in each hop is a measure of the total time needed to establish a connection. By default, it outputs the result of each hop and the final results. It sends out three packets and proceeds unless all three packets are lost more than twice. If this happens, the connection will be considered lost; therefore, the route/path cannot be evaluated. By default, `traceroute` uses UDP.

`traceroute` is available at the Windows command prompt as `tracert`, but unfortunately, it is not part of most default Linux installations. However, it is available from the repositories. You can obtain it from a standalone package (`traceroute`); you can also obtain it as part of the `inetutils-traceroute` utilities.

The output of `traceroute` is simple: the first column displays the hop count, and the last column displays the IP address and hostname. The middle three columns display the RTT of each of the three packets sent. The only required parameter for this utility is the hostname or IP address of the destination host.

You can also invoke `traceroute` from the pfSense web GUI, which you can do by navigating to **Diagnostics** | **Traceroute**. You can enter the hostname or IP address in the **Hostname** field, and you can select the protocol in the **IP Protocol** drop-down box. The source address of the trace can be set in the **Source Address** drop-down box. You can also set the maximum number of hops and enable DNS lookup. You can even change the protocol used by traceroute from UDP to ICMP. When you are done configuring the session, you can click on the **Traceroute** button.

netstat

netstat is a network utility that displays a variety of statistics relating to network connections on the system on which it is running. For example, it displays incoming and outgoing connections, routing tables, and much more. It is still available in Windows, but in Linux, **netstat** is considered deprecated. You are advised to use **dss**, part of the **iproute2** package, instead. **netstat** may still work under Linux, depending on which distribution you are using.

If you do not specify any command-line arguments for **netstat**, it will display a list of active sockets for each network protocol. Under Linux, netstat will also display a list of active Unix domain sockets. As with **pfTop**, **netstat** uses abbreviations at the top of its columns. **Proto** stands for protocol; 6 denotes use of IPv6. **Recv-Q** indicates how many packets have not yet been copied from the socket buffer by the application using the socket, whereas **Send-Q** tells you how many packets have been sent, but for which ACK packets have not yet been received. **Local Address** indicates the IP address/hostname and port of the local end of the connection. **Foreign address** indicates the IP address/hostname and port of the remote end. State indicates the state of the socket.

Active Unix domain sockets will have several additional columns of information. **RefCnt**, or reference count, is the number of attached processes connected via this socket. The **Flags** column, as you may have guessed, contains a number of flags used on both connected and unconnected sockets. The **Type** column indicates the type of socket access; **DGRAM** (datagram) is a socket in connectionless mode; **STREAM** indicates the socket is a connection socket; and **RAW** indicates a raw socket. The **State** column indicates the state; **FREE** is an unallocated socket; and **LISTENING** is a socket listening for a connection request. **CONNECTING** means the socket is about to establish a connection. **CONNECTED** indicates the socket is already connected. Finally, **DISCONNECTING** indicates that the socket is disconnecting. The **I-Node** and **Path** columns show both the inode and path of the file object the represents the process which is attached to the socket.

A troubleshooting scenario

Now that we have outlined the process for troubleshooting network problems, as well as discussing a number of utilities available to help us in our diagnosis, it is time to consider a real-world example of a networking problem—something that you might well encounter if you were a network administrator. We will then apply our seven-step approach to troubleshooting to solve the problem.

A user cannot connect to a website

This is a common end user problem. The user cannot connect to a website, and they consistently get the same error message. This illustrates how important it is to gather information because without knowing more about the problem, we do not know which of many causes may be in play here:

- **User error**: Did the user mistype the URL or make a similar mistake?
- **Computer configuration issue**: This may be the case if new software/hardware was installed recently
- **Network connection issue**: Does the user's computer have network connectivity?

If the problem is with our internet connection or the website, then the problem is beyond our control. However, other likely causes are more likely to be within our sphere of control; even if the problem is something that requires escalation to another tier within our support team.

Referring back to our basic troubleshooting procedure, we want to spend some time gathering information. We might question the user and ask them what error message they received when they tried to access the website. If the user cannot remember, we can ask them to recreate the problem. As an example, they may try to access the website again and receive a **Server Not Found** error page.

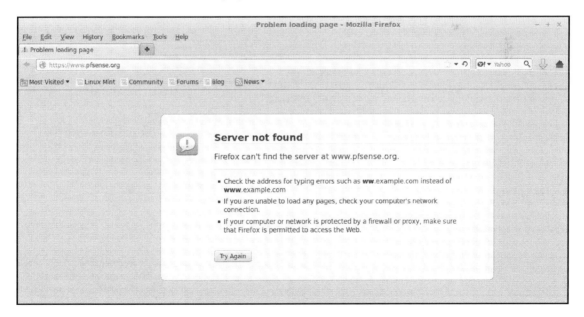

An error message such as this can have several causes. The web server to which the user is trying to connect may be down. Also, the user's internet connection may be down, or DNS resolution may not be working. Further, the user may be connecting to the website through a proxy, and the proxy may be down or misconfigured. It might be helpful to begin with the most wide-ranging possibilities first because they are the easiest to prove or disprove. Thus, we might begin by considering the possibility that the user's internet connection is down.

Most organizations have shared internet connections. Therefore, the end user's system will connect to a switch that connects to a router that connects to an ISP. There are several problems that could occur:

- There may be a problem with the router's connection to the ISP, or the ISP's connection to the internet. This is a problem beyond our control, and there would be little we could do about it, other than reporting it to the ISP.
- The problem may be within our network—for example, a bad network cable or a misconfigured switch or router. Finding out the number of users affected by the problem might help us zero in on the problem. For example, a misconfigured switch will likely affect several users, whereas a bad network cable between our user's computer and the switch will only affect that user.
- The user's computer might be the source of the problem. There may be a problem with the network card, the networking software, or the computer's configuration. If so, our user will likely be the only person affected by the problem.

Let us assume that no other users have reported any networking problems. If this is so, it is unlikely that we have a malfunctioning router or switch, as we would likely have multiple users reporting issues. Still, we can easily eliminate this as a possibility by accessing a website using a separate computer using the same internet connection. Doing so will help us narrow down the source of the problem. We can begin to focus on the user, their computer, the way they access the site, or the computer's connection to the network.

If we find that we are unable to access the internet via another computer connected to the network, then we may need to change our focus. A component we used to access the Internet could be broken, such as a switch, cable, or another component. It could also be the connection between our router and the ISP, and as mentioned before, then it would be beyond our control.

If users on your network are accessing the web through a proxy such as Squid, this could be the source of the problem. If you think it is the source of the problem, then this becomes your theory of probable cause. You can test the theory by temporarily disabling the proxy and seeing if you can access websites. If you can, then you have likely isolated the cause of the problem or at least one of the causes.

If you were able to access the internet via another computer and thus have narrowed down the source of the problem to either the user or the user's computer, then you should continue the process of trying to isolate the cause of the problem. You could ask the user to access a different website. If the user can do that, then the network, router, and internet connection are functioning; the problem is likely either a website that is down or user error.

If the user cannot access any other website, then you should ask the user to open another network client application and use it to try to connect to the internet. The application could be an email or FTP client. If the user can connect to the internet using another application, then we have likely isolated the cause of the problem: the web browser software on the user's computer. If we cannot connect to the internet at all from the user's computer, we are left trying to determine what element of the computer's networking setup is at fault.

One possibility we should consider is that the computer's DNS configuration is wrong. As you know, hosts rely on DNS servers to resolve hostnames to IP addresses. If the user's computer is not configured with one or more valid DNS servers to which it can connect, name resolution will fail. An easy way of detecting likely DNS problems is to try to ping an IP address rather than a hostname. If you can ping a site when entering the IP address, but pings fail when you enter the hostname, there is a significant chance that you have a DNS issue. You will thus want to have the user check his computer's DNS settings. In most cases, we will have configured pfSense to act as a DNS server or at least have specified upstream DNS servers in the settings. Therefore, resolving the issue may be as simple as having the user click on **Obtain DNS server address automatically** so that they use the DNS server specified by the upstream router.

If we cannot ping an IP address of a site on the internet, then DNS misconfiguration either isn't an issue—or at least, isn't the only issue. There could be another configuration issue. An incorrect gateway may have been specified, in which case the user will only have access to the local subnet. We might try pinging a host on the same network, then ping a computer on a different network and see what the result is. If the user can access the local network but not another network, there is a good chance the issue is a network configuration issue, such as an incorrect gateway specified. If even a ping to a local host fails, however, we should consider whether the problem is the computer hardware.

If we suspect that the network card is at fault, we could try pinging the loopback (127.x.x.x) address. If this fails, then there is a good chance the network card drives may need to be reinstalled. The network card itself may be broken as well. If we can ping the loopback address, then it is likely the network card is functioning, and we might consider checking the cabling instead.

Once you have identified the problem, you still have to formulate a plan of action. In this case, the user will likely want to have the issue resolved as soon as possible. Therefore, you can begin working on fixing the problem right away. In other cases, implementing a solution may affect many users. If so, it is good practice to inform such users and also to follow any procedures your organization has for performing such maintenance. When you test the solution, you may not have success at first. For example, what if we replace the network card, only to find we still cannot access the internet from the computer. There may have been two or more causes preventing the user from accessing the internet, and we may have only solved one of them. We would have to go back to step one, gather more information, and formulate a new theory of probable cause. Even if your tests are successful, you will want to verify system functionality and document what you have done.

As you can tell by our relatively brief discussion of this troubleshooting scenario, even a simple problem can have many possible causes. Nonetheless, by employing the troubleshooting procedure we outlined in the first section, we can work toward eliminating many of these possibilities and move toward a solution.

Summary

In this chapter, we covered troubleshooting fundamentals, including a basic troubleshooting procedure you can employ in any networking troubleshooting scenario. We covered some common problems and troubleshooting tools you can use. We also put these fundamentals into practice by considering a real-world networking problem.

Needless to say, we have really only laid a foundation here for understanding diagnosis and troubleshooting of networks. There are many resources available for learning how to troubleshoot networks, not the least of which are networking professionals who can provide invaluable expertise on many issues. Of course, there is no substitute for practical experience, and as you become more skilled in building and maintaining networks, you will become more skilled at troubleshooting.

Questions

1. What is the final step in troubleshooting a networking problem?
2. A site can be reached by pinging the IP address, but pinging the hostname fails. What is the likely cause?

3. We cannot reach the internet from a computer, but we can access other nodes on the local network. Assume that we have isolated the problem to this computer. What is the likely cause?
4. Name a wireless standard that uses the 5 GHz range (there are four).
5. Which wireless encryption standard sends challenges in the clear and is generally considered insecure now?
6. Name a utility that can be used to monitor the pfSense state table and can be used from the console or within the web GUI.
7. What problem might we encounter if we try to ping hosts on networks not under our control?
8. What protocol does traceroute use by default?

Further Reading

- **Top 10 Basic Network Troubleshooting Tools Every IT Pro Should Know (Good overview of the software utilities available for troubleshooting. Ping is #10 on the list)**: https://www.pluralsight.com/blog/it-ops/network-troubleshooting-tools
- **Basic network troubleshooting (Network troubleshooting tips from Computer Hope)**: https://www.computerhope.com/issues/ch000445.htm

Assessments

Chapter 1

1. FreeBSD.
2. Packet filter.
3. t1n1wall, SmallWall, OPNsense, ShoreWall (any one of these is acceptable).

Chapter 2

1. Physical, Data Link, Network, Transport, Session, Presentation, Application
2. (a) The network layer. (b) The transport layer.
3. Class A: 10.0.0.0 to 10.255.255.255; Class B: 172.16.0.0 to 172.31.255.255; Class C: 192.168.0.0 to 192.168.255.255.
4. Unicast, broadcast, and multicast.
5. No (pfSense 2.4 and later will not run on 32-bit processors).
6. UFS and ZFS.
7. When the WAN interface has been configured, but the LAN interface has not yet been configured.
8. Configure a static IP address that is on the LAN network for the PC.
9. By navigating to System | Setup Wizard.
10. Because private networks should not be routed through the public Internet.

Chapter 3

1. 2001:ba::3257:652.
2. (a) Unicast, multicast, anycast. (b) fec0::/10
3. Using a public/private key pair.
4. Static DHCP mappings.
5. The range of IP addresses must be valid IP addresses for the subnet for which DHCP is enabled.
6. Yes.

7. At the console and in the web GUI.
8. 802.1Q.
9. (a) 1 to 4094. (b) Yes; by using QinQ tagging.
10. A managed switch.

Chapter 4

1. Because it is crowded and full of interference from other devices.
2. User manager authentication, voucher authentication, RADIUS authentication
3. Disable concurrent user logins (also could set Maximum concurrent connections to 1).
4. The portal page.
5. Voucher authentication or RADIUS MAC authentication with the MAC authentication secret set.
6. RADIUS authentication.
7. DHCP service.
8. No; pfSense is the RADIUS client.

Chapter 5

1. (a) A; (b) AAAA; (c) PTR.
2. (a) Cache poisoning can occur. (b) Deploy DNSSEC.
3. (a) DNS Resolver and DNS Forwarder. (b) DNS Resolver.
4. (a) 53; (b) UDP.
5. Host Overrides.
6. DDNS and RFC 2136.
7. You are validating certificates; you are running pfSense on an embedded system that does not have a battery for the clock; you want the correct time stamp on logs.
8. ntpq.
9. (a) Agents; (b) network management station.
10. Agents are unable to communicate with the SNMP daemon.

Chapter 6

1. This means that pfSense keeps track of active connections and allows return traffic through the firewall automatically.
2. Ingress and egress filtering.
3. Because the logs will fill up quickly.
4. (a) Floating rules can apply to more than one interface, and can be used on traffic either entering or leaving the interface. (b) The Quick option.
5. No; we must create a firewall rule to allow the traffic as well.
6. (a) No; (b) Yes
7. 1:1 NAT.

Chapter 7

1. (a) VoIP applications; (b) video streaming applications. (b) FTP client; filesharing application.
2. Priority queuing (PRIQ), class-based queuing (CBQ); Hierarchical Fair Service Curve (HFSC)
3. Penalty box.
4. CoDel Active Queue.
5. Because TCP uses the number of dropped packets as a criteria for adjusting the rate at which packets are sent, and with large buffers, packets won't drop until the buffers are almost full.
6. Pass, Block, Reject, Match.
7. UDP.
8. p2p Catch All.

Chapter 8

1. Peer-to-peer and client-server.
2. (a) IPsec; (b) OpenVPN; 9c) OpenVPN.
3. 500.
4. Mobile Client Configuration.
5. (a) None; (b) Challenge Handshake Authentication Protocol, MS-CHAP, and Password Authentication Protocol (PAP).

6. ECDH Only, to enable Elliptic Curve Diffie-Hellman.
7. OpenVPN Client Export Utility.
8. 4500.

Chapter 9

1. Service Level Agreement (SLA).
2. We likely did not configure DNS for the secondary WAN connection.
3. Failure to correctly configure the monitor IP for the secondary WAN; failure to create firewall rules or to change outbound NAT rules to send traffic to the gateway group.
4. We didn't configure latency settings for the secondary WAN to allow for the greater amount of latency a satellite connection would have.
5. (a) Because policy-based routing does not work with traffic that originates with pfSense, like DNS traffic. (b) Make the upstream DNS server the monitor IP, and pfSense will create an implicit static route to it.
6. Enable State Killing on Gateway Failure.
7. (a) Set both to Tier 1. (b) Set one to Tier 1 and one to Tier 2.
8. (a) pfSense will think the gateway is up when it should be down. (b) The remote site's administrator may interpret our pings an an attack and block them. When our pings fail, pfSense will mark the gateway as down.

Chapter 10

1. (a) Layer 2; (b) Layer 3.
2. Distance-vector and link-state protocols
3. (a) routed and Quagga OSPF; (b) FRR and Quagga OSPF.
4. (a) 15; (b) 15.
5. No; if one is installed, pfSense will automatically uninstall the other one if it is already installed.
6. STP (Spanning Tree Protocol) and RSTP (Rapid Spanning Tree Protocol).
7. A firewall rule must be created allowing DHCP traffic on the bridged interface.
8. Looping.

Chapter 11

1. Documenting the problem and solution.
2. A DNS failure.
3. An incorrect gateway configuration.
4. 802.11a, 802.11g, 802.11n, 802.11ac.
5. Wired Equivalent Privacy (WEP).
6. PfTop.
7. The remote network may have blocked ICMP traffic; therefore, we cannot ping the host.
8. UDP.

Other Books You May Enjoy

If you enjoyed this book, you may be interested in these other books by Packt:

Mastering pfSense - Second Edition
David Zientara

ISBN: 978-1-78899-317-3

- Configure pfSense services such as DHCP, Dynamic DNS, captive portal, DNS, NTP and SNMP
- Set up a managed switch to work with VLANs
- Use pfSense to allow, block and deny traffic, and to implement Network Address Translation (NAT)
- Make use of the traffic shaper to lower and raise the priority of certain types of traffic
- Set up and connect to a VPN tunnel with pfSense
- Incorporate redundancy and high availability by utilizing load balancing and the Common Address Redundancy Protocol (CARP)
- Explore diagnostic tools in pfSense to solve network problems

Network Security with pfSense
Manuj Aggarwal

ISBN: 978-1-78953-297-5

- Understand what pfSense is, its key features, and advantages
- Configure pfSense as a firewall
- Configure pfSense for failover and load balancing
- Connect clients through an OpenVPN client
- Configure an IPsec VPN tunnel with pfSense
- Integrate the Squid proxy into pfSense

Leave a review - let other readers know what you think

Please share your thoughts on this book with others by leaving a review on the site that you bought it from. If you purchased the book from Amazon, please leave us an honest review on this book's Amazon page. This is vital so that other potential readers can see and use your unbiased opinion to make purchasing decisions, we can understand what our customers think about our products, and our authors can see your feedback on the title that they have worked with Packt to create. It will only take a few minutes of your time, but is valuable to other potential customers, our authors, and Packt. Thank you!

Index

59148799R00192

Made in the USA
Middletown, DE
09 August 2019